For more information about the *Straight to the Heart series*, please go to **www.philmoorebooks.com**.

You can also receive daily messages from Phil Moore on Twitter by following **@PhilMooreLondon**.

*This book is dedicated to the church in Europe, from Portugal
to Russia, and from Iceland to Cyprus. May it start to enjoy
the fruits of the radical surgery of the Lord.*

Text copyright © 2021 Phil Moore
This edition copyright © 2021 Lion Hudson IP Limited

The right of Phil Moore to be identified as the author of this work has been
asserted by him in accordance with the Copyright, Designs and Patents Act 1988.

Published by
Lion Hudson Limited
Wilkinson House, Jordan Hill Business Park
Banbury Road, Oxford OX2 8DR, England
www.lionhudson.com

ISBN 978 0 8572 1988 6
e-ISBN 978 0 8572 1981 7

First edition 2021

Acknowledgments
Scripture quotations taken from the Holy Bible, New International Version (NIV).
Copyright © 1979, 1984, 2011 Biblica, formerly International Bible Society. Used
by permission of Hodder & Stoughton Ltd, an Hachette UK company. All rights
reserved. "NIV" is a registered trademark of Biblica. UK trademark number
1448790. Both 1984 and 2011 (Anglicised) versions are quoted in this commentary. Scripture quotations marked The Living Bible are taken from The Holy
Bible, Living Bible Edition, copyright © Tyndale House Publishers 1971.
All rights reserved.

Every effort has been made to trace copyright holders and to obtain permission
for the use of copyright material. The publisher apologizes for any errors or
omissions and would be grateful to be notified of any corrections that should
be incorporated in future reprints of this book.

A catalogue record for this book is available from the British Library

Printed and bound in the UK, February 2021, LH26

STRAIGHT TO
THE HEART OF

Jeremiah
and Ezekiel

60 BITE-SIZED INSIGHTS

Phil Moore

MONARCH
BOOKS

CONTENTS

LAMENTATIONS: RESPONDING TO SURGERY

EZEKIEL 1–32: FURTHER SURGERY IS NEEDED

EZEKIEL 33–48: THE RESULTS OF SURGERY

About the
Straight to the Heart
Series

On his eightieth birthday, Sir Winston Churchill dismissed the compliment that he was the "lion" who had defeated Nazi Germany in World War Two. He told the Houses of Parliament that *"It was a nation and race dwelling all around the globe that had the lion's heart. I had the luck to be called upon to give the roar."*

I hope that God speaks to you very powerfully through the "roar" of the books in the *Straight to the Heart* series. I hope they help you to understand the books of the Bible and the message that the Holy Spirit inspired their authors to write. I hope that they help you to hear God's voice challenging you, and that they provide you with a springboard for further journeys into each book of Scripture for yourself.

But when you hear my "roar"', I want you to know that it comes from the heart of a much bigger "lion" than me. I have been shaped by a whole host of great Christian thinkers and preachers from around the world, and I want to give due credit to at least some of them here: Terry Virgo, Dave Holden, Guy Miller, John Hosier, Adrian Holloway, Greg Haslam, Lex Loizides, Malcolm Kayes and all those who lead the Newfrontiers family of churches; friends and encouragers, such as Stef Liston, Joel Virgo, Stuart Gibbs, Scott Taylor, Nick Derbridge, Phil Whittall, and Kevin and Sarah Aires; Joshua Wells at Lion Hudson Ltd; the pastors and congregation that serve alongside me at Everyday Church in London; my great friend Andrew Wilson – without all of your friendship, encouragement and example, this series would never have happened.

I would like to thank my parents, my brother Jonathan, and my in-laws, Clive and Sue Jackson. Dad – your example birthed in my heart the passion that brought this series into being. I didn't listen to all you said when I was a child, but I couldn't ignore the way you got up at five o'clock every morning to pray, read the Bible and worship, because of your radical love for God and for his Word. I'd like to thank my children – Isaac, Noah, Esther and Ethan – for keeping me sane when publishing deadlines were looming. But most of all, I'm grateful to my incredible wife, Ruth – my friend, encourager, corrector and helper.

You all have the lion's heart, and you have all developed the lion's heart in me. I count it an enormous privilege to be the one who was chosen to sound the lion's roar.

So welcome to the *Straight to the Heart* series. My prayer is that you will let this roar grip your own heart too – for the glory of the great Lion of the Tribe of Judah, the Lord Jesus Christ!

Introduction:
Only Radical Surgery
Can Save This Patient

"I will slay in my anger and wrath…
I will bring health and healing."

(Jeremiah 33:5–6)

A few years ago, an Australian woman stabbed me. She had planned her move so carefully that I was powerless to stop her. First, she arranged for her friend to drug me so that I became disorientated. Then she stabbed me with a sharp knife, slicing a great chunk of flesh out of my leg. Her blade was only inches away from a major artery.

Sounds pretty shocking, I know. But what if I told you that I had been diagnosed with a suspected melanoma? What if I told you that the Australian woman was a gifted surgeon who had been tasked with removing the suspicious tissue from my body? What if I told you that her scalpel enabled me to sit here writing this devotional commentary for you, cancer-free? It would transform your perspective, and I want you to think the same way about Jeremiah and Ezekiel. They are two of the greatest writers of the Old Testament, and two of the most neglected. They share a common message. They both address the same spiritual cancer that is spreading across the southern kingdom of Judah, and they both reveal God's diagnosis: *Only radical surgery can save this patient.*[1]

---

[1] The twelve tribes of Israel had split into two kingdoms in 930 BC. The northern kingdom of Israel had already been destroyed by this spiritual cancer in 722 BC. Jeremiah and Ezekiel address the southern kingdom of Judah in order to rescue it from the fate of its northern neighbour.

9

Jeremiah 1–25 explains why **radical surgery is needed**. These early chapters are the reason why, in modern English, we still refer to any speech that outlines a long list of problems as a jeremiad. They are why modern politicians dismiss those who point out problems with their policies as the Jeremys of this world. Granted, these chapters can make for difficult reading in places, but that's precisely the point. Nobody likes to be sat down by their doctor and informed that they have cancer, but it would be far worse for their doctor to pretend that everything was looking fine and rosy when it wasn't. Jeremiah describes the sin that is destroying God's people and he calls his listeners to lie down gladly on God's operating table before it spreads to their entire body. At a time when many churches are in decline and when our experience of Christianity seems quite distant from the triumphs of the book of Acts, we need to read these chapters carefully. They help us to recognize the spiritual cancer that still destroys God's people. They invite us to embrace God's scalpel in our own lives and in our own churches today.

Jeremiah 26–52 informs us that **radical surgery has begun**. The Lord has heard his people's response to his diagnosis, and he has begun his life-saving operation. These chapters are full of horror, as many people close their ears to the doctor's warnings and become part of the infected tissue that needs to be removed from the body. But these chapters are also full of glorious hope, as others face up to the dire diagnosis and find deliverance. The Lord uses these chapters to describe the bright future which lies on the other side of surgery for anybody who is willing to surrender to the truth of his Word.

Lamentations is a collection of poems that teach us healthy ways of **responding to surgery**. Although the five poems are anonymous, we will discover later that the prophet Jeremiah probably penned them and so we will take a brief look at them in our tour through Jeremiah and Ezekiel. He teaches us how to weep for the sin inside our churches and for the catastrophic pain that it inevitably causes. He encourages us that the Lord wounds us in order to heal us, so long as we respond well to his scalpel.

Ezekiel 1–32 informs us sadly that **further surgery is needed**. Ezekiel was a teenager in 605 BC, when the Babylonians first besieged Jerusalem and carried away thousands of captives, including Daniel and his friends. Ezekiel therefore witnessed first-hand the stubborn refusal of the Jewish leaders to surrender to the surgeon's hand of God. He was in his twenties when the Babylonians captured Jerusalem for a second time, in 597 BC, and he found himself among the group of captives taken into exile. These chapters record his prophecies in Babylonia during the eleven years that led up to the total destruction of Jerusalem in 586 BC. Ezekiel confronts the spiritual cancer that still lingers on in Judah and in its capital city of Jerusalem, pleading with God's people to surrender to the surgeon's blade while they still have a chance. Otherwise their nation will need to be ruined so that its spiritual recovery can begin.

Ezekiel 33–48 is a glorious proclamation of **the results of surgery**. After Jerusalem is destroyed and Judah is swallowed up into the Babylonian Empire, the Jewish exiles start hearing promises of a glorious future for their fallen nation. Even now, Ezekiel prophesies that if they repent of their rebellion against the Lord, he will bring them back to their land and recommence their nation's great salvation story. These chapters take us back to the creation of Adam and Eve in the Garden of Eden, encouraging the Jewish survivors to believe that the Lord's surgery has been successful and that the best days for God's people now lie ahead of them. These chapters are full of mighty promises about what God has in store for those who willingly embrace his radical surgery.

So, well done for deciding to read these books of the Bible and thank you for allowing me to guide you through them in this devotional commentary. Jeremiah, Lamentations and Ezekiel are some of the least-read books of the Bible, but they are also some of the most rewarding. They are still the words God speaks to his backslidden people today.

It doesn't take much insight to spot that the church in the West has problems very similar to those of Jerusalem and Judah, as described by Jeremiah and Ezekiel. Some time ago, a headline in *The Independent* newspaper predicted that the church would be dead within 40 years.[2] A few years later, an Anglican bishop admitted to *The Daily Telegraph* that he felt it hard to see the church surviving more than another 30 years.[3]

So let's not treat these three books as somebody else's mail, dismissing them as too gloomy or too difficult for us to understand. These three books of the Old Testament are still God's Word to his people today. Full of solemn warnings and glorious promises, they still warn believers in our own generation that only radical surgery can save this patient.

---

[2] *The Independent* is published in London, UK, and ran this headline on 16 April 2000.
[3] *The Daily Telegraph* is also based in London and ran this article on 27 June 2009.

Jeremiah 1–25:

Radical Surgery is Needed

You Go First
(Jeremiah 1:1–19)

"Get yourself ready! Stand up and say to them whatever I command you. Do not be terrified by them, or I will terrify you before them."

(Jeremiah 1:17)

One of the best lines in the movie *Shrek* comes when the evil Lord Farquaad sends his soldiers off on a near-impossible mission. He informs them grandly but callously that some of them may have to die – but that it's a sacrifice that he is willing to make![1]

The opening verses of the book of Jeremiah reassure us that the prophet is nothing like Lord Farquaad. He does not merely inform other people that *radical surgery is needed*. He is the very first to lie down gladly on the Lord's operating table.

Jeremiah is introduced to us as *"one of the priests at Anathoth"*, a town three miles to the northeast of Jerusalem that was synonymous with sin and corruption. Not only was the town named after the Canaanite war goddess Anath, but it was also home to a family of priests that had been spiritually sidelined for the sins of its ancestors. The family had been cursed because Eli tolerated wickedness within among his sons, and the family had been exiled to Anathoth as a result of Abiathar's treachery towards King Solomon.[2] Jeremiah had therefore grown up in a family that tried to keep its nose clean in the hope of being reprieved, so when the Lord called him to pronounce a dire

---

[1] *Shrek* (DreamWorks Pictures, 2001).

[2] Joshua 21:17–18, 1 Samuel 2:27–36 and 1 Kings 2:26–27.

diagnosis over the disobedient nation of Judah, he was asking him to surrender all hope of ever being restored to the ranks of the respectable.[3] Preaching such a message would make the prophet so unpopular that even the disgraced priests of Anathoth would seek to murder him in 11:21–23. Nobody likes to be given bad news, so the Lord warns Jeremiah upfront that serving as his prophet will cost him everything. In order to preach that only radical surgery can save the nation of Judah, Jeremiah must be the first to submit to God's surgeon's scalpel.

These opening verses inform us that Jeremiah preached his unpopular message for over forty years. He started in 627 BC, in the thirteenth year of King Josiah. He carried on throughout the reigns of the last four kings of Judah, then continued to prophesy even after the destruction of Jerusalem in 586 BC.[4] Jeremiah expresses his frustration over this in 25:3, while still only halfway through his marathon of ministry. He would suffer *physically* when the kings of Judah tortured him and threw him into prison. He would suffer *emotionally* when the Lord forbade him from marrying, even though all the other priests in his family had married.[5] He would suffer *spiritually* when his insights made him weep for his unrepentant nation. Unlike Lord Farquaad, Jeremiah completely practises what he preaches. Not for nothing is he known as *The Weeping Prophet*. The Lord calls Jeremiah to embrace this cost and to lead the way in surrendering to his surgeon's scalpel. He encourages him

---

[3] Jeremiah's father was named Hilkiah, which means *The Lord Is My Portion* and which was also the name of the high priest in Jerusalem (2 Kings 22:8). Although their cursed family had been barred from the Temple, the priests of Anathoth still longed to rejoin the other priestly families in Jerusalem.

[4] Josiah reigned 640–609 BC, Jehoahaz reigned 609 BC, Jehoiakim reigned 609–598 BC, Jehoiachin reigned 598–597 BC and Zedekiah reigned 597–586 BC. We do not know how Jeremiah died, but Jewish tradition says that he was stoned to death by some of the Jewish survivors in Egypt after the fall of Jerusalem.

[5] Jeremiah's call to singleness would be a prophetic sign to his hearers (16:1–4), as was Hosea's call to marry a prostitute and Ezekiel's call not to grieve after his wife died (Hosea 1:2 and Ezekiel 24:15–24).

that his life is brimfull of destiny. Before he was conceived in his mother's womb, the Lord had already chosen him to serve as his prophet to the nations (verse 5).[6] This is very good news. It reminds us that our salvation and significance derive from God's unsolicited grace towards us and not from our own attempts to win his favour.[7] But it didn't sound like good news to Jeremiah at the time.[8] He tries to postpone his operation to another day, protesting (verse 6), *"Alas, Sovereign Lord, I do not know how to speak; I am too young."*[9] The Lord responds by pledging to stand alongside him at all times to protect him and to give him wisdom beyond his years. The Lord fortifies Jeremiah still further by doing something that he knows will remind him of the commissioning of the prophet Isaiah. One of the interesting features of the book of Jeremiah is how often it echoes the other Old Testament prophets. He is even saved from death row in 26:17–19 when some of Judah's leaders notice how similar his words sound to those of the prophet Micah. When the Lord touches Jeremiah's mouth, it is therefore a deliberate echo of the way in which he commissioned the prince of prophets back in Isaiah 6:6–7. Whenever Jeremiah feels lonely and isolated, this action will remind him that he is merely the latest soldier in a great prophetic army.

The Lord offers Jeremiah a third encouragement through some clever wordplay. If the second syllable of the name Jeremiah comes from the Hebrew verb *rūm*, then his name

---

[6] Jeremiah is not just called to prophesy to the nation of Judah, but also to the Gentile nations. He does this in chapters 46–51, and also in his proclamation of God's new and better covenant for everyone who believes.

[7] The Apostle Paul echoes this in Romans 9:10–16 and Ephesians 2:8–10.

[8] *"Before I formed you in the womb I knew you"* is still greeted by many as bad news today, since it answers the question of when human life begins. It stands alongside Psalm 22:10, Luke 1:41–44 and Galatians 1:15 in declaring that life begins at conception and that to terminate a pregnancy is therefore to take a life.

[9] This is a poor excuse, since the priests of Anathoth had all been cursed with never living to old age (1 Samuel 2:32). Jeremiah was already in his teens or twenties, so the sooner he started, the better!

means *The Lord Lifts Up* or *The Lord Raises Up*, but if it comes from the Hebrew verb *rāmāh* then his name means *The Lord Throws Down* or *The Lord Razes to The Ground*. God uses this ambiguity to encourage Jeremiah in verse 10 that both are true. His words will tear down the wicked in their arrogance and they will build up the humble in their salvation. He will preach the gospel that is later likened to a double-edged sword.[10]

The Lord encourages Jeremiah further by giving him some quick visions to kickstart his prophetic ministry. The Hebrew words for *almond tree* and for *watching* are *shāqēd* and *shōqēd*, so Jeremiah's first picture is a simple promise that the Lord is watching to ensure that everything that Jeremiah speaks will be fulfilled. The vision of a pot of boiling water poured out from the north against Jerusalem is a first hint at which nation the Lord will use as his surgeon's scalpel to operate on his people.[11]

The Lord therefore ends this commissioning chapter by calling Jeremiah to go first. *"Get yourself ready! Stand up and say to them whatever I command you. Do not be terrified by them, or I will terrify you before them.*[12] *Today I have made you a fortified city, an iron pillar and a bronze wall to stand against the whole land ... They will fight against you but will not overcome you, for I am with you and will rescue you."*

The people of Judah may not like Jeremiah's prophecies but, when they watch him gladly go first onto the Lord's operating table, some of them will start to believe his message that only radical surgery can save their nation.

---

[10] Hebrews 4:12. Four out of the six things that God speaks over Jeremiah in 1:10 are about tearing down. Only two are about building up. If we want to preach for salvation, we need to preach against sin.

[11] Jeremiah started prophesying in 627 BC, around the same year that Babylon threw off Assyrian rule in the north and began amassing its own empire. Still, God insists in 1:10 that Jeremiah is the real nation-changer.

[12] The great antidote to the fear of people is to fear the Lord instead. The Lord essentially warns Jeremiah: *Do not be afraid of these people, or I will give you good reason to be afraid in front of them!*

Head Down
(Jeremiah 2:1–3:5)

"They followed worthless idols and became worthless themselves."

(Jeremiah 2:5)

An old Persian proverb warns us that *"A fish rots from the head down."*[1] Whenever a nation or an organization goes bad, the problem can always be traced back to the top. In this first prophecy in his collection, the prophet Jeremiah agrees. He traces the heart of Judah's problem right back to the heart of Judah's problematic leaders.

The twelve tribes of Israel were always meant to look to the Lord as their true leader. In 2:1–3, the Lord reminisces fondly about the early days after the Exodus when that was briefly true. The Israelites looked to him as their Deliverer and they loved him with all of the excited affection of a newlywed bride. In 2:4–6, the Lord recalls that this honeymoon period did not last very long. The Israelites quickly began grumbling that they were thirsty in the desert. Instead of looking to the Lord to help them, they built a golden calf and looked to pagan deities instead. One of the big themes of the Bible is that we become like what we worship. To choose our god is to choose our destiny, because a fish rots from the head down. *"They followed worthless idols and became worthless themselves."*[2]

---

[1] The thirteenth-century Persian poet Rumi first shared this proverb in his poem *Masnavi* (3.144).

[2] The Bible states this principle both negatively and positively. As we look to idols, we become corrupted (2 Kings 17:15 and Romans 1:18–32). As we look to Jesus, we become glorious (2 Corinthians 3:16–18).

In 2:7–8, the Lord recalls how he called their bluff. The Israelites had blamed him for their many hardships in the desert, so he transformed their poverty into prosperity. He empowered them to dispossess the Canaanites and to gain possession of some of the most fertile farmlands in the region. He gave them the Law as a written record of his character and of his constant mercies towards their sinful nation. He gave them priests to preach the Law to them and prophets to speak fresh words from the throne of heaven. He gave them leaders to rule as regents for the Lord as King. Since the Israelites had disobeyed him in their poverty, this was a test of whether they would serve him gladly in times of prosperity. It was a test that Israel failed. They became even more rebellious in the good times than in the bad. Their priests stopped preaching about him, and their prophets started claiming that the Canaanite rain god Baal was the true architect of their prosperity.[3] Their leaders turned their backs on God, and the rest of Israel followed. A fish rots from the head down. Evil gods produced evil leaders and an evil nation.

In 2:9–13, the Lord adopts the tone of a prosecuting lawyer and calls the skies to bear witness that no other nation has betrayed its national gods as Israel has betrayed him. The skies can testify that nowhere – from the marauding seafarers of Cyprus in the far west to the nomadic Arabs of Kedar in the far east – has any other nation ever done such a vile thing. In verse 13, the Lord therefore repeats the double-accusation that he made against the nation of Judah in 1:16. *"My people have committed two sins: They have forsaken me, the spring of living water, and have dug their own cisterns, broken cisterns that cannot hold water."* This is one of the most famous verses in the book of Jeremiah, comparing the Lord to a spring that endlessly gushes forth the water of life, and the pagan idols to

---

[3] The Hebrew word for *fertile land* in 2:7 is *carmel*, which was meant to remind the people of Judah that Baal had been unmasked as a deceiving demon by the prophet Elijah on Mount Carmel in 1 Kings 18.

empty wells that demand heavy lifting but that prove powerless to deliver on their promises.[4]

In 2:14–19, the Lord alerts the people of Judah to the work of his surgeon's scalpel. The ten northern tribes of Israel have already paid the price for their refusal to allow God to operate on their sin. In 722 BC, the Assyrians destroyed their cities and turned their fertile fields into a wasteland, carrying the few survivors into exile as their plunder. In 609 BC, the Egyptians killed King Josiah in battle and, three months later deposed Jehoahaz as his successor to install Jehoiakim as their puppet ruler instead.[5] Even a fool could see that this was a direct result of Judah having chosen to worship Assyrian and Egyptian idols instead of the God of Israel. It was God's surgeon's scalpel operating on their sin. *"Your wickedness will punish you; your backsliding will rebuke you."*

In 2:20–30, the Lord confronts the nation that he rescued from slavery in Egypt for being so foolish as to go back to its former slave masters in search of freedom. It is all about leadership, because a fish rots from the head down. It is the *kings*, the *officials*, the *priests* and the *prophets* who have led the southern tribes astray into worshipping the gods of wood and stone that proved so fatal to the northern tribes.[6] It is Judah's leaders who have turned the devoted bride of 2:2 into the adulterous prostitute of 2:20.[7] It is Judah's leaders who have trained God's people to lust after foreign idols like a camel

---

[4] See also Jeremiah 17:5–8 and 17:13, Ezekiel 47:1–12, and John 4:10–15 and 7:37–39.

[5] 2 Chronicles 35:20–36:4. *Memphis* was the capital city of Egypt, and *Tahpanhes* another of its major cities. Though undated, these verses show us that Jeremiah must have prophesied these words in 609 or 608 BC.

[6] The leaders of Judah murdered the true prophets of the Lord (2:30). Instead of using their leadership positions to teach the people how to serve God, they became servants of the roaring lion, Satan (1 Peter 5:8).

[7] *High hills* and *leafy trees* were the choice sites for pagan altars (1 Kings 14:23, 2 Kings 17:10 and Ezekiel 6:13).

or a donkey in mating season.[8] Yet now, those same leaders dare to blame the Lord for their defeat at the hands of the Egyptian army. Let their idols deliver them![9] Better still, let them turn back to the Lord and plead with him to cut away the fatal cancer of their sin.[10]

In 2:31–3:5, the Lord uses the nation of Judah's own laws to condemn them. Deuteronomy 24:1–4 forbade a Jewish man from divorcing his wife in order to have sex with another woman, only to take her back without having technically committed adultery. If their own law courts outlawed such moral trickery, then how can the leaders of leaders imagine that they can cast the Lord aside to worship foreign idols and oppress the poor, before insisting in his Temple courtyards that *"I am innocent"* and *"I have not sinned"*?[11] How dare they still address the Lord as their *"Father"* and *"Friend"*? He has sent a drought upon their land to show them that he has witnessed their Baal-worship and made plans to judge them as he judged the wicked King Ahab of Israel.

This prophecy is the first in Jeremiah's collection because it goes straight to the heart of Judah's problems. A fish rots from the head down. The leaders of Judah have led their nation astray and they must lead it back to the Lord in repentance. They must lead the way in surrendering to God's surgeon's scalpel, because radical surgery is required.

---

[8] The *valley* in 2:23 is the Valley of Ben Hinnom, the site of a shrine where the people of Judah murdered their children as sacrifices to the false god Molek. King Josiah had destroyed the shrine, but it appears that it was quickly rebuilt by his successors (2 Chronicles 28:3 and 33:6, and 2 Kings 23:10).

[9] The Lord still says the same thing to backslidden churches today: Let your clever modifications to my gospel stem your decline! You rejected my Word long ago, so I will do nothing to keep your religious social club open!

[10] Jeremiah 2:22 echoes Isaiah 1:18. There is no detergent (Hebrew *bōrîth*) that can cleanse those who break God's covenant (Hebrew *berîth*). The only detergent strong enough to cleanse away sin is the blood of Jesus.

[11] 1 Corinthians 4:4 warns that we can fall for this too. Believing we are innocent does not make us innocent.

Real Repentance
(Jeremiah 3:6–25)

"Judah did not return to me with all her heart, but only in pretence," declares the Lord.

(Jeremiah 3:10)

If you enjoy movies that have a non-linear narrative, then you will love the book of Jeremiah. If, on the other hand, you find it difficult to follow films such as *Memento*, *Dunkirk* and *Eternal Sunshine of the Spotless Mind*, then you will struggle unless you understand how the book of Jeremiah was compiled.

Jeremiah prophesied for over forty years, but we are told in chapter 36 that he was over twenty years into his ministry before he started to collate those prophecies into the book of the Bible that bears his name. In 605 BC, just before Jerusalem fell to the Babylonian army for the first time, the Lord warned Jeremiah that his freedom to prophesy openly was about to come to a sudden end. In order to avoid being silenced by his enemies, he needed to write up the past two decades of warnings into a single scroll. Jeremiah hired a scribe named Baruch to complete the task, who appears to have been the Christopher Nolan of the ancient world. For reasons known only to him and the Holy Spirit, Baruch decided to collate Jeremiah's words by theme, rather than in the order that he prophesied them. This gives the book a decidedly non-linear narrative, worsened by the fact that King Jehoiakim burned the original scroll, forcing poor Baruch to begin his work of collation all over again. But don't give up in frustration. Baruch gives us plenty of clues to help us date the different sections of Jeremiah. We just need to read each passage carefully.[1]

One of the clues can be found in 3:6, which informs us that Jeremiah prophesied the words in 3:6–6:30 before Pharaoh and his Egyptian army killed King Josiah in battle in 609 BC. The prophet therefore spoke 3:6–6:30 before he spoke 2:1–3:5, since the first prophecy in this collection was given in late 609 or early 608 BC, after Pharaoh took King Jehoahaz into exile and replaced him with his own puppet ruler King Jehoiakim instead.[2]

That's why the message of 3:6–11 is so shocking. It was given at a time when Judah appeared to be doing well. Josiah had restored God's Temple and destroyed the pagan shrines throughout his kingdom. He had come to real repentance through studying the Law of Moses, and in 622 BC he attempted to lead the nation of Judah into real repentance too.[3] Sadly, the Lord declares a disappointing verdict over what appeared to be one of the greatest spiritual revivals in the Old Testament. *"Judah did not return to me with all her heart, but only in pretence"* (verse 10). The people of Judah went through the motions of repentance in order to curry favour with their ruler, but their tears were about as sincere as a used car salesman's smile. They hadn't really learned from the destruction of their northern neighbour. They were the little sister of Israel in every way but one.[4] At least Israel never attempted to disguise its idolatry,

---

[1] A chronological reading of Jeremiah would probably be 1:1–19, 3:6–7:15, 2:1–3:5, 26:1–24, 7:16–20:18, 25:1–38, 46:1–51:64, 36:1–8, 45:1–5, 36:9–32, 35:1–19, 21:1–24:10, 27:1–31:40, 34:1–7, 37:1–10, 34:8–22, 37:11–38, 39:15–18, 32:1–33:26, 38:14–39:14, 40:1–44:30, 52:1–30 and 52:31–34. Don't be put off by this complexity. The Holy Spirit inspired Baruch to collate these prophecies by theme, so we can trust him to speak to us through their order.

[2] Jehoahaz (609 BC) and Jehoiakim (609–598 BC) were brothers, both sons of King Josiah (640–609 BC).

[3] You can read about Josiah's attempt at revival in 2 Kings 22:1–23:25 and 2 Chronicles 34:1–35:19.

[4] Ezekiel will expand on this picture of Israel and Judah being two promiscuous sisters in Ezekiel 23.

whereas Judah served the Lord in public as its national God, while continuing to worship foreign idols on the sly. The Lord therefore pronounces that *"Faithless Israel is more righteous than unfaithful Judah."* [5] These shocking verses are echoed by Revelation 3:15, where Jesus warns half-hearted Christians that *"you are neither cold nor hot. I wish you were either one or the other!"*

In 3:12–25, the Lord cries out to the survivors of the northern kingdom of Israel: Come back, all is forgiven! The fact that they have lost their land and been carried off to serve as slaves throughout the Assyrian Empire does not mean that the God of Israel has forgotten them. Their salvation depends on the Lord's faithfulness, not on their own, so it is not too late for them to ask him to perform his radical surgery on them. If they acknowledge their sin and rebellion for what it really is – spiritual adultery – then the Lord promises in 3:22 to slice away their cancer and cure their nation. The same husband who "divorced" them by sending them into exile in 3:8 will take them back in 3:14 as a beloved bride.[6] He will reveal himself once more as *"the salvation of Israel"* (verse 23) by rescuing a remnant of the northern kingdom alongside anyone who really repents in Judah.[7]

These are difficult verses to read, echoing the message of Hosea by likening the idolatry of God's people to spiritual adultery.[8] But beneath the talk of judgment lies an astonishing

---

[5] Verse 11. Zephaniah also prophesied during the reign of Josiah that the people of Judah were worshipping God in public and their pagan idols in secret, reneging on their pledge to serve the Lord alone (Zephaniah 1:4–6).

[6] The Lord is not expressing any lack of knowledge in 3:7 and 19–20. He is simply stating that repentance was the only logical path for Israel to take when it felt his scalpel. Persisting in sin was crass stupidity.

[7] In the Hebrew text of 3:12, the Lord says literally, "*I will not cause my face to fall on you.*" His presence is so glorious that sinful flesh cannot survive before his utter holiness (Leviticus 10:1–3 and 2 Samuel 6:6–7).

[8] It is clear from 3:9 that the adultery described here is primarily spiritual. Judah lusted after idols made of *stone and wood*, just as we can lust after polymer banknotes, bricks and mortar, and metal and rubber.

offer from a rejected husband. The breakaway northern kingdom had never had a godly king, yet the Lord promises to give them *"shepherds after my own heart, who will lead you with knowledge and understanding"* (verse 15). The northern tribes had failed to travel south over the border to worship the Lord at his Temple in Jerusalem, yet he promises to do more than simply bring them back to Zion. He will do away with the physical Temple altogether. *"People will no longer say, 'The ark of the covenant of the Lord.' It will never enter their minds or be remembered; it will not be missed, nor will another one be made."* Instead, as the prophet Ezekiel will explain in much more detail later, God will fill all of his followers with his Holy Spirit, transforming them into a new and living Temple.[9]

Jerusalem will not just be rebuilt with bricks and mortar. The Lord will create a living, breathing New Jerusalem out of all those who love and serve him – throughout Judah, throughout Israel and throughout the pagan nations of the world. Together, this New Jerusalem will be known as *The Throne of the Lord*. Babylon may appear to be on the rise, but God is planning to rule the world through the New Jerusalem. These verses are the New Testament in miniature.[10]

No wonder Jeremiah puts words in the mouths of the survivors of the northern kingdom in 3:22–25, encouraging them to turn back as a nation to the Lord.[11] Judah had merely play-acted at revival in the days of King Josiah, but now the Lord describes the fruit of real repentance. It is better than anything that Israel and Judah have ever known.

---

[9] The ark of the covenant was where God's presence dwelt (Exodus 30:6, Numbers 7:89). Now that God's presence dwells within every believer, it is irrelevant (1 Corinthians 3:16–17 and 2 Corinthians 6:16).

[10] That's why the Devil hates us reading Jeremiah. He wants the church to feel weak and helpless, instead of stepping into its true calling to be *the Throne of the Lord*, extending the Kingdom of God throughout the earth.

[11] The Hebrew word for *deception* in 3:23 is *sheqer*, the same word the Lord used to describe Judah's *pretence* in 3:10. False gods make empty promises, but salvation belongs to the Lord.

Sharp Blade, Soft Hearts
(Jeremiah 4:1–6:30)

*"Break up your unploughed ground… circumcise
your hearts, you people of Judah and inhabitants of
Jerusalem."*

(Jeremiah 4:3–4)

Charles Finney seemed to see spiritual revival wherever he
went. When he preached at Rochester, New York, in 1830, the
city underwent a total transformation.

> *The whole community was stirred. Religion was the
> topic of conversation in the house, in the shop, in the
> office and on the street. The only theatre in the city
> was converted into a livery stable; the only circus into
> a soap and candle factory. Grog shops were closed; the
> Sabbath was honoured; the sanctuaries thronged with
> happy worshippers; a new impulse was given to every
> philanthropic enterprise; the fountains of benevolence
> were opened, and men lived to good.*[1]

Charles Finney made no secret of his methods. He constantly
quoted from Hosea 10:12 – *"break up your unploughed ground;
for it is time to seek the Lord, until he comes and showers his
righteousness on you."*[2] Hard hearts can no more respond to

---

[1] Rochester resident Charles P. Bush, quoted in Raymond Edman's book
Finney Lives On (Wipf and Stock Publishers, 1971).
[2] Both of the quotations in this chapter come from the third of Charles Finney's
Lectures on Revival (1835).

God's offer of salvation than hardened soil can absorb rainfall. Whether we call it a ploughshare or a scalpel, revival starts when we say "yes" to God's call for us to place our hearts on his operating table.

Jeremiah 4:3-4 is a deliberate echo of Hosea 10:12. Having called the survivors of the northern kingdom of Israel to repentance in 4:1-2, the Lord now turns back to the southern kingdom of Judah, pleading with its people to embrace his surgeon's scalpel too. If they will allow him to plough up their hard hearts – or, to use the language of Deuteronomy 10:16 and 30:6, to circumcise their souls as they have done to their bodies – then they will enjoy the same blessings that he has just described for repentant northerners.[3] God will use all twelve tribes of Israel to call the nations to repentance too.[4]

In 4:5-31, the Lord explains how he softens hard hearts. Having already warned us in 1:13-16 that he will use a northern city as his surgeon's scalpel, he now takes the lion, one of the symbols of the city of Babylon, and declares that Judah will need to feel the sharpness of a lion's claws before its hard hearts are softened before the Lord.[5] It will take a national humiliation of some magnitude to convince Judah that the prophets of peace are preaching a pack of lies and that their true prophets are Zephaniah, Habakkuk and Jeremiah.[6] Only by a lightning series of Babylonian invasions will Judah be shaken out of its

---

[3] This picture is repeated in Jeremiah 9:25–26 and Romans 2:28–29. Paul explains in Colossians 2:11–12 that circumcision was a prophetic picture of our dying to sin so that we can be raised to new life with Christ.

[4] The salvation of non-believers is linked to the obedience of God's people. The extent to which the promise of 3:14–18 will be fulfilled throughout the earth is linked to how fully we respond to God's call in 4:1–4.

[5] They are clueless at doing good and ambidextrous at doing evil (4:22). They will not find repentance easy.

[6] Zephaniah prophesied from 640–628 BC, Habakkuk from 605 BC and Jeremiah from 627–585 BC. Ezekiel 23 will pick up on the language of 4:30, presenting Israel and Judah as two promiscuous sisters.

fatal complacency.[7] The Lord loves the people of Judah, so he is prepared to apply his surgeon's blade to their calloused hearts.[8]

In 5:1–31, the Lord repeats his determination to operate on the hard hearts of Judah. Note the echo of Abraham's prayer for Sodom in Genesis 18:20–33 as the Lord searches for a single sincere believer in the entire southern kingdom. Note the desperation also in Jeremiah's voice as he grasps with horror that the leaders and the people are equally stony-faced towards the Lord. Note the intensification of his warning, as he realizes that there is no guarantee that Judah will repent, even in the face of foreign invasion.[9] He turns the *lion* of chapter 4 into a *lion*, *wolf* and *leopard* in chapter 5 to convince the southern kingdom that it really has no other choice but major surgery.[10] The one who holds back the oceans on the beaches will not hold back Babylon forever. The one who sends rain on their farmlands will not tolerate their worship of the Canaanite imposter rain god Baal. The one who rules the world with justice will not ignore the way in which their rich oppress the poor.[11] The one who appoints priests and prophets will no longer stand for the way in which Judah's priests and prophets serve only themselves.[12]

---

[7] *Dan* was the northernmost city of Israel and the *hills of Ephraim* its southernmost region. Jeremiah 4:15 and 20 therefore predict Babylon's three speedy blitzkrieg invasions of Judah, in 605, 597 and 586 BC.

[8] Despite the fierce language in this chapter, the Lord's love comes through in 4:14, 19 and 27. Although he appears to undo his work of creation in 4:23–26, he has not forgotten the covenant he made with Abraham.

[9] Revelation 16:10–11 warns that the Lord's discipline only leads to repentance if it is met with humility.

[10] We see this love in 5:10, 18 and 25. Although Judah despises God's Word as a restrictive *yoke* and *chains* (5:5), his yoke is easy and it delivers us from the far heavier chains of sin (Proverbs 5:22 and Matthew 11:30).

[11] The Law of Moses calls down curses on the twelve tribes of Israel if they oppress the poor. Note how much God's judgment in 5:15–17 mirrors the curses that are described in Deuteronomy 28:49–51.

[12] Jesus appears to be quoting from Jeremiah 5:21 in Mark 8:18 when he warns his disciples that the first-century leaders of Israel are as misguided as the priests and prophets in the days of Jeremiah.

In 6:1–15, the Lord steps up his warning even further.[13] He will do whatever it takes to soften the hard hearts of the people of Judah.[14] Having warned them in 4:5–6 to flee the countryside into Jerusalem and its fortified cities, he now warns that Jerusalem and its fortresses are equally doomed to destruction.[15] *"This city must be punished"* because it is riddled with the cancer of sin yet refuses to listen to the Word of God. It believes the lies of its false prophets, who deny that radical surgery is needed. *"They dress the wound of my people as though it were not serious. "Peace, peace," they say, when there is no peace."*[16]

In 6:16–30, the Lord warns Judah that, not only will their cities be destroyed by the Babylonian army, but there will also be slaughter in the countryside for anyone who tries to flee. Their only hope of salvation is to look back to the days when their ancestors followed the Lord gladly and lived under his blessing. *"Stand at the crossroads and look; ask for the ancient paths, ask where the good way is, and walk in it."* Only then will they grasp how unimpressed the Lord is with their insincere sacrifices of expensive incense and of burnt offerings at his Temple.[17] Only then will they learn to weep over their sin as bitterly as a man grieving the death of his only son, fasting with dust on their

---

[13] Jeremiah echoes 4:4 by declaring literally in the Hebrew text of 6:10 that the ears of Judah are *uncircumcised* towards the Lord. Stephen picks up on this in Acts 7:51, just as Jesus picks up on Jeremiah 6:16 in Matthew 11:29.

[14] The Lord emphasizes this in 6:3–4 by using Hebrew words to describe the Babylonians that are normally reserved for God's people. Babylon's leaders are *shepherds* who *sanctify* their troops in readiness for battle.

[15] Jeremiah loves Hebrew wordplay, a great example of which can be found in 6:1–3. He calls for the trumpet (*tāqōa'*) to sound (*tāqa'*) in Tekoa (*teqōa'*) because the Babylonians are about to pitch (*tāqa'*) their tents there.

[16] Verse 14. The Lord makes this same accusation again in 8:11, 14:13 and 23:17, as well as in Ezekiel 13:10. God is looking for preachers who will proclaim the truth, even when it is unpopular: *Radical surgery is needed.*

[17] *Frankincense* and *calamus* were key ingredients of the sacred incense and anointing oil that the Lord had stipulated must be used in his Temple worship (Exodus 30:22–38).

heads and with sackcloth on their bodies. Only then will their hard hearts be ploughed up and softened so that their faith will pass the test in the crucible of Babylonian invasion.

Charles Finney insisted in one of his "Lectures on Revival" that *"My experience has taught me that the value of a revival to any community depends on the thoroughness with which the fallow ground is broken up in the hearts of Christians."* Jeremiah feels the same. He tells the people of Judah that the Lord will do what it takes to soften their hard hearts. He will even wield the sharp blade of Babylon.

Talisman
(Jeremiah 7:1–8:3)

"Do not trust in deceptive words and say, 'This is the temple of the Lord, the temple of the Lord, the temple of the Lord!'"

(Jeremiah 7:4)

Legend has it that the Tower of London will never fall while ravens live in its courtyards. Another legend says that Britain will never lose Gibraltar to Spain while monkeys live on its rock. On the estate where I holidayed in the Scottish Highlands last summer, there is a legend that the lairds will never lose their land while its waterfall keeps flowing. We can add another legend to this list from the book of Jeremiah. The people of Judah were convinced that Jerusalem would never fall while the Lord's Temple was still standing.

The third of the prophecies in the book of Jeremiah is perhaps the most famous. Chapters 7–10 are known collectively as the *Temple Sermon*. Just think for a moment how scary it must have been for Jeremiah to stand in the gateway of the Temple, from which his own disgraced priestly family had been excluded, in order to expose a cherished Jewish legend as a lie. Although these chapters are undated, there are such close parallels between chapters 7 and 26 that we can tell how viciously the crowds reacted to his words. Jeremiah almost lost his life by prophesying what is recorded for us here.[1]

In 7:2–11, Jeremiah warns the people of Judah that they are trusting in the Temple in vain. The Lord is *"the God of Israel"*

---

[1] Jeremiah prophesied these words at the New Gate, which connected the outer and inner courtyards of the Temple, sometime between 609 and 598 BC (26:10 and 36:10). He was therefore trapped by the angry crowds.

but he didn't shrink back from plunging his surgeon's blade into the corrupted northern kingdom when it was carried off into exile in 722 BC.[2] That ought to temper their trust in their own local legend: *"This is the temple of the Lord, the temple of the Lord, the temple of the Lord!"* Since Judah is worshipping the same foreign gods that scuppered the ten northern tribes, they ought not to imagine that their Temple is a lucky talisman, a guarantee of their protection by the Lord.

One of the big messages of the Bible is that disobedience in our daily lives renders our worship unacceptable to God.[3] Jeremiah therefore tells the people of Judah that God has witnessed their mistreatment of immigrants, orphans and widows. He has seen them steal from one another, lie to one another and be violent towards one another.[4] He does not regard their Temple worship services as gatherings of the faithful, but as safe spaces for scoundrels. *"Has this house, which bears my Name, become a den of robbers to you?"*[5]

I find these verses terrifying – not simply because I have been to the Temple Mount in Jerusalem and witnessed that the Temple is no longer there, but because Jesus quotes from these verses when confronting religious fakery many centuries later. As he overturns the tables of the moneychangers in the Temple courtyards, he quotes from 7:11 to declare that any religious gathering can become *"a den of robbers"*.[6] It makes me wonder what he makes of some of our church services today and how

[2] Jeremiah often refers to the Lord as *the God of Israel* in order to underline the fact that the southern kingdom consists of two tribes that have survived out of an original twelve.

[3] We may prefer to dismiss the sobering message of Proverbs 28:9 and Isaiah 1:13 as "a bit Old Testament", but the New Testament says it too. See 1 Timothy 2:8, James 3:9–10 and 5:16, and 1 Peter 3:7.

[4] The people of Judah break five of the Ten Commandments in 7:9 alone!

[5] Verse 11. The Lord speaks these words in love. He does not command the people of Judah to repent in order to restrict their lives. He says in 7:6 and 19 that worshipping false gods is only ever *to our own harm*.

[6] Jesus contrasts Jeremiah 7:11 with Isaiah 56:7 in Matthew 21:13, Mark 11:17 and Luke 19:46.

much of the church's decline in Europe and America is the work of the same surgeon's scalpel that operated on sinful Judah. After all, the only person who ever shuts down a church in the Bible is Jesus, not the Devil. Jesus warns us that he is sickened by fake Christianity.[7]

Nobody is more aware of this than Jeremiah. He is one of the priests of Anathoth, cursed and exiled from the Temple through the misdeeds of his ancestor Eli. Eli was both high priest and the thirteenth judge of Israel, yet he had led God's people very badly. He had turned a blind eye to the sins of the priests and worshippers at the Lord's Tabernacle in Shiloh. He had encouraged the people of Israel to treat the ark of the covenant as a lucky talisman, even taking it onto the battlefield against the Philistines in the futile belief that the Lord would never let his people lose with such a holy golden trinket in their hands. In 7:12–15, Jeremiah therefore draws on his own troubled family history to speak God's Word to Judah: *"Go now to the place in Shiloh where I first made a dwelling for my Name ... what I did to Shiloh I will now do to the house that bears my Name, the temple you trust in."*[8]

Prayer is so powerful that, in 7:16–20, the Lord has to forbid Jeremiah from praying that the Temple will be spared.[9] Far from offering any sanctuary to the religious hypocrites of Judah, the Lord announces that the Temple has become the epicentre of his anger.[10] He is so determined to destroy their lucky talisman that he doesn't want the prophet's prayers to get

---

[7] Revelation 2:5 and 3:16. I also find these two verses quite encouraging. If the Lord shuts down churches, not the Devil, then he is more than able to revive any church that surrenders to his surgeon's scalpel.

[8] Shiloh was a city in the hill country of Ephraim. After capturing the ark of the covenant, the Philistines destroyed the Tabernacle at Shiloh. See Joshua 18:1, 1 Samuel 1:9 and 4:1–22, and Psalm 78:60–64.

[9] God forbids Jeremiah from praying again, in 11:14 and 14:11–12, so that he can carry out his plan.

[10] There is a suggestion in 1 Peter 4:17 that the same may be true of corrupted churches today.

in the way of the operation. He has decreed that his surgeon's scalpel needs to fall.

In 7:21-29, the Lord calls Jeremiah to get up on the operating table too. Since the crowds refuse to listen to Jeremiah, he must take a knife to his own hair and throw his shorn locks away as a prophetic picture of what the Lord will do to Judah unless its people grasp that the Law of Moses is as much about obedience as it is about burnt offerings.[11] If they refuse to listen to the Word of God, either written in the Jewish Law or spoken by the prophets, then they will be cut off and rejected alongside their Temple talisman.[12]

In 7:30-8:3, the Lord points out that the Temple worshippers have filled the Temple Mount with idols, and that just below it, in the Valley of Ben Hinnom, they are murdering their own children as sacrifices to the evil idol Molek! They have no right to protest when the Lord says that he has decided to rename it the Valley of Slaughter and to fill it with their own corpses when the Babylonian army destroys their city and its Temple. Nor can it surprise them that he will punish Judah from the head down. The bones of their *kings*, *officials*, *priests* and *prophets* will be laid out on the top of the pile.[13]

It appears from chapter 26 that at this point Jeremiah was almost lynched by the indignant Temple worshippers, so let's see this as a natural pause. Before we move on, let's take a moment to reflect on our own worship. Let's take some time to identify our own lucky talismans and to surrender our own hearts completely to the Lord.

---

[11] The Hebrew word *nēzer* in 7:29 means literally *consecrated hair*. It may refer to the part of Jeremiah's hairstyle that identified him as a priest, proving his disdain for priesthood at this worthless Temple. Alternatively, since the Hebrew for *your* is feminine, it may speak punishment over adulterous Jerusalem.

[12] I find these verses surprisingly encouraging. The success of Jeremiah's ministry was not dependent on whether or not people listened to him. It depended on whether or not he kept on preaching faithfully.

[13] The Valley of Ben Hinnom is *Gehenna* in Greek, a name that Jesus used for *hell* (Matthew 5:22-30 and Mark 9:43-48). *Topheth* means *Fire Pit* and was the part of the valley where children were burned (Isaiah 30:33).

Get Real
(Jeremiah 8:4–10:25)

"They dress the wound of my people as though it were not serious. 'Peace, peace,' they say, when there is no peace."

(Jeremiah 8:11)

Jeremiah's famous *Temple Sermon* consists of three separate speeches. It is possible that he gave them on different occasions and that Baruch grouped them together for the sake of theme but, reading the narrative that accompanies these speeches in chapter 26, it seems more likely to me that Jeremiah was interrupted twice by the angry crowd.

We are told in chapter 26 that at the end of Jeremiah's first speech, in 7:1–8:3, the Temple worshippers attempted to lynch him. He was only saved when some of the elders of Judah noticed how similar his words sounded to those spoken by the prophet Micah before the destruction of Israel. As a result, the crowds withdrew in fear.

The second and third speeches, in 8:3–9:26 and 10:1–25, are marked out as separate speeches by a brief word of introduction. Having escaped from the clutches of the mob, Jeremiah did not go into hiding. He reassumed his place in the gateway of the Temple and carried on warning the people of Judah that it was time for them to get real.

In 8:4–13, he urges them to get real about their relationship with the Lord. People who fall down get up, and birds that migrate in winter come back in summer, but with Judah it is non-stop backsliding all the way. They fool themselves that they are wise, but they are not even smart enough to notice that their priests are manipulating the Law of Moses so that it says whatever their sinful listeners want to hear.[1] I find these verses very challenging, for there are plenty of Christian preachers who make a career out of explaining away certain Bible passages. How many sermons do we hear on Sunday that confront the sins of our flesh and call us to surrender to the Spirit of God alive inside us? How many of our preachers dare to warn us that radical surgery is needed? How many of them sound suspiciously similar to the preachers of Judah? *"They dress the wound of my people as though it were not serious. 'Peace, peace,' they say, when there is no peace."*

This is an important question, which repeats an earlier warning in 6:14. The Lord warns us literally in the Hebrew text of 8:13 that, whenever preachers seek to grow their congregations by smoothing over truth and speaking soothing lies, then *"I will gather away their gatherings."* The Lord promises that he will decimate deceitful churches.

In 8:14–17, Jeremiah calls those who dwell in the countryside to get real about their future. They will have to flee into the fortified cities of Judah. The hostile reaction of the crowd to this *Temple Sermon* is making the Babylonian invasion so inevitable that they can almost hear the snorting of its chariot horses among the ruins of Dan, the northernmost city of Israel before its destruction. Jeremiah declares that the God who sent a plague of snakes against the sinful Israelites in the desert has resolved to send the Babylonians against them now, serpents whose snakebite cannot be charmed away.[2]

In 8:18–9:2, Jeremiah weeps over a nation that refuses to weep for itself. He had hoped that the death of King Josiah in battle and the exile of King Jehoahaz to Egypt would jolt the people of Judah into repentance, but *"The harvest is past, the*

---

[1] The Lord declares in 8:8–9 that, whenever *scribes* or *teachers of the law* or *Bible teachers* twist the Scriptures to make it say what they want them to say, they are guilty of rejecting the Bible as the Word of God.

[2] Numbers 21:4–9. We are told in John 3:14–21 that the only serum for their venom is the blood of Jesus Christ.

summer has ended, and we are not saved." He had hoped that his countrymen would surrender gladly to the Lord's scalpel, so *"Why then is there no healing for the wound of my people?"*[3] These verses at the beginning of chapter 9 are some of the ones that earned Jeremiah his nickname, The Weeping Prophet. *"Oh, that my head were a spring of water and my eyes a fountain of tears! I would weep day and night for the slain of my people."* Don't misunderstand his longing to live in the desert, far away from the people of Judah. He loves the people of Judah, but he detests the sin that is destroying them.

As a result of his love for them, Jeremiah argues their case before the Lord in full earshot of the crowds of Temple worshippers. In 9:3-9, the Lord declares that they are liars through and through.[4] They do not sin out of laziness and passivity. They have worn themselves out learning active rebellion. Surely Jeremiah can see that their destruction is well deserved. The prophet protests in 9:10 that it seems excessive. Dissatisfied with the Lord's response in 9:11, he protests a second time in 9:12, so the Lord enumerates the sins of Judah a little further in 9:13-16. They have broken the Law of Moses and they have worshipped false idols, as even Jeremiah is forced to concede.[5]

In 9:17-22, the Lord pleads with the women of Judah who will be raped and widowed. In 9:23-26, he begs the wise men and the warriors and the wealthy to stop relying on their own strength. Let them boast instead in their willingness to accept his surgeon's scalpel. Let them place

---

[3] Verse 22. The resin of the balsam trees of Gilead, to the east of the River Jordan, was used as medicine all over the world (Genesis 37:25). Jeremiah knows deep down that the problem lies with the patient, not the doctor.

[4] The Hebrew word for *deceiver* in 9:4 is the root of the name *Jacob*. The Lord therefore says literally that *"every brother Jacobs like Jacob"*. They have become a nation like their forefather at his worst, in Genesis 27.

[5] Jeremiah 9:15 deliberately echoes Deuteronomy 29:18. Because the leaders of Judah have failed to recognize that idolatry is *bitter food* and *poisoned water*, they will have their fill of both during their exile in Babylon.

their complete confidence in his *loving kindness*, in his *justice*, in his *righteousness* and in their willingness let him circumcise their hearts, as they have done to their bodies, as a sign of their commitment to live as his happy worshippers.[6]

The start of chapter 10 indicates that Jeremiah was interrupted a second time by the crowd. When he resumes, it is to point out the enormous difference between the Lord and the foreign idols that are cluttering his courtyards. God created humans; humans create idols. God speaks to his people; idols are as silent as a scarecrow in a vegetable field. God carries his people; idols force people to carry them.[7] God is the eternal King who created all nations; idols are lifeless, carved out of materials that rot and decay with time. Jeremiah speaks all of his prophecies in Hebrew, except for a single verse 10:11, which he speaks in Aramaic, the international language of the day, in order to proclaim to every nation of the world that the God of Israel is far greater than their idols.[8]

In 10:19–25, Jeremiah gets real himself. He finally accepts that the spiritual cancer within Judah is incurable unless God operates on it using the scalpel of Babylon. He no longer prays for the Lord to hold back his surgery, but prays instead for the Lord to remove only as much flesh as is absolutely necessary. He also prays that the Lord will deal with the pagan nations, so that he can quickly restore the fortunes of Judah.

The *Temple Sermon* is over. The Lord has got real with Judah, and Jeremiah has got real with the Lord. As silence falls again over the Temple courtyards, the only question is how many of the people of Judah will humble themselves and get real with the Lord too.

---

[6] These verses echo 4:3–4 and 6:10. Paul quotes from them in 1 Corinthians 1:31 and 2 Corinthians 10:17. He also explains in Romans 2:25–29 and Colossians 2:11–12 that Jewish circumcision of the body was meant to be a prophetic picture of our dying to sin and self-confidence in order to be raised to new life with Christ.
[7] The Lord carries his worshippers in Exodus 19:4, Deuteronomy 1:31 and Jeremiah 29:14. Idols force their worshippers to carry them in Isaiah 46:1 and 7.
[8] Note how much Jeremiah 10 echoes the words of Isaiah 40 and Psalm 115.

Covenant
(Jeremiah 11:1–17)

"Listen to the terms of this covenant and tell them to the people of Judah and to those who live in Jerusalem."

(Jeremiah 11:2)

By the time most readers arrive at the beginning of Jeremiah 11, they are feeling pretty punch-drunk. We have only read three of the ten speeches that make up the first section of Jeremiah, but such relentless repetition of the same dire diagnosis can leave us feeling like a boxer on the ropes.[1] If that describes how you are feeling, then well done. It means that you are grasping the message of Jeremiah. You are meant to feel that way.

Baruch's decision to collate the prophecies of Jeremiah according to their theme, rather than the order in which he prophesied them, was quite literally inspired. The Holy Spirit led him to do this, because the Lord is more concerned about evoking an emotional response to the words of Jeremiah than sketching out a detailed chronology. That's one of the reasons why most of its chapters are much longer than those of the other books of the Bible. Psalms and Isaiah contain more chapter divisions but, word for word, the book of Jeremiah is the longest book in the Bible. Baruch could have abridged these prophecies, but he chose not to do so in order to make us feel punch-drunk now. It required such a tirade to make us stop to consider whether we need radical surgery too.

---

[1] Jeremiah's ten speeches are 2:1–3:5, 3:6–6:30, 7:1–10:25, 11:1–13:27, 14:1–15:21, 16:1–17:18, 17:19–27, 18:1–20:18, 21:1–24:10 and 25:1–38.

In June 2015, the British magazine *The Spectator* ran a feature on the Western church that could have come straight out of the history books of Judah.

> *It's often said that Britain's church congregations are shrinking, but that doesn't come close to expressing the scale of the disaster now facing Christianity in this country. Every ten years the census spells out the situation in detail: between 2001 and 2011 the number of Christians in Britain fell by 5.3 million – about 10,000 a week. If that rate of decline continues, the mission of St Augustine to the English, together with that of the Irish saints to the Scots, will come to an end in 2067. That is the year in which the Christians who have inherited the faith of their British ancestors will become statistically invisible... [They are] one generation away from extinction."*

The Spectator is by no means a Christian publication, but it places its finger on the church's problem. A fish rots from the head down. *The Spectator* calls on church leaders to lead their congregations back to radical obedience to God's Word:

> *They're led by middle-managers who are frightened of their own shadows. They run up the white flag long before the enemy comes down from the hills... It can't be stressed too often that the secularization that happens inside churches is as important as the sort that happens outside them.*[2]

That's why we mustn't tire of the long parade of prophecies in this first section of Jeremiah. We are not reading somebody else's

[2] Damian Thompson, *2067: The End of British Christianity* (*The Spectator*, 13 June 2015).

mail. The Lord still says these things to Christians all around the world today. The key concept in Jeremiah's fourth speech, which runs from 11:1–13:27, is that of *covenant* – the Hebrew word *berīth* was used to describe a *peace treaty* between two feuding warlords, an *alliance* between two rulers or a *marriage* between a man and a woman. The Lord asks Jeremiah to re-examine the terms of the covenant he made with Israel at Mount Sinai, because it was a mixture of all three.

It was like a marriage covenant because both parties pledged themselves to one another. The Lord became *"the God of Israel"* and the Israelites became the people of God. During King Josiah's failed revival, the southern kingdom of Judah had renewed its marriage vows towards the Lord in the Temple courtyards in 2 Kings 23:1–3, which is why the Lord accuses them so often of committing spiritual adultery.

It was also like a peace treaty and a military alliance, since he cleansed his people from the sin that set them at odds with him, and his people declared that they were now siding with God in waging war against their sin.[3] They even called down blessings and curses on themselves in the final chapters of Deuteronomy, based on how much they remained true to their treaty promise never again to regard any foreign god or any cherished sin as their true friend and ally.

All of this forms the background to 11:1–8, where the Lord tells Jeremiah to remind Judah of the terms of his covenant with them. Obedience to God was not in the small print. It was written in large letters. The Law is therefore no more a lucky talisman for Judah than is their Temple. Flaunting the Lord's covenant with their nation will only curse them, never save them.[4]

---

[3] This is why Jeremiah echoes Deuteronomy 4:20 and 1 Kings 8:51 by describing Israel's time in Egypt as an *iron-smelting furnace*. Witnessing the dire consequences of idolatry had helped the Israelites to affirm their alliance with God.

[4] Paul repeats this in Romans 3:20 and Galatians 3:10–14, explaining in Romans 10:4 that we can only be saved through faith that Jesus has fulfilled all of the terms of God's covenant on our behalf.

In 11:9–13, the Lord tells Jeremiah to explain why. The Hebrew word *pārar* in 11:10 indicates that the Lord's covenant with the people of Judah has been *broken* or *violated,* or *rendered null and void* as a result of their spiritual adultery. They have run after the false gods of both Egypt and Canaan, of both their old home and their new. They have bowed down to as many idols as there are towns in Judah and they have built as many shrines to Baal as there are streets in Jerusalem.[5]

In 11:14–17, the Lord therefore forbids Jeremiah a second time from praying against the destruction of Jerusalem. God has already made up his mind to use the Babylonians as his surgeon's scalpel, so the prophet's prayers must not get in the way of his operation.[6] He reassures Jeremiah that Judah is still his *beloved*, but he warns that it will take far more than offering consecrated meat on the altar at their Temple to save them. His blade will need to slice into their own flesh before they offer real repentance towards the Lord.

Once they do so, however, they will immediately discover the true purpose of the Law of Moses. When King Josiah studied its chapters, in 622 BC, the terms of God's covenant brought his heart to real repentance. We are told in 2 Kings 22 that *"When the king heard the words of the Book of the Law, he tore his robes"*, and that the Lord was quick to forgive him when he did so. *"Because your heart was responsive and you humbled yourself before the Lord when you heard what I have spoken against this place and its people – that they would become a curse and be laid waste – and because you tore your robes and wept in my presence, I also have heard you, declares the Lord."*

When the people of Judah study the terms of God's covenant, they will find that the Lord is still eager to teach people real repentance and to forgive them for their many sins.

---

[5] Jeremiah 11:13 echoes 2:28 and 2 Chronicles 28:24.

[6] Jeremiah 7:16 and 11:14 are very encouraging. Our prayers must be very powerful for the Lord to need to tell Jeremiah not to pray so that he will be unhindered in his plan to revive his people.

Covenant-Breakers (Jeremiah 11:18–13:27)

"This is your lot, the portion I have decreed for you,"
declares the Lord, "because you have forgotten me
and trusted in false gods."

(Jeremiah 13:25)

Over the years, I've had some pretty hostile feedback to my preaching. I've been heckled in the street. I've been trolled on Twitter. I've been no-platformed by the government. But I have never experienced anything like the reaction that Jeremiah received when he began to prophesy about God's covenant. Members of his own family tried to kill him.

In 11:18–23, we discover that the priests of Anathoth were far from pleased when one of their own number began prophesying that only radical surgery could save their nation. Eventually they decided that the only way to silence such prophecy was to murder the prophet. Chop down a tree and its fruit stops growing. Chop down a prophet and there is no more talk of surgeon's scalpels and of operating tables. But it isn't easy to plot against a prophet who receives revelations from the Lord. Instead of being easy to kill, like a lamb at the slaughterhouse, Jeremiah turns and prophesies against their plan.[1] He declares that, even for a family cursed through Eli and exiled through Abiathar, this latest conspiracy represents a new low. It proves that they are amongst the vilest covenant-breakers in Judah, and God is about to call time on their cursed family.

---

[1] Jeremiah commits his cause into the Lord's hands instead of fighting his own corner, both here in 11:20 and in 20:12. Expect to be hated for proclaiming the gospel, and never lash out at those who hate you.

In 12:1–4, Jeremiah complains to the Lord that he is surrounded by covenant-breakers.[2] How can the Lord allow such wicked people to prosper all around him in the land? Jeremiah models something for us here by asking this question with great humility, taking the default position that the Lord's ways must be right and that his own misgivings must be wrong.[3] *"You are always righteous, Lord ... yet ... why?"*[4]

In 12:5–17, the Lord responds. His opening statement says it all. *"If you have raced with men on foot and they have worn you out, how can you compete with horses?"*[5] It's a poetic way of telling Jeremiah that he hasn't seen the half of the problem! If he is confused that the Lord should allow his own family members to plot against him, then how will he cope when Lord allows the sinful Babylonians to destroy the Temple and to turn the Promised Land into a wasteland?[6] How will he feel when Judah's neighbours exploit the situation by invading its territory, and when the sinful Babylonians go on to annex those nations too? Perhaps worst of all, how will he cope when God decides to save many of the survivors of those pagan nations and to offer them a place among his holy people?[7]

---

[2] The difference between the godly and the wicked is not in what they say. Jeremiah points out that the Lord's name is forever on the lips of his enemies – it's just that their actions prove he is not their Lord at all.

[3] Jeremiah is a great man of prayer, whose painfully honest prayers are meant to serve as models for our own prayers. See especially 1:6, 4:10, 10:23–25, 11:20, 12:1–6, 14:19–22, 15:15–18, 17:14–18, 18:19–23 and 20:7–18.

[4] The books of Job, Psalms and Habakkuk are full of such confused questions. They reassure us that God's silence never means that he is oblivious to injustice and to people's sin (Psalm 50:21).

[5] The second half of this verse is perhaps best translated, *"If you only feel secure in a land of peace then how will you cope when the River Jordan is in flood?"*

[6] The Lord explains to us in 12:11 that churches fail *"because there is no one who cares"*. The issue is not so much the sins of the majority, but the lack of a faithful praying minority. See also Ezekiel 22:30.

[7] This is normal Christianity. One of the clues that the Lord gives us in 12:13 that a church may be backslidden is that it wears itself out to win converts but finds it reaps very little fruit for all its exertions.

In 13:1–11, the Lord commands Jeremiah to act out a prophetic drama about how God regards the covenant-breakers of Judah. Jeremiah is to buy a belt made of linen, the material that was used to create a priest's robes and which represents Judah's commitment to God's covenant and its call for them to serve him as a nation of priests, displaying his renown and honour to the pagan world.[8] Jeremiah is told to wear the linen belt for several days before hiding it in a crevice in the rocks down by the River Euphrates on the way to Babylon.[9] Sometime later, he is told to retrieve his mouldy belt so that its corruption can serve as a vivid picture of how useless covenant-breakers are to God's plan to reveal his glory to the world by blessing them.

In 13:12–14, the Lord inspires Jeremiah to prophesy that wineskins are meant to be full of wine. When the people of Judah protest that he is stating the obvious, Jeremiah warns that it is equally obvious that they will soon all be drunk on the cup of the Lord's anger. He will prophesy in much greater detail about this terrible cup in chapter 25.

In 13:15–27, the Lord ends this speech about covenant-breaking by confronting the rebellious kings of Judah. This prophecy is undated, but the reference in 13:18 to a king ruling alongside a *queen mother* points us to 2 Kings 24:8, where we are told that Queen Nehushta, the widow of King Jehoiakim (609–598 BC), remained the true power behind the throne during the three-month reign of her eighteen-year-old son, King Jehoiachin (598–597 BC). Jeremiah therefore calls both King Jehoiachin and his mother to take their crowns off their heads, to come down from their high thrones and to lead their covenant-breaking nation back to the Lord in real repentance.

Jeremiah knows that they will refuse to do so. The new king is too busy boasting about how many subjects he has,

---

[8] Exodus 19:5–6, Leviticus 16:3–4 and Revelation 19:8.

[9] The Hebrew word *perāth* could potentially refer to a city named Perath, but in every other occurrence of the word throughout the Old Testament, it always refers to the River *Euphrates*.

comparing himself to a shepherd with countless sheep in his sheepfolds. Jehoiachin has no time to consider his nation's covenant with Lord because he has struck his own peace treaty with King Nebuchadnezzar and the generals of Babylon. The Lord laughs at the idea of a "special relationship" in 13:21. A covenant with Babylon cannot help them if they break their covenant with the Lord. Sure enough, we are told in 2 Kings 24:8–15 that the Babylonian army invaded suddenly from the north, deposing King Jehoiachin and dragging both him and his mother into exile in Babylon.

Jeremiah therefore ends this prophecy by declaring that the royal family of Judah are even greater covenant-breakers than the rest of Judah.[10] *"Can an Ethiopian change his skin or a leopard its spots?"* Of course they can't, and nor can King Jehoiachin and Queen Nehushta change their sinful habits now. They have broken the covenant that God made with their nation, so God's covenant is now about to break them.

---

[10] The Hebrew for *you* in 13:20–23 alternates between the plural and the feminine singular. Some readers assume it must refer to Jehoiachin and Nehushta (based on 13:18), while others assume it must refer to the city of Jerusalem (based on 13:27). Both might be true, because both were inveterate covenant-breakers.

Rain God
(Jeremiah 14:1–15:21)

*This is the word of the Lord that came to Jeremiah
concerning the drought.*

(Jeremiah 14:1)

The philosopher George Santayana famously argued that *"Those
who cannot remember the past are condemned to repeat it."*[1]
Like Adolf Hitler, invading Russia and losing an empire in the
exact same way as Napoleon, we forget the lessons of the past at
a heavy price. I know that. You know that. But, sadly, the leaders
of Judah didn't seem to know it at all.

Two hundred and fifty years before the prophet Jeremiah
began his ministry, King Ahab had come to the throne of Israel.
Married to a Canaanite princess named Jezebel, he soon started
worshipping the Canaanite rain god Baal. When he tried to turn
Baal into the national god of the northern kingdom, the Lord
sent the prophet Elijah to confront him with his sin. Since Baal
was supposedly the rain god, the Lord would expose him as a
worthless idol by ensuring that not a drop of rain would fall on
Israel for three years. This would spell short-term disaster for
the agrarian economy of Israel, but it would bring about their
long-term deliverance. The drought would serve as a surgeon's
scalpel to slice away their idolatry. Sure enough, when they
repented, the rains began to fall.[2]

The leaders of Judah had forgotten this, so Jeremiah
delivers the fifth of the ten speeches in part one of his book in

---

[1] George Santayana says this in volume one of *The Life of Reason* (1905).
[2] 1 Kings 16:29–18:46. The Apostle Paul explains that idols are both *deceiving
demons* and at the same time *nothing at all* (1 Corinthians 8:4 and 10:19–21).

the midst of a similar drought.[3] The rain had stopped falling on the land of Judah. Its wells were empty. Its fields were dry, cracked and cropless. Even the animals were abandoning their young so that they could keep whatever precious little food they discovered to themselves. As in the days of Ahab and Elijah, the rain god Baal had proved to be a false friend, a very idle idol.

In 14:7-9, Jeremiah prays for the Lord to have mercy on his thirsty people, but note what he says in his prayer.[4] He makes no attempt to deny his nation's sinfulness and rebellion – this terrible drought is totally deserved – but he reminds the Lord that his global reputation is inextricably bound up in the fortunes of the land that bears his name. Every foreigner knows that another name for Yahweh is *"the hope of Israel"* and that, against all odds, he saved his people from the army of Assyria in the days of King Hezekiah. If that same nation now dies for lack of rainfall from the heavens, where Yahweh dwells, then those foreigners will naturally conclude that the God of Israel has become *"a warrior powerless to save"*. If the Babylonian army sweeps across the border and finds the thirsty army of Judah wasting away in its barracks, then will they not regard him as *"a man taken by surprise"* – not so much the Lord as an absentee landlord?[5]

In 14:10-12, the Lord gives his prophet a very sobering reply. First, he calls the people of Judah *"this people"*, instead of *"my people"*. Second, he quotes verbatim from Hosea 8:13 in order to pass the same sentence on idolatrous Judah as he passed on idolatrous Israel. Next, he tells Jeremiah to stop

---

[3] The ten speeches in part one of Jeremiah are 2:1–3:5, 3:6–6:30, 7:1–10:25, 11:1–13:27, 14:1–15:21, 16:1–17:18, 17:19–27, 18:1–20:18, 21:1–24:10 and 25:1–38.

[4] Jeremiah is not disobeying the Lord's command to him in 7:16 and 11:14. He is not praying that judgment will not fall on Judah, but that the Lord will come near to rescue his people out of it.

[5] This fifth speech is undated, but the drought must have occurred before 592 BC, when Ezekiel says God's presence left the land of Judah. For now, at least, Jeremiah can still pray: *"You are among us, Lord"* (verse 9).

praying for the well-being of Judah. He has already forbidden him from praying that Judah will not fall (7:16) and that its Temple will be spared (11:14), so now he forbids him even from praying for respite from its pain.[6] Judah will not repent unless it feels the surgeon's scalpel, since only radical surgery can save this patient. To emphasize this, for the first time the Lord uses the phrase *"sword, famine and plague"*– a terrible trio that appear together fifteen times in the book of Jeremiah.

In 14:13, Jeremiah protests that the people of Judah have no idea that this drought is punishment from the Lord. Their prophets have told them that he is happy with them, promising peace and prosperity. The drought will not foster repentance, but rebellion.

In 14:14–18, the Lord says that the purpose of the drought is to root out such liars. The drought will expose such false prophets to be liars, consigning them to the scrapheap, like the prophets of Baal that Elijah put to the sword on Mount Carmel. One of the curses in the covenant that the Lord made with Israel at Mount Sinai was that drought would come upon the disobedient, so Judah will be forced to confess that no sweet-talking prophet can remove Leviticus 26:18–20 and Deuteronomy 28:22–24 from the Bible.

In 14:19–22, Jeremiah prays, not for respite from God's judgment, but a prayer of genuine repentance for Judah's sin. He reminds the Lord that the covenant that he made with Israel at Mount Sinai can wash away his people's guilt, so let the Lord not become a covenant-breaker too! Jeremiah confesses freely that Baal is not the real rain god. The Lord alone sends the rains. He is the true hope of Israel.

In 15:1–9, the Lord responds, and what he says is not encouraging. He declares that, even if the great intercessors Moses and Samuel convened a prayer meeting for Judah, he

---

[6] We can tell that the Lord is not forbidding Jeremiah from praying at all, because he prays in 14:19–22! The Lord is telling him to pray in line with his own perfect will – not for respite, but for real repentance.

would not change his mind about destroying her.[7] Saving the southern kingdom from the army of Assyria during the days of King Hezekiah had merely paved the way for his successor, King Manasseh, to fill the Temple courtyards with foreign idols and to sacrifice his children in the fire to Molek. The Lord has performed enough minor operations on Judah to prove that only radical surgery can save this patient.[8] In 15:10, we discover how right he is, when Jeremiah complains about people's angry reaction to these words of warning. Even in the midst of drought, they still refuse to listen.[9]

In 15:11–21, the Lord therefore uses Jeremiah as a model of how he will treat anyone who finally listens to his Word. Jeremiah has sinned, so he will feel God's judgment (15:11–14), but the Lord has noticed how different he is from his neighbours. Deep down, he delights in obedience to God's Word (15:15–18). If Jeremiah leads the way for Judah by repenting of his own sin, then the Lord promises to deliver him from the destruction of Jerusalem so that he can lead his nation back to the true God of Israel (15:19–21).[10]

---

[7] See Exodus 32:11–14, Numbers 14:13–20, 1 Samuel 7:5–10, Psalm 99:6, and Ezekiel 14:14 and 20.

[8] God had promised Abraham that he would make Israel as numerous as the grains of sand on the seashore (Genesis 22:17). Saying the same thing about Judah's widows in 15:8 is a terrible inversion of that blessing.

[9] Gospel preachers need to be prepared to feel people's hatred before they see people's repentance. We will only see the fruit of Matthew 24:14 if we are willing to endure the hatred of Matthew 24:9.

[10] The Hebrew for you in 15:11–14 and 19–21 is masculine singular. It cannot refer to Jerusalem (feminine) or Judah (plural). Jeremiah is to show Judah what it truly means to bear the name of the Lord (14:9 and 15:16).

Radical Decision
(Jeremiah 16:1–17:18)

This is what the Lord says: "Cursed is the one who trusts in man… But blessed is the one who trusts in the Lord."

(Jeremiah 17:5, 7)

Aron Ralston is famous for one thing. He didn't shrink back when he saw that a radical decision was needed. If you have ever watched the Danny Boyle movie *127 Hours*, then you know what Ralston did after a canyoneering accident in Utah in April 2003. Finding that his right arm had become trapped beneath an immoveable boulder, and knowing that he was too hidden away for anyone to come and rescue him, he broke the bones in his own arm and cut it off with his pocket knife in order to save himself from dying in the canyon. In his autobiography, he writes about the euphoria of that radical decision. He describes the world as feeling like a different place. He describes an exhilarating sense of freedom. He remembers staring back at the wall of the canyon, where he had etched "RIP" and his name underneath, and excitedly shouting "I am free!"[1]

Jeremiah's sixth speech is all about making similar, radical decisions. If the Lord insists that major surgery is needed, then following him means behaving as Aron Ralston did.

In 16:1–4, the Lord commands Jeremiah not to get married like all of his friends. This would be sad in our own culture, but for the marriage-obsessed ancient world it must have felt like

---

[1] Aron Ralston in *127 Hours: Between a Rock and a Hard Place* (Simon and Schuster, 2004).

a death sentence. An unmarried, childless man was regarded as an outcast from society, a rejected soul, the walking dead. Instead of arguing, however, the prophet embraces this as a way of proving to people that he truly believes what he is preaching. The women and children of Judah really are about to fall to plague, famine and sword.[2]

In 16:5-7, the Lord forbids Jeremiah from entering any house where there is mourning, since those who die now will turn out to be the lucky ones.[3] In 16:8-9, he also forbids Jeremiah from entering any house where there is feasting, since there is nothing left to celebrate in Judah. This effectively rings a death knell over the prophet's social life, but he accepts God's call to isolation. If the Lord wants him to become a loner as well as a singleton, then he will make that radical decision even more quickly than Aron Ralston made his.

In 16:10-18, the Lord assures Jeremiah that such radical separation from his neighbours will gain the greatest hearing for the message of salvation that has been entrusted to him. When people see how seriously he takes his own words, they will begin to take them seriously too. They will ask him to tell them more about the imminent destruction of Judah and about the Lord's promise to bring any repentant exiles home.[4]

Martyn Lloyd-Jones believes that this is a vital lesson for us to learn from Jeremiah. He argues that:

---

[2] Perhaps it is a sign that we are equally marriage-obsessed that we preach very little on the words of Jesus and of the Apostle Paul – both single men – which state that God often calls people to singleness in order that they might be able to serve him better. See Matthew 19:10–12 and 1 Corinthians 7:1–40.

[3] Isaiah 57:1. In the Jewish Law, the Lord had already forbidden the pagan practices of shaving heads and of self-harming as an expression of grief for the dead (16:6, Deuteronomy 14:1–2).

[4] Repaying Judah *double* for its sins in 16:18 and 17:18 does not indicate unfairness, but restitution. See Exodus 22:9, Isaiah 40:2 and Revelation 18:6. Note also that the promise of 16:14–15 is repeated almost verbatim in 23:7–8. Babylon will become a second Egypt for God's people, but with an even greater Exodus.

The glory of the gospel is that when the Church is absolutely different from the world, she invariably attracts it. It is then that the world is made to listen to her message, though it may hate it at first. That is how revival comes. That must also be true of us as individuals. It should not be our ambition to be as much like everybody else as we can, though we happen to be Christian, but rather to be as different from everybody who is not a Christian as we can possibly be. Our ambition should be to be like Christ, the more like Him the better, and the more like Him we become, the more we shall be unlike everybody who is not a Christian.[5]

Suddenly, the Hebrew text turns from prose to poetry. In 16:19–20, Jeremiah prays that the Lord will save the pagan nations along with the exiles of Judah.

In 16:21–17:4, the Lord replies that this is precisely what he plans to do. But since sin has been engraved on the hearts of the people of Judah in the same way that a scribe engraves words on a stone tablet with his metal chisel, the Lord first needs to scrape away those deep-seated sins from their hearts with his metal surgeon's scalpel.[6]

In 17:5–8, the Lord calls Jeremiah's hearers to make their own radical decision. Will they *trust in man* and be cursed with poverty, even in the good times, along with anybody else who relies on the forces of this world instead of on God's Spirit? Or will they *trust in the Lord* and be blessed with fruitfulness, even during drought, along with anybody else who walks by faith in God and not by earthly wisdom?[7] How we answer this question

---

[5] Martyn Lloyd-Jones in his *Studies in the Sermon on the Mount* (IVP, 1959).

[6] The Apostle Paul does not quote directly from 17:1 in 2 Corinthians 3:3, but he appears to have it in mind when he says that Jesus writes on our hearts by his Holy Spirit. Jeremiah 17:3–4 is largely a repeat of 15:13–14.

[7] This is an amazing promise. Even amidst national church decline, repentant churches will still grow.

is vital. The Lord would have us repent, not just of our sin, but of our self-confidence too.[8]

In 17:9–10, the Lord warns that *"The heart is deceitful above all things and beyond cure. Who can understand it?"* We do not merely need to repent of reliance upon human strength, but also of reliance on human intellect.[9] Only the Lord can tell what is truly happening in our lives, so being saved requires us to repent of our own second-guessing and to accept his perfect verdict instead. It isn't the wise that God prospers, but the humble.[10]

In 17:11–18, Jeremiah therefore ends with prayer. He makes his own radical decision. He will not be like his neighbours, who cling so foolishly to the things of this world, like a partridge hatching another bird's eggs and then wondering why the chicks fly away. Jeremiah is prepared to serve the Lord alone if need be. He is determined to look to him as *"the hope of Israel"* and to drink from his Spirit as *"the spring of living water"*.[11] Like Aron Ralston in his secluded canyon, the prophet says "yes" to the surgeon's scalpel. He asks the Lord to do whatever it takes to heal him of his share in the corrupted flesh of Judah.

Nineteenth-century philosopher Henry David Thoreau encourages his readers that, *"If a man does not keep pace with his companions, perhaps it is because he hears a different drummer. Let him step to the music which he hears, however*

---

[8] This is one of the Bible's biggest themes. See Judges 7:1–7, Isaiah 40:29–31 and 2 Corinthians 12:7–10.

[9] The Hebrew word for *deceitful* in 17:9 is the root of the name *Jacob*, just as the Hebrew word for *man* in 17:5 is the root of the name *Adam*. We can only find true wisdom and true strength in Jesus Christ.

[10] This is also one of the Bible's biggest themes. See Matthew 11:25, Romans 1:22 and 1 Corinthians 1:17–2:16.

[11] Jeremiah 17:13 looks back to 2:13 and forward to Ezekiel 47:1–12, John 4:10–15 and John 7:37–39.

measured or far away."[12] Jeremiah has resolved to march to the beat of a very different drum, and he calls us to join him in his radical decision to serve the Lord.

RADICAL DECISION (JEREMIAH 16:1–17:18)

---

[12] Henry David Thoreau says this in his book *Walden* (1854).

*"Keep the Sabbath day holy by not
doing any work on it."*

(Jeremiah 17:24)

56

The seventh of the ten speeches that form the first section of
the book of Jeremiah is by far the shortest. Its message is also
the simplest. The Lord tells Jeremiah to put some flesh on his
call for the people of Judah to make a radical decision. They can
tell very easily whether or not they have repented of the self-
reliance that the Lord condemns in 17:5–8. He has created a
weekly test for them, and its name is *the Sabbath*.

The Hebrew word *shābath* means simply *to rest*. It is used
right at the start of the Bible, when the Lord declares that Day
Seven of Creation will be a rest day to enable all of his creatures
to enjoy what he has made. Even before he made his covenant
with the Israelites at Mount Sinai, the Lord explained that this
was to be an enduring principle for all those who follow him.
Later, one of the Ten Commandments was a call to rest from
work on the seventh day of each week.[1] As a result, by the
time of Jeremiah, the idea of Sabbath was hardwired deep into
the consciousness of Judah. But that didn't mean that people
actually observed it. They hadn't repented of their self-reliance
at all.

In 17:19, the Lord sends Jeremiah down to each of the
busy gateways through which people enter and exit the walls of
Jerusalem. We do not know for certain which gate was known

---

[1] Genesis 2:2–3, and Exodus 16:19–30, 20:8–11 and 31:12–17.

as the Gate of the People, but it doesn't really matter because the Lord tells Jeremiah to *"stand also at all the other gates of Jerusalem"*. These were the busy highways used by traders to bring their wares in and out of the city, so the prophet's message is equally relevant to any of the gates that are open on the Sabbath. The people of Jerusalem are failing God's weekly test to reveal whether they are relying on their own strength or on his. By conducting trade on the Sabbath, they are revealing that they have forgotten its sacred meaning, described in Psalm 46:10: *"Be still, and know that I am God."*

Many modern readers assume that such talk about the Sabbath has no relevance to us. After all, Christians are no longer under the Jewish law. Jesus declared that *"The Sabbath was made for man, not man for the Sabbath."*[2] But that's precisely Jeremiah's point. The Lord did not create the Sabbath to be observed in the manner of the first-century Pharisees. Their nit-picking definitions of what constituted "work" actually made observing the day of rest more exhausting than the other six days! God did not create man to be burdened by the Sabbath, but he created the Sabbath as a way of relieving him from carrying on his own shoulders a burden God alone can carry. It was a weekly reminder, a litmus test of whether or not a person had surrendered his proud self-reliance to the Lord.

Jeremiah informs the kings, merchants and people of Judah that they are failing this simple test every weekend. They are too afraid to pause their labours on the seventh day because, deep down, they believe their provision and prosperity depend on the strength of their own hands. They are among those the Lord curses in 17:5: *"Cursed is the one who trusts in man, who draws strength from mere flesh and whose heart turns away from the Lord."*

These verses ought to make us feel rather uneasy too. While it isn't clear that Scripture commands us to treat Sunday as the Christian equivalent of the Sabbath, Scripture is clear that

---

[2] Mark 2:27, Romans 6:14, Galatians 5:18 and Colossians 2:14–17.

we must continue to observe the Sabbath principle.[3] It teaches us that the God who never needs to take a lunch break, or a recovery day, or a good night's sleep, has created us to require all three.[4] He did so in order to give us daily, nightly and weekly opportunities to down our tools as an expression of our reliance upon the Lord for our daily needs. Our willingness or unwillingness to embrace the God-given limits of our existence is a test of whether or not we are among those that he blesses in 17:7: *"Blessed is the one who trusts in the Lord, whose confidence is in him."*

We live in one of the most stressed-out, crazy-busy generations in history. It has never been easier to grab a quick lunch on the go, to fix some coffee that will help us to pull an all-nighter, and to make our weekends even busier than our weekdays. Despite the fact that I have tucked myself away to write this book, every few minutes my watch and phone and tablet vibrate to inform me that yet another message has arrived. I find it hard to be still and know that God is God, and I am not, when my devices are constantly flattering me about how much I am needed. Kevin DeYoung describes it this way:

> *Because we* **can** *do so much, we do* **do** *so much. Our lives have no limits. ... As much as we must pray against the devil and pray for the persecuted church, in Jesus' thinking the greater threat to the gospel is sheer exhaustion. Busyness kills more Christians than bullets. ... Going to sleep is our way of saying, "I trust you, God. You'll be okay without me."*[5]

[3] Sunday was a workday in the ancient world. It simply makes sense for most Christians to take it as their Sabbath in order to enable us to meet together as churches (Acts 20:7 and Hebrews 10:25).

[4] Isaiah 40:28 and Psalm 121:4. A literal translation of the Hebrew words translated *be careful* in 17:21 is actually: *Guard your souls!* If we refuse to accept the limits of our humanity, we damage our very selves.

[5] Kevin DeYoung in his book *Crazy Busy* (2013). Used by permission of Crossway, a publishing ministry of Good News Publishers, Wheaton, IL 60187, www.crossway.org

Back at the gateways of Jerusalem, the prophet Jeremiah explains what will happen to the people of Judah if they continue to fail their weekly Sabbath test. They are at a crossroads. If they are willing to down tools to prove that they are looking to the Lord as their true Provider, then they will experience the blessings of 17:8: *"They will be like a tree planted by the water that sends out its roots by the stream."* They will come in and out of these gateways for many years to come, as happy creatures in the hand of their Creator.

But if they refuse to down tools, thereby demonstrating that they are relying on their own strength to meet their daily needs, then they will come under the curse of 17:6: *"That person will be like a bush in the wastelands; they will not see prosperity when it comes."* As a result of their refusal to serve the Lord and his seventh-day rhythm, they will be condemned to serve as slaves to their enemies in Babylon. They will no longer enter and exit the gateways of Jerusalem. Its mighty walls will be pulled down and burned.

What Jeremiah says in his brief seventh speech is therefore very simple. So is the response that it demands. Take some time out today to be still before the Lord and to confess that he is God, and you are not, and that this is remarkably good news. Thank the Lord that he is your true Resting Place and Provider. Ask him to help you live under his Sabbath blessings, not under the curse that befalls the stressed-out and crazy-busy.

The book of Hebrews encourages us: *"There remains, then, a Sabbath-rest for the people of God; for anyone who enters God's rest also rests from their works, just as God did from his."*[6]

---

[6] Hebrews 4:9–10. As you spend time resting in God today, it may help you to read and reflect on Hebrews 3:7–4:11.

Pottery
(Jeremiah 18:1–20:18)

*"Go down to the potter's house, and there
I will give you my message."*

(Jeremiah 18:2)

Jeremiah was a brilliantly gifted communicator. To write the longest book in the Bible, he needed to be. Think about the variety of ways in which he has essentially said the same thing for the past seventeen chapters: *Only radical surgery can save this patient.*

He has talked about distraught dads and weeping widows and leaping lions. He has contrasted brides with prostitutes, fertile fields with wastelands, gushing springs with broken wells, lions with camels, and leafy trees with arid bushes. In order to hold our attention, he has made use of every verbal weapon in the preacher's arsenal.

Whenever creative wordplay was not enough to hold our attention, Jeremiah has also made use of visual aids. The Lord inspired him to cut off his hair in the Temple courtyards as a sign to Judah that their lucky talisman was running out of time. The Lord told him to bury his linen belt among the rocks by the River Euphrates so that he could retrieve it several weeks later as a prophetic picture of Judah's corruption. Now the Lord inspires him to employ another visual aid. He sends him to a local pottery.

In 18:1–10, Jeremiah obeys the Lord and visits the house of a friendly potter. It provokes the eighth of the ten speeches that form this first section of Jeremiah.[1] Doesn't a potter have the right to shape and reshape a lump of clay however he wishes?[2] Doesn't the Lord, therefore, have the same right to reconsider the plans and promises that he has made to Judah if its people persist in their rebellion against him?[3]

In 18:11–17, the Lord inspires Jeremiah to explain further what he learned from his trip to the local pottery. Some of his wordplay is lost in English, since the Hebrew word for God *devising* plans against Judah (*yātsar*) is linked to the Hebrew word for *potter* (*yōtsēr*). Jeremiah essentially prophesies that, like a potter, the Lord is reshaping his plans for the nation of Judah. Instead of living under God's blessing, they are now hurtling towards disaster, one that is very well-deserved. The melting snows on the lofty mountaintops of Lebanon provide cool streams all year round for northern Israel, so the people of Judah are more inconstant than its snow. They have left their God to run after idols. How can they complain if he goes back to the potter's wheel and reshapes them for destruction?

In 18:18, the people of Judah refuse to listen. They prefer the soothing voices of their lying priests and wise men and prophets. In 18:19–23, Jeremiah therefore cries out to the Lord against them. He is sick of interceding for such people. They plot against him every time he turns his back, so let the Potter hasten the disaster as he has promised!

In 19:1–13, the Lord commands Jeremiah to go back to the pottery.[4] This time he is to take some of Judah's priests and

---

[1] Once again, the Lord refers to Judah as *Israel* in order to emphasize that, unless the southern kingdom repents, it will be destroyed in the same manner as the northern kingdom.

[2] Paul quotes from Isaiah 29:16 and 45:9 in Romans 9:19–21, but he also seems to have these verses in mind when he argues that the Lord has as much right to shape human affairs as a potter has to shape his clay.

[3] This is good news as well as bad news. Jonah 3 says God also reconsiders his threats whenever we repent.

[4] Although Matthew 27:9–10 quotes from Zechariah 11:12–13 when Judas Iscariot's blood money is used to buy a potter's field, Matthew drops a clue that he is also thinking about Jeremiah 19:1–13 and 32:6–9.

elders with him. He is to purchase a clay jar from the potter and take it down to the East Gate of Jerusalem, the one that looks out onto the Valley of Ben Hinnom.[5] From here, Jeremiah can see Topheth, meaning *Fire Pit*, the shrine of the evil idol Molek who demanded that his worshippers sacrifice their children to him in the flames. Looking out across the valley, he can also see the shrine of Baal, who these verses suggest had begun to demand child sacrifices too. The Hebrew word for *clay jar* (*baqbuq*) sounds like the Hebrew word for *ruin* (*bāqaq*), so Jeremiah declares that Judah's ruin is now set in stone, liked fired clay. He hurls down the jar and smashes it into dozens of fragments of pottery. That's how the Lord will destroy Jerusalem, he declares to the priests and elders.[6] This place will no longer be known as the Valley of Ben Hinnom. It will become known as the Valley of Slaughter.[7]

In 19:14–15, the Lord commands Jeremiah to continue preaching on this theme in the Temple courtyards. There is nothing so adaptable as a clay pot in the making and nothing so unalterable as a clay pot once made. The people of Judah therefore have an urgent choice to make. Will they be soft-hearted or hard-hearted towards the Lord?

In 20:1–18, Jeremiah receives an immediate answer. Pashhur is the priest in charge of the Temple guard, which makes him second only to the high priest in terms of seniority.[8] He arrests Jeremiah, beats him and places him in the stocks, a wooden chair designed to confer public humiliation on a

---

[5] *Potsherd Gate* in 19:2 means *Broken-Piece-of-Pottery Gate*. The East Gate presumably gained this nickname as a result of Jeremiah's vivid prophecy in this chapter.

[6] Jeremiah repeats much of what he said in 2:23 and 7:30–34, but there is new detail in 19:9. The people of Jerusalem will become so hungry during its final 2½-year siege that they will even eat their own children.

[7] Jewish corpses would be left to rot in the valley in 586 BC. After the city's reconstruction, it would serve as a rubbish tip so, using its Greek name *Gehenna*, Jesus makes its never-ending fires a graphic picture of hell.

[8] Jeremiah 29:25–26 and 52:24. See also Acts 4:1 and 5:24.

prisoner.[9] He leaves the prophet in the stocks for an entire day in the busy passageway at the Upper Gate of Benjamin.[10] When Jeremiah is finally released, he continues prophesying – this time to predict what will happen to the captain of the guard. God no longer calls him Pashhur. He has a new name – *Māgōr Missābīb*, which means *Terror On Every Side* – since he will be one of the first to be surrounded and captured by the Babylonian soldiers when all of these pottery prophecies are fulfilled.[11]

Jeremiah still speaks these pottery prophecies to you and me. Will we say "yes" to the Lord and let him shape us however he sees fit, or will we harden our hearts towards him? The Christian writer Pete Greig encourages us not to respond like stubborn Pashhur:

> *By saying "no" to God's leadership in your life you will miss out on the actual reason for which you were born. You will quietly live a second-rate life... without knowing why. When you become a Christian you take your first step out of futility and into your destiny.*[12]

[9] This is the first time that he has been referred to as *"Jeremiah the prophet"*. This is meant to intensify our shock that one of the Temple priests should treat God's anointed servant in such a shameful way.

[10] The Upper Gate of Benjamin was in the Temple courtyards and the Lower Gate of Benjamin was in the city walls (37:13, 38:7). Both names reflected how near Jerusalem was to the tribal lands of Benjamin.

[11] Pashhur's new name is echoed by 6:25, 20:10, 46:5 and 49:29, as well as by Lamentations 2:22. He must have been captured when Jerusalem fell to the Babylonians for a second time, in 597 BC, since we are told in 29:25–26 that two men named Jehoiada and Zephaniah held his role between then and its final fall, in 586 BC.

[12] Pete Greig says this in his book *Dirty Glory* (© NavPress 2016). Used by permission of NavPress, represented by Tyndale House Ministries. All rights reserved.

The Inner Ring
(Jeremiah 20:1–18)

I am ridiculed all day long; everyone mocks me.

(Jeremiah 20:7)

I was a worshipper long before I began to follow Jesus. The name of my false god was Popularity. I was desperate for people to like me. I craved their approval and would do anything to remain a member of the in-crowd. If you do not consider Popularity to be a god, then listen to C.S. Lewis. He regards it as one of the most subtle idols of them all.

> *The prophecy I make is this. To nine out of ten of you the choice which could lead to scoundrelism will come, when it does come, in no very dramatic colours. Obviously bad men, obviously threatening or bribing, will almost certainly not appear. Over a drink, or a cup of coffee, disguised as a triviality and sandwiched between two jokes, from the lips of a man, or woman, whom you have recently been getting to know rather better and whom you hope to know better still – just at the moment when you are most anxious not to appear crude, or naïf or a prig – the hint will come. It will be the hint of something which the public, the ignorant, romantic public, would never understand: something which even the outsiders in your own profession are apt to make a fuss about, but something, says your new friend, which "we" – and at the word "we" you try not to blush for mere pleasure – something "we always do".*

And you will be drawn in, if you are drawn in, not by desire for gain or ease, but simply because at that moment, when the cup was so near your lips, you cannot bear to be thrust back again into the cold outer world. It would be so terrible to see the other man's face – that genial, confidential, delightfully sophisticated face – turn suddenly cold and contemptuous, to know that you had been tried for the Inner Ring and rejected. And then, if you are drawn in, next week it will be something a little further from the rules, and next year something further still, but all in the jolliest, friendliest spirit... Of all the passions, the passion for the Inner Ring is most skilful in making a man who is not yet a very bad man do very bad things.[1]

Perhaps the best indicator that we might be trying to worship both Christ *and* Popularity is how little we discuss the many verses in which Jesus warns us that siding with him means being hated by the world. It means renouncing the false god Popularity.

Jeremiah leads the way for us here. In the run-up to this chapter, he has been heckled, hated and arrested. His own family members have attempted to kill him. Instead of giving him a cheery pep talk, the Lord has warned him that worse is yet to come: *"They will not listen to you; when you call to them, they will not answer."*[2] The Hebrew word that is used here for Pashhur putting Jeremiah in the *stocks* means literally *the twister*, indicating that it was an instrument of torture as well as a pillory that enabled passers-by to spit and jeer and throw things at the prisoner. Reading these verses ought to make us ask ourselves why God would allow his anointed prophet to be

---

[1] This comes from an essay entitled "The Inner Ring" in the C.S. Lewis book, *The Weight of Glory* (© C.S. Lewis Pte Ltd. 1949). Extract reprinted by permission.
[2] Jeremiah 7:27. See also 1:17–19 and 18:11–12.

beaten and subjected to an entire day contorted in the twister, while exposed to the naked hostility of the crowd.

One answer might be that suffering for Jesus draws us closer to him. We don't like to dwell on this thought in case he asks us to do so, but the book of Jeremiah keeps suggesting that it's true. Jeremiah is called to live as a singleton in a married man's world. So was Jesus. Jeremiah discovers that the priests are conspiring to kill him. So did Jesus. Jeremiah is arrested by the captain of the Temple guard. So was Jesus. Jeremiah says that he feels *"like a gentle lamb led to the slaughter"*. So did Jesus. All of this ought to stir our hearts to reflect very carefully on what the Apostle Paul means when he says, *"I want to know Christ – yes, to know ... participation in his sufferings, becoming like him in his death."*[3]

Another answer might be that suffering for Jesus produces his character within us. Rejection and unpopularity for the sake of gospel can become the surgeon's scalpel that cuts away at our fleshly ambition and our desire for this world's praise. One of the clearest messages of Jeremiah is that faithfulness and fruitfulness are not the same thing. God commands us to proclaim his Word, even when he knows that people will throw it back in our faces, not just because he wants to give non-believers a chance to respond, but because he wants to give us a chance to discover how much our Christian ministry is an act of worship and how much of it is an attempt to feel that we are living useful lives.

In 20:7–18, Jeremiah discovers that he still needs to feel the surgeon's scalpel in his own soul. This complaint may seem like a rather depressing way to end his eighth speech, but I am grateful for the prophet's honesty. Whenever I am abused and rejected by people as a result of the gospel, I tend to react the

---

[3] Philippians 3:10. Jeremiah 11:19 is a deliberate counterpart to Isaiah 53:7.

same way![4] *"You deceived me, Lord,"* the prophet complains. *"I am ridiculed all day long; everyone mocks me... the word of the Lord has brought me insult and reproach all day long."* Even as Jeremiah vents his anger to God, he realizes that his inner joy at preaching God's Word is not dependent on whether or not he is fruitful. *"His word is in my heart like a fire, a fire shut up in my bones. I am weary of holding it in; indeed, I cannot."*[5] Liberated from his lust to feel successful, Jeremiah is able to resolve to keep on preaching for the sake of God's glory alone.[6] He confesses his conviction that God is *"a mighty warrior"* and the *"Lord Almighty"* (verses 11 and 12). He will ensure that his Word bears fruit through Jeremiah, even if that fruit is quite well hidden now.

Perhaps a final answer might be that suffering for Jesus is the strongest evidence for our listeners that what we are proclaiming about him is true. The final five verses of this chapter find Jeremiah at his very lowest. We know that lamentations in the ancient world employed hyperbole (he doesn't really want to remove his birthday from the calendar or to curse his father's friend for not having murdered him at birth!) but the prophet's pain is visible and real.[7] It is one of the reasons why he wins a few important converts in the second section of Jeremiah. The French philosopher Blaise Pascal argued that this is also why the persecuted early Christians won so many converts across the Roman Empire. *"I only believe the stories of witnesses who get their throats cut."*[8]

---

[4] Jeremiah has prayed prayers of complaint before in 11:18–23, 12:1–4, 15:10–21, 17:12–18 and 18:19–23. Note that 20:12 is an almost verbatim repetition of 11:20.

[5] Paul says something very similar in 1 Corinthians 9:16. This is how we are all to feel about the gospel.

[6] The Hebrew that is translated *"Terror on every side"* in 20:10 is *Māgōr Missābīb*, the name that God gave to Pashhur in 20:3.

[7] For a similar example, see Job 3:1–16. We can lament like this too, but better still is Acts 16:22–25!

[8] This is the 593rd of Blaise Pascal's *Pensées* (1670).

So make your decision now. Would you rather cling to your acceptance by the Inner Ring or join the circle of faithful witnesses who have suffered pain as a result of their radical obedience towards the Lord? The Apostle Paul warns us categorically that *"Everyone who wants to live a godly life in Christ Jesus will be persecuted."*[9] The book of Jeremiah challenges us that the word everyone means everyone – including you and me.

---

[9] 2 Timothy 3:12. See also Matthew 5:10–12 and 10:22–25, Luke 14:26–27, John 15:19–21 and Acts 14:22.

The Last King of Judah (Jeremiah 21:1–23:8)

"The days are coming," declares the Lord, "when I will raise up... a King who will reign wisely... The Lord Our Righteous Saviour."

(Jeremiah 23:5–6)

Jeremiah prophesied for over forty years during the reigns of the last five kings of Judah.

> Josiah (640–609 BC)
> Jehoahaz (609 BC)
> Jehoiakim (609–598 BC)
> Jehoiachin (598–597 BC)
> Zedekiah (597–586 BC)

King Josiah was the last of Judah's godly kings, but he was dead. His impressive-looking revival had proved short-lived and superficial. His pride had led him onto the battlefield against an Egyptian army that was on its way to fight off Babylon. His death at the Battle of Megiddo in 609 BC signalled the beginning of the end for the kings of Judah.

His son Jehoahaz had ruled for only three months when Pharaoh Necho deposed him, dragged him off into exile in Egypt and installed the brother of Jehoahaz as a puppet ruler instead. Jehoiakim reigned for eleven years, but after burning the first edition of the book of Jeremiah, he became a violent casualty of the tug-of-war between Egypt and Babylon. His son Jehoiachin was king for only three months before the Babylonian army arrived in Jerusalem and carried him off into exile, replacing a puppet ruler for Egypt with a puppet ruler for Babylon. King Zedekiah was the third of Josiah's sons to reign. Sadly, he was every bit as sinful as his brothers. He provoked the final destruction of Jerusalem at the hands of the Babylonian army. He became the last king of Judah.

The ninth speech of Jeremiah addresses this sordid royal saga. In 21:1–14, King Zedekiah requests help from the Lord during the final siege of Jerusalem.[1] Instead of being flattered to be asked, Jeremiah prophesies that the siege is God's judgment on the sinful *"house of David"* and on the corrupted *"royal house of Judah"*. The prophet risks his life to declare that the Lord is fighting for the Babylonians – Zedekiah and his subjects are about to be slaughtered and Jerusalem destroyed.[2] Their only hope of survival is to submit gladly to God's surgeon's scalpel by surrendering and going willingly into exile.[3]

In the next chapter, Jeremiah prophesies similar things about the other last kings of Judah. In 22:1–12, the Lord tells people to stop weeping over the death of King Josiah. Those who have died are the lucky ones.[4] They should weep instead for the sinful King Jehoahaz, who will never return from his exile in Egypt.[5] This prophecy appears to have been given before the one in chapter 21, but it unpacks the same theme. Jeremiah is

---

[1] Pashhur son of Immer had been taken into exile in 597 BC and replaced as captain of the Temple guard by Zephaniah son of Maaseiah. The royal messenger, Pashhur son of Malkijah, would prove as sinful as his namesake, also launching an attack on Jeremiah in 38:1.

[2] Zedekiah ignored God's warnings not to listen to Egyptian promises of help if he rebelled against Babylon (Ezekiel 17:11–21). By rebelling, he provoked his own exile and the death of all his sons (52:10–11).

[3] Although many people talk as if patriotism were the supreme virtue, it is a vice if it means disobeying God.

[4] This echoes 16:5–7 and Isaiah 57:1. Jeremiah had written a song of lament for Josiah and his death had provoked unprecedented national mourning (2 Chronicles 35:23–25 and Zechariah 12:11).

[5] *Shallum* took the throne name Jehoahaz when he became king (22:11 and 1 Chronicles 3:15).

sent *"to the palace of the king of Judah"* to call time on the *"kings who sit on David's throne"*. The Lord has decreed that they will be the last kings of Judah.[6]

In 22:13-19, Jeremiah prophesies the same thing against the sinful King Jehoiakim. The Lord has witnessed his injustice and his insatiable greed.[7] The Babylonians will kill him and throw his body out onto the road. Even a donkey will have a better burial than he does.[8]

In 22:20-30, Jeremiah prophesies along the same theme to Jehoiachin, the remaining king of Judah. He may feel secure in the magnificent royal palace of his father, but he and the queen mother will both die in exile in Babylon.[9] Although he boasts of his many children, he is in fact as good as childless, since none of them will ever sit on his throne to rule over Judah.[10] God has called time on David's depraved dynasty.

All of this is the build-up to what this ninth speech is really all about. The Lord is about to prophesy something truly astonishing in 23:1-8.[11] He announces that the reason why he is calling time on these four lousy leaders of Judah is to make way

---

[6] The Hebrew word *qādash* is used throughout the Old Testament to describe God *sanctifying* his people. He aims to shock us, therefore, by using it in 22:7 to describe *sending* the Babylonian army to destroy Jerusalem.

[7] We are given an example of Jehoiakim's injustice in 26:20-23. He executed the godly prophet Uriah. The Lord fumes in 22:16: *Don't you know that those who truly know me always defend the cause of the poor and needy?*

[8] In his *Antiquities of the Jews*, the first-century Jewish historian Josephus Flavius confirms that this is indeed what King Nebuchadnezzar of Babylon did to Jehoiakim's body (10.6.3).

[9] Jeremiah 22:23 is refering to the Palace of the Forest of Lebanon, the seat of Judah's kings (1 Kings 7:2), rather than the kingdom to the north of Israel and Judah.

[10] 1 Chronicles 3:17-18. Born *[Je]Koniah*, he took the throne name Jehoiachin, just as Shallum, Eliakim and Mattaniah took the throne names Jehoahaz, Jehoiakim and Zedekiah.

[11] These verses are full of Hebrew wordplay. God will bestow punishment (*pāqad*) on the evil (*ra'*) shepherds (*rō'ī*) who bestow no care (*pāqad*). Jesus will rule in righteousness (*tsedāqāh*) instead of Zedekiah (*tsidqīyāh*).

for a true and better Last King of Judah.[12] *"The days are coming,"* he declares, *"when I will raise up from David's line a righteous Branch, a King who will reign wisely and do what is just and right in the land."* Jehoiachin would never return from exile, but one day his grandson Zerubbabel would lead the survivors of Judah back home. Zerubbabel would not be crowned king, but many centuries later one of his direct descendants would be born in a stable at Bethlehem and crowned King on a cross at Calvary. David's down-and-out dynasty will not end in failure. It will end with the one whose name is *Yahweh Tsidkēnū*, which is best translated *The Lord Who Makes Us Righteous*.[13] This Messiah will not be a self-serving monarch. He will be the true Shepherd of Israel, leading them on a spiritual Exodus from sin to salvation, and reigning forever as the true Last King of Judah.[14]

This massive turnaround for David's dynasty also marks a massive turnaround in the book of Jeremiah. The message of section one is that *radical surgery is needed*, but now we begin to catch a glimpse of what that surgery will achieve. These verses set us up for section two of the book, which declare that *radical surgery has begun*. The surgeon's scalpel that we have read so much about will finally bring healing to God's people.

We will discover in section two of the book of Jeremiah that God is also planning to rename his people *Yahweh Tsidkēnū* too. He is cutting out the cancer of sin from his people so that he can make them holy preachers of salvation to every nation of the world.[15]

---

[12] The Lord calls these leaders *shepherds* or *pastors.* These verses are echoed in Acts 20:28 and 1 Peter 5:1–4.

[13] We might have expected the name of Jesus in these verses to be *The Righteous Lord*, in contrast to the sinful kings of Judah. But this name speaks of something far greater. He is *The Lord Who Makes Us Righteous.*

[14] This incredible turnaround begins in 52:31–34 and is completed in Matthew 1:1–17, 27:29 and 27:37.

[15] Jeremiah 23:7–8 repeats 16:14–15 and it echoes Isaiah 4:2, 11:1 and 53:2. Jeremiah 23:5–6 is repeated with slight changes in 33:15–16 as a declaration that we now bear the name *The Lord Who Makes Us Righteous* too!

Clean-Up Operation
(Jeremiah 23:9–24:10)

"So will I deal with Zedekiah king of Judah, his officials and the survivors from Jerusalem."

(Jeremiah 24:8)

Every day, an enormous clean-up operation takes place under our noses. I live in London, which produces 3.7 million tonnes of rubbish every year, or enough to fill 1,500 Olympic-sized swimming pools.[1] We don't tend to think much about the refuse lorries on our streets, but we would notice very quickly if they paused their clean-up operation.

That's what this ninth speech of Jeremiah is all about. In 21:1–23:8, the Lord informed us that he was cleaning out the royal palace of Judah in order to make way for the true and better King of Judah. Now he continues in 23:9–24:40, sending his bin men out from the palace into the streets of Jerusalem to clean up the filth across the rest of the city.

In 23:9–15, the bin men make their first stop at the Temple. This is where they ought to find the priests and prophets pointing out to the people of Judah that idolatry is a form of spiritual adultery that brings on people all the curses listed in the Law of Moses. Instead, in the name of tolerance, they are helping the prophets of Baal to lead the people astray. The Lord describes them as *"the prophets of Samaria"*, because their toxic message will prove as fatal to the southern kingdom as it did to

---

[1] Taken from a London Assembly report entitled *Waste: The Circular Economy* (2017).

the northern kingdom.[2] As for *"the prophets of Jerusalem"*, they do not deserve to be called prophets of the Lord because their lives are as filthy as the lives of those to whom they prophesy. Their self-seeking and idolatrous agenda sounds more loudly than any of their sermons, reassuring people that they are not in any real danger of judgment.[3] They strengthen people's hands in wickedness, transforming Jerusalem into Sodom and Gomorrah.[4]

In his classic book, *The Reformed Pastor*, Richard Baxter warns that Christian leaders promote the same pollution in their own cities whenever they compromise with sin.

> *All that a minister does is a kind of preaching; and if you live a covetous or a careless life, you preach these sins to your people by your practice ... They take it as if you said to them, "Neighbours, this is the life you should all live; on this course you may venture without any danger" ... Is that man then likely to do much good, or fit to be a minister of Christ, that will speak for him an hour on the Sabbath, and, by his life, will preach against him all the week?*[5]

In 23:16–24, the bin men continue on their rounds to the houses of Jerusalem, reminding us how much polluted preaching contaminates people's daily lives. Confronting sin is difficult. It is always easier to tell people what they want to hear – *"The Lord says: you will have peace ... No harm will come to you."*

---

[2] Samaria was the capital city of the northern kingdom and home to King Ahab and Queen Jezebel.

[3] Jeremiah 23:14 echoes 2 Samuel 12:13–14, Ezekiel 13:22–23 and Romans 2:24. Jeremiah 23:15 is a repeat of 9:15.

[4] Genesis 18:16–19:29, Isaiah 1:10, Ezekiel 16:44–58 and Revelation 11:8.

[5] The Richard Baxter quotations in this chapter come from *The Reformed Pastor* (1655).

But whenever we do so, we are not loving them but hating them.[6] The Lord is deadly serious when he threatens judgment, so unless we warn people then we are killing them with kindness. How will they ever be convinced to turn back to God if we do not warn them that their hour of judgment is near?[7] The Lord warns the people of Judah that their prophets are preaching *"false hopes"* out of their own imaginations. The tragedy here is that God's Word is so powerful that, had they only taken time to listen, the prophets could have brought salvation to Judah.[8] Richard Baxter warns us again:

> *You shall be judged... and what sin more heinous than the betraying of souls? ... I am afraid, nay, I have no doubt, that the day is near when unfaithful ministers will wish that they had never known the charge of souls; but that they had rather been colliers, or sweeps, or tinkers, than pastors of Christ's flock, when, besides all the rest of their sins, they shall have the blood of so many souls to answer for. O brethren, our death, as well as our people's, is at hand, and it is as terrible to an unfaithful pastor as to any.*[9]

In 23:25–40, the bin men complete their rounds, stopping at the houses of the *prophets*, the *priests* and the *people*. Prophetic dreams are causing quite a stir in the houses of Jerusalem, but the Lord declares that these are nothing more than the delusions of a prophet's mind. They plagiarize their prophecies from one

---

[6] This is one of the repeated messages of Jeremiah. See 6:14, 8:11 and 14:13, as well as Ezekiel 13:10.

[7] This is the force of 23:23. The Lord is both immanent and transcendent, both near and far away.

[8] The Hebrew word *sōd*, which is translated *council* in 23:18 and 22, describes the deep friendship we can enjoy with God by attending to both his Spirit and his Word (Job 29:4, Psalm 25:14 and Acts 20:27).

[9] We need to take this warning seriously. We are far quicker to quote from 29:11 (*"I know the plans I have for you ... plans to prosper you"*) than we are from 21:10 (*"I have determined to do this city harm and not good"*).

another, telling reckless lies that serve to harden sinful hearts, whereas the true Word of God is *"like fire and like a hammer that breaks a rock in pieces."*[10] The Lord therefore tells the prophets of Jerusalem to stop pretending that their so-called revelations are *"a message from the Lord"* (verse 34).[11] Their words have got about as much in common with God's Word as straw has with chaff. He is *"The Living God"*, *"the Lord Almighty"* and *"our God"*, so let nobody dare to speak in his name without first listening to what he says.[12]

In 24:1–10, the Lord gives Jeremiah a genuine vision to cause a real stir in the houses of Jerusalem. It is 597 BC, and King Nebuchadnezzar of Babylon has just defeated Judah for a second time, carrying off a second wave of captives into exile.[13] Everybody in Jerusalem has assumed that those captives are the infected flesh that Jeremiah has been saying needs to be cut away by God's surgeon's scalpel. That's what makes Jeremiah's vision so surprising. He sees two baskets of figs – one full of good figs that are ready for eating and one full of figs that are so rotten as to be only ready for the bin men. Now for the big surprise. The Lord announces that those who have been taken into exile are the "good figs" that the Lord will use to plant a new orchard in Judah. Those who have been left behind are the "rotten figs", who are misunderstanding God's clean-up operation.[14]

The prophet Ezekiel was among the "good figs" who

---

[10] Verse 29. This chapter makes pretty sobering reading for Christian preachers, but this should encourage us. God's Word is so powerful that it needs no helping hand. It is the most powerful weapon in the universe.

[11] The Hebrew phrase translated *"The Lord declares"* in 23:31 is used 364 times in the Old Testament, half of which are in the book of Jeremiah. He took this statement as seriously as the false prophets took it lightly.

[12] These three names of God in 23:36 are meant to fill us with awe. We are to be eager to prophesy (23:28–29 and 1 Corinthians 14:39), whilst never forgetting that to prophesy falsely is far worse than not to prophesy at all.

[13] *Egypt* is mentioned in 24:8, not just because some had gone into exile there with King Jehoahaz in 609 BC, but because some of the survivors of the slaughter of 586 BC would later flee there (41:17–18 and 43:7).

[14] Jeremiah refers to this vision in 29:17 in a letter to the exiles in Babylon.

were taken into exile in 597 BC. King Zedekiah and his corrupt officials were among those who stayed. The Lord had begun his plan to purify the pathway for the real King of Judah to come. He had also begun his plan to plant and purify a new people of Judah after his clean-up operation.[15]

---

[15] 3,023 men were taken into captivity in 597 BC, along with their wives and children (52:28). They joined Daniel and the 7,000 families who had been exiled in 605 BC (52:28 subtracted from 2 Kings 24:14). Only 1,577 of the men left behind in Jerusalem would survive its final destruction in 586 BC (52:29–30).

The Cup
(Jeremiah 25:1–38)

"Take from my hand this cup filled with the wine of my wrath and make all the nations to whom I send you drink it."

(Jeremiah 25:15)

I find the ten speeches in the first section of the book of Jeremiah a little bit like a Top Ten countdown. I love the speeches in the first few chapters, but the Lord seems to me to save the best till last. The final two speeches contain the most glorious music of them all. In 21:1–24:40, God reveals that he is clearing the way for his Messiah to rule over a freshly planted kingdom. In 25:1–38, he shares the timing for that turnaround and explains how the sinful Jewish exiles can be transformed into the holy people of God.

In 25:1–7, Jeremiah declares that section one of his book is coming to an end. He is speaking in 605 BC, which marked a turning point in history for two reasons. First, it was the year in which Babylon defeated Egypt and its allies at the Battle of Carchemish, shifting the balance of power in the Middle East to make the entire region Babylon's for the taking. Second, it was the year in which Nebuchadnezzar came to the throne. His generalship at Carchemish had left nobody in any doubt that he was clever and ruthless enough to ram home the advantages of his victory.[16] Jeremiah therefore points out to the people of Judah that he has been prophesying to them for almost a quarter of a

---

[16] Nebuchadnezzar was the undisputed master of the world – yet in 25:9 God describes him as *"my servant"*.

century.[17] They have refused to listen to the message of part one of his book – that *radical surgery is needed* – so they are about to feel the message of part two – that *radical surgery has begun*.[18]

In 25:8–11, Jeremiah prophesies that the destruction of Jerusalem is close at hand. Before the end of the year, the Babylonian army would conquer Judah's neighbours and would arrive at the gates of its capital city. The first group of Jewish exiles would be taken off to Babylon. We tend to view this event a bit too neutrally, since we know that the city survived for two more decades and that Daniel and his friends had a bright future ahead of them in Babylon. But for the Jews who first heard these words, it was a devastating blow. It meant that everything that Jeremiah had prophesied was coming true.

In 25:12–14, Jeremiah reveals God's timescale for the captivity of his people in Babylon. He repeats what he just said in verse 11 – that at the end of *"seventy years"* the Lord will bring about the fall of Babylon and the repatriation of his repentant people.[19] The city of Babylon would be devastated so completely that, unlike Jerusalem, it would never rise again. Acting as God's surgeon's scalpel didn't mean its misdeeds would go unpunished. After using Babylon to judge the nations, the Lord would then judge Babylon.[20]

If you know the Bible well, then these verses will make you think of Daniel 9, where this prophecy from Jeremiah prompts Daniel to pray. Having been taken into exile with the first group of exiles, in 605 BC, Daniel becomes excited when he does the maths in 538 BC. In the wake of the fall of Babylon, these verses

---

[17] The Hebrew way of counting treated part years as whole years, so *twenty-three years* in 25:3 is 627–605 BC.

[18] We catch a hint of the editing process in 25:18, where the scribe Baruch adds much later, *"as they are today."*

[19] Babylon fell to the Persians in 539 BC and King Cyrus of Persia sent the Jewish exiles home shortly after. It took them until 516 BC to rebuild the Temple, however, so Jeremiah's *seventy years* refer to the years that the Temple would lie fallen. See Zechariah 1:12, which was prophesied in 519 BC.

[20] God was merciful to Babylon. It was only destroyed completely in a second Persian campaign in 516 BC.

give him faith to pray for the exiles to be sent home.[21] Before the end of the year, Daniel's prayers are answered.

This leaves a big question unanswered. On what basis could the Jewish exiles be permitted to return home? The Bible insists that without the shedding of blood there is no forgiveness, so what could seventy years in the doghouse achieve for them?[22] How could God be just in his judgments and yet extend love and mercy towards the Jewish exiles in Babylon? That's the question that occupies the final half of this chapter.

In 25:15–38, the Lord begins to preach the Christian gospel through Jeremiah. He asks his listeners to consider *"this cup filled with the wine of my wrath"*, which will be drunk by all those slaughtered by the Babylonians (the people of Judah, Egypt, Uz, Philistia, Edom, Moab, Ammon, Tyre, Sidon, Dedan, Tema, Buz, Arabia, Elam and Media – the list goes on[23]) and then drunk finally by Sheshak – a codename for Babylon.[24] The Lord says that there will be something sacrificial about all of this slaughter. The sword of Babylon will be *"the sword I will send among them."* The cup of God's wrath will be a goblet of justice, somehow bringing recompense for all of the injustice and idolatry and murder in the ancient world, *"for the Lord will bring charges against the nations; he will bring judgment on all mankind and put the wicked to the sword."* There will be nothing secular about the Babylonian slaughter. It will be an expression *"of the Lord's fierce anger"* falling down on those who are *"slain by the Lord"*. It will be his Day of Judgment,

---

[21] Daniel was presumably also stirred to pray by Jeremiah 29:10.

[22] Leviticus 17:11 and Hebrews 9:22.

[23] The *"coastlands across the sea"* are probably Cyprus and Crete. After listing Judah's immediate neighbours, Jeremiah lists the nomadic tribes of Arabia (Dedan, Tema and Buz) and kingdoms in modern-day Iran (Elam and Media). *"The people left at Ashdod"* recognizes that much of the city had already been destroyed by Egypt.

[24] Jeremiah explains in 51:41 that *Sheshak* is a codename for Babylon. Since Jerusalem was about to fall to the Babylonians in 605 BC, he thought twice about predicting the fall of Babylon too openly.

when his surgeon's scalpel exacts terrible amends for all the sins of the world.

But this has not fully answered our question. It might explain how the violence surrounding the creation of the Babylonian Empire dealt justly with the sins of the slaughtered, but it does not explain how forgiveness could be extended to the Jewish exiles. For the answer to that question, we need to flick forward many pages to a conversation between Jesus and his Father on the night before he was crowned King of Judah on a cross at Calvary. Many readers do not stop to consider the strange language in the prayer he prayed three times in the Garden of Gethsemane – *"My Father, if it is possible, may this cup be taken from me. Yet not as I will, but as you will."* They do not realize that Jesus is referring back to these verses and to this crucial prophecy from Jeremiah.[25]

The Jewish exiles would be permitted to return home without being slaughtered for their sin because Jesus would one day drink the cup of God's judgment so that they didn't have to drink it for themselves. They would be spared the Day of Judgment because Jesus would one day bear it for them. Because he died and rose again for his people, the repentance and renewed faith of the Jewish exiles meant that God could be both just and merciful towards them. It meant that he could view Babylon as Judah's *tomb* and the return from Babylon as their *resurrection day*. It meant that they could be forgiven through the blood of the Messiah that Jeremiah praises in 23:6 as *Yahweh Tsidkênû – The Lord Who Makes Us Righteous.*

Jeremiah therefore ends the first section of his book in triumph. So can we, since the Saviour of Judah drank this cup of the wine of God's wrath for us too. He still says to us what he said to his disciples at the Last Supper:

---

[25] Matthew 26:39. See also Psalm 75:8, Isaiah 51:17, Lamentations 4:21, Ezekiel 23:31–34, Habakkuk 2:15–16, Matthew 20:22 and John 18:11.

"Then he took the cup, gave thanks and offered it to them, saying, 'Drink from it, all of you. This is my blood of the covenant, which is poured out for many for the forgiveness of sins.'"[26]

---

[26] Matthew 26:27–28. In the parallel account of the Last Supper in Luke 22:20, Jesus calls it the cup of his *"new covenant"*, echoing the prophet's additional words of explanation in Jeremiah 31:31–34.

Jeremiah 26–52:

Radical Surgery Has Begun

Action Story
(Jeremiah 26:1–28:17)

Ahikam son of Shaphan supported Jeremiah, and
so he was not handed over to the people to be put
to death.

(Jeremiah 26:24)

I love climbing mountains with my family. The way up is usually hard, and we have to spur each other on with the thought of an amazing view at the top of the mountain. The way down, however, is a whole lot easier. It is the same with the book of Jeremiah.

Section one of Jeremiah feels like climbing a mountain. The view from the top is phenomenal – the prophet's ninth and tenth speeches contain some of the most glorious promises in the Old Testament – but it doesn't stop the climb from feeling pretty difficult at times. You'll be pleased to know that section two of Jeremiah is relatively easy in comparison. The long speeches give way to quickfire encounters. The pages of poetry give way to pages of prose. Jeremiah turns into an action story, filled with dates and names and life-or-death decisions, as the people of Jerusalem are forced to take sides. The structure of the book of Jeremiah can be described simply:

1	God commissions Jeremiah
2–25	The *Book of Judgment* against Judah
26–29	Action story
30–33	The *Book of Comfort* for Judah
34–45	Action story

In 26:1–24, the action story gets underway. This narrative accompanies the *Temple Sermon* that we studied together in chapters 7–10, where we noted that Jeremiah's arrest and release probably took place between 8:3 and 8:4. It is the first of the events that Baruch collates in this second section to emphasize that everybody needs to pick a side.[2] The priests, prophets and people choose to fight against Jeremiah's prediction that their Temple will be destroyed like the Tabernacle at Shiloh, along with the rest of their city. In doing so, they follow King Jehoiakim's earlier choice, at the start of his reign, when he executed the godly prophet Uriah.[3] Jeremiah is spared a similar fate by some of the king's officials, who decide that *"This man should not be sentenced to death! He has spoken to us in the name of the Lord our God"* (verse 16). It turns out that there are still a few believers left in Judah. The Lord has found a few "good figs" that he can put into his basket for Babylon.

Faith is contagious. Having spent this chapter siding with the priests and prophets, baying for Jeremiah's blood, many of the people of Judah now switch sides. They are convicted by this rebuke from the court officials. Some of their elders even pipe up (verses 17–18) that Jeremiah's words sound a lot like Micah 3:12.[4] Instead of executing Micah, King Hezekiah had repented

85

---

[1] Isaiah and Ezekiel have a single *Book of Judgment* for both Judah and the nations. Jeremiah splits his in two. The *Books of Judgment* and the *Book of Comfort* are mainly poetry, while the rest is mainly prose.

[2] The Lord does not expect Judah to repent as a whole in 26:3. He is looking for any "good figs" that remain.

[3] The Bible tells us nothing more about Uriah but, as he was from the small town of Kiriath Jearim, he was possibly the descendant of a former custodian of the ark of the covenant during the days of Samuel and Saul (1 Samuel 7:1–2).

[4] This is the final verse of Micah's own *Book of Judgment*. He probably prophesied these words before Hezekiah became king, but he kept on prophesying throughout the reign of Hezekiah.

and saw the Lord deliver Jerusalem from the Assyrian army at its walls. Surely King Jehoiakim ought to think about doing the same thing now?[5]

For a moment, Jeremiah's life hangs in the balance. His refusal to backpedal on his words before the elders is likely to provoke King Jehoiakim to execute another prophet from the Lord. But Jeremiah's life is saved when one of the leaders of King Josiah's short-lived revival steps into the fray. Ahikam, son of Shaphan, is an elder statesman of Judah, whose own spiritual revival was evidently sincere. None of the crowd dares to argue with such a senior politician. Jeremiah is saved, and the Lord has found a few more "good figs" that he can put into his basket for Babylon.[6]

In 27:1-22, this action story continues to force people to choose sides.[7] The Lord tells Jeremiah to visit each of the foreign ambassadors to Jerusalem with a wooden yoke on his shoulders as a sign that they should tell their kings to submit gladly to the expanding rule of Babylon.[8] They must not be deceived by their pagan prophets who preach pipedreams about resistance. They must listen, instead, to the God of Israel and accept his surgeon's scalpel at work in their nations. Last, Jeremiah repeats the same instruction to King Zedekiah (verses 12-14), warning him not to listen to those who prophesy lies about a speedy recovery of the plunder that was taken from the

---

[5] The priests and prophets were supposed to preach from God's Word to the elders and the people. Ironically, they had backslidden so badly that the elders had to preach God's Word to them instead!

[6] 2 Kings 22:12-14 and 2 Chronicles 34:20. Later, Ahikam's brother, Gemariah, (36:10-12 and 25) and Ahikam's son, Gedaliah, (40:5-16) would prove to be "good figs" within Judah too.

[7] Some Hebrew manuscripts of 27:1 talk about the reign of *Jehoiakim*, but the context makes it clear that the correct manuscripts are those that read *Zedekiah*.

[8] Jeremiah is not just being negative. He tells the people to surrender because he believes firmly that the Lord has set a day to destroy Babylon (27:7) and to bring any repentant exiles home (27:22).

Temple in 605 and 597 BC.[9] Unless he surrenders willingly to Nebuchadnezzar, his Temple talisman will fall![10]

In 28:1–17, one of the false prophets of Judah chooses the wrong side. Infuriated by Jeremiah's talk of surrender, Hananiah repeats his pipedream promise that the plunder of 605 and 597 BC will very quickly be returned. Tearing the yoke from Jeremiah's shoulders, he angrily breaks it as a prediction that Nebuchadnezzar's power is on the wane. The Lord accepts Hananiah's choice and inspires Jeremiah to pass sentence on him. Within two months, the false prophet was dead.

Do you see what I mean about section two of Jeremiah being much faster-paced than the first section? It is an action story compiled by Baruch from the prophet's writings in order to call each of us to choose sides. It tells us that the Lord has begun his radical surgery and that he is calling us to a decision: Will we embrace his surgeon's scalpel willingly or will we cling onto pipedream promises of prosperity?

There is an interesting epilogue to these chapters in the book of Acts, which reminds us that the need to choose sides has not gone away. The name Hananiah means *The Lord Is Gracious*, and in Greek it became Ananias. In Acts 5, we meet an Ananias who chooses to lie to the Holy Spirit and drops down dead. In Acts 9, we meet another Ananias who chooses to risk everything in obedience to the Lord. In other words, this action story isn't ancient history. It still carries on in our churches today. God's radical surgery on his people has begun, and he still calls each one of us to choose sides.

---

[9] Ominously, God calls Nebuchadnezzar *"my servant"* in 27:6. He would use him to destroy their talisman.

[10] The remaining Temple vessels would indeed be stolen (52:17), but they would prove to be the downfall of Babylon (Daniel 5:1–6, 23–30). They would eventually be returned to Jerusalem (Ezra 1:7–11).

Long-Distance Letter
(Jeremiah 29:1–32)

This is the text of the letter that the prophet Jeremiah sent from Jerusalem to… Babylon.

(Jeremiah 29:1)

It is said that Billy Graham communicated with more people in his lifetime than anybody else in history. If that's true, then it is largely because he was willing to use whatever media was available to him. Although many despised him as a "mass evangelist" for preaching to hundreds of millions of people via radio and television, he smiled back: *"This is not mass evangelism, but personal evangelism on a mass scale."*[1]

Jeremiah had no radio, no television and no internet, but he made the most of whatever media was available to him. He had a pen, some ink, a scroll and some friends who were travelling to Babylon as part of one of King Zedekiah's delegations. He therefore decided to write down the message that God had called him to preach across Jerusalem. A long-distance letter would enable the exiles to take part in his action story too.[2]

The deportations of 605 and 597 BC have already taken place. There are now around ten thousand Jewish families in Babylon. The deposed King Jehoiachin is among them. So is the queen mother, along with many elders, priests, prophets and craftsmen. Jeremiah puts pen to paper because he wants to change the way in which they view what God is doing to

---

[1] Quoted in his obituary in the *New York Times* (21 February 2018).

[2] This letter calls the Jewish exiles out of passivity and into action. If the Lord has sent them to Babylon for a purpose, then they need to *build* and *plant* and *seek* and *pray* and *find* (verses 5 and 7).

their troubled nation. When things go wrong in our lives, it is all too easy for us to assume that our hopes have failed and God has finished with us. Jeremiah writes this letter to reassure the exiles that what has happened to them is all part of God's perfect plan for Judah. It is simply proof that his radical surgery has begun.

In 29:4–9, Jeremiah repeats the words he spoke in 27:8–12. The Jewish exiles must submit gladly to the yoke of their new masters in Babylon. They should make long-term plans – building houses, planting gardens, finding spouses for their children, becoming grandparents and earning money by doing all they can to help their new adoptive city prosper.[3] The key message behind these verses is that the Lord is sovereign over world events, even the brutal conquests of the Babylonians. Twice in these verses, the Lord refers to the recipients of Jeremiah's letter as *"those I carried into exile from Jerusalem to Babylon."*

In 29:10–14, Jeremiah repeats the words he spoke in 25:11–14. The Lord has a perfect timescale for bringing the Jewish exiles back home. He is the one who set the date when they were taken into exile (4:9 and 17:16), and he has set the date when Babylon will fall and its exiles will return home (27:22). He has determined the exact time-frame for their exile at *seventy years*.[4] They can settle down in Babylon and make the most of the next few decades, because God has got their future covered.[5]

---

[3] This is Babylon of all places. Yet God's people must not despise their pagan homelands. Although Christians are citizens of heaven (Philippians 3:19–20 and Hebrews 11:13), they ought to be among the best citizens of their earthly nations too. Churches are to bless their cities, not just use their cities.

[4] Daniel 9:1–2 looks back to 25:11–14 and 29:10. The exiles would return roughly seventy years later, in 538 BC. It would be precisely seventy years from the destruction of the Temple in 586 BC to its grand reopening in 516 BC.

[5] The Hebrew phrase in 29:14 can either be translated *"bring you back from captivity"* or *"restore your fortunes"*. It will be repeated seven times in the *Book of Comfort* (30:3, 30:18, 31:23, 32:44, 33:7, 33:11 and 33:26).

In 29:15-19, Jeremiah repeats the words he spoke in 24:1-10. He confronts the false prophets who are misleading the Jewish exiles in Babylon into thinking that those they left behind in Jerusalem were the lucky ones.[6] He informs the exiles that this is a gross misreading of the situation. The exiles are the "good figs" that the Lord has stored away in Babylon in order to replant the Jewish nation in days to come. King Zedekiah and his cronies are the "bad figs", not the lucky ones. Jerusalem is about to be destroyed.

This brings us to the two most famous verses in this chapter. They are favourites for Christian greeting cards, and you will hear them preached more often in churches than the rest of Jeremiah put together. They are wonderful verses, so read them slowly. In verse 11, the Lord promises, *"I know the plans I have for you ... plans to prosper you and not to harm you, plans to give you hope and a future."* The second glorious promise comes only two verses later, in verse 13: *"You will seek me and find me when you seek me with all your heart."* Now I don't want to detract from these verses. Both are magnificently true, but we need to read them in the context of this chapter. What the Lord is actually saying is that these things are only true for those who submit themselves to his perfect purposes, instead of pursuing an agenda of their own.[7]

In order to emphasize this, the Lord declares in 29:20–23 that he also knows the plans he has for two of the false prophets in Babylon. Ahab and Zedekiah have refused to surrender to God's agenda, insisting that he must do things their way. The Lord's plans for them are not therefore hope and a future, but

---

[6] The Lord's damning indictment of the false teachers in Babylon in 29:9 is simply: *"I have not sent them."* Genuine Christian leaders are never self-appointed. They can only ever be God-appointed.

[7] This lies at the heart of the second promise. God wants us to know him and his agenda for our lives. Such a friendship is ours for the seeking. See also 33:3, 2 Chronicles 15:2 and Matthew 7:7.

being burned to death in the fiery furnace of Nebuchadnezzar.[8]

In case we miss this correction to our Christian greeting cards, the Lord also declares in 29:24–32 that he has plans for a man named Shemaiah, who tried to silence Jeremiah by sending a copy of his letter back to Jerusalem with a demand that he be arrested for encouraging collaboration with the enemy.[9] The Lord's plans for Shemaiah are not hope and a future either. They are to scupper his plans through the sudden death of his children.[10]

This long-distance letter is therefore a call for us to submit to the Lord's perfect plans, even if they appear far from perfect to us. They are a warning against trying to force God to do things our way, using Bible verses like fortune-cookies to reassure ourselves that "faith" will ensure God does as we please. If we manipulate these verses, then we will find ourselves thwarted like the false prophets. But if we surrender ourselves gladly to God's surgeon's scalpel, then we will find these promises to be gloriously true:

"'For I know the plans I have for you," declares the Lord, "plans to prosper you and not to harm you, plans to give you hope and a future. ... You will seek me and find me when you seek me with all your heart."

---

[8] We can read about Nebuchadnezzar's fiery furnace in Daniel 3. Unlike Daniel's friends, these two false prophets would find no deliverer from the flames.

[9] Zephaniah son of Maaseiah was the captain of the Temple guard. He may also have been the brother of the false prophet Zedekiah. Unlike his predecessor Pashhur, he chooses to side with Jeremiah.

[10] Shemaiah *the Nehelamite* may refer to his hometown, but it can also be translated as Shemaiah *the Dreamer*.

Enjoy The View
(Jeremiah 30:1–31:40)

> *"The days are coming," declares the Lord, "when I will make a new covenant with the people of Israel and with the people of Judah."*
>
> (Jeremiah 31:31)

If reading the book of Jeremiah can feel like climbing up and down a mountain, then these two chapters offer some of the greatest views on the way back down the mountain. From the summit, in chapters 21–25, we saw the Lord clearing a pathway for his Messiah to come and to confer the righteousness of God on sinful people. As we head back down the mountain, we arrive at Jeremiah's *Book of Comfort*, in chapters 30–33, and are invited to reflect on what the coming of the Messiah will achieve. From our own vantage point in AD history, these chapters invite us to rejoice in what Jesus has now done for us.

In 30:1–3, the Lord tells Jeremiah for the first time to gather his prophecies into a book. The timing of this is important, because God is revealing to Jeremiah that his ministry is not just to his own generation. He is creating views that will be enjoyed by people from every nation and generation – by anyone who puts their faith in the Jewish Messiah.[1]

The first viewing platform is 30:4–11. The Lord promises that, although the fall of Babylon will be terrifying, he will protect the Jewish exiles from the slaughter and grant them favour with

---

[1] The Lord refers to Israel and Judah as *"my people"* in 30:3, not *"my peoples"*. These views are not just for the northern or the southern kingdom, but for everyone who becomes part of this renewed people of God.

their new Persian masters.[2] He will call time on their captivity and bring them home to serve him again in the Promised Land.[3] Since Jehoiachin's grandson Zerubbabel would merely become governor of the Persian province of Judea, *"David the king"* (verse 9) must refer to someone greater. After the exiles returned home, their Messiah would come. Returning home from Babylon would only be the start of God's salvation.[4]

The second viewing platform is 30:12–17. The Lord comes back to the theme of section one of Jeremiah – that *radical surgery is needed* – in order to remind the Jewish exiles that their city was destroyed to rid the world of its guilt and sin. Its wrongdoing was *"incurable"* and *"beyond healing"*, because sin is a disease for which humanity has *"no remedy"* and *"no healing"* and *"no cure"*. That's why the Lord needed to come personally to drink the cup of his own judgment towards us. It was only through the perfect life, death and resurrection of Jesus in the future that the Jewish exiles could now be made right with God. *"'I will restore you to health and heal your wounds,' declares the Lord."*

The third viewing platform is 30:18–24. The Lord promises to restore to the Jewish exiles everything they have lost. They will regain the city and palace and houses destroyed by the Babylonians and, even better, they will also regain what their nation lost long before the Babylonians invaded. The Messiah will retrain them in how to be the people of God.[5] Note the echo of 23:19–20, as the Lord invites us to rejoice over what

---

[2] God's promise to protect the exiles in 30:11 echoes his promise to protect Jeremiah in 1:8, 1:19 and 15:20.

[3] Jeremiah 30:11 speaks of God's perfect timing. He will not bring them home until his scalpel has completed its work. The Jewish exiles needed to come to real repentance before they could come back home.

[4] The Hebrew word *ābad* is used in 30:8 and 30:9 to describe both *slaving* for the Babylonians and *serving* the Lord. The gospel sets us free, not to live for ourselves, but as slaves of God (Romans 6:22).

[5] Jeremiah 30:22 is like the renewal of a marriage vow. It points us back to Exodus 6:7, Leviticus 26:12 and Hosea 2:23, and forward to Revelation 21:3. Jeremiah will repeat this promise again in a moment, in 31:33.

his surgeon's scalpel will eventually achieve for his eternal purposes.

The fourth viewing platform is 31:1–22. The Lord announces that even the northern tribes of Israel, which have rejected him for centuries, will come to a place of repentance and be restored. Whatever breathtaking views you and I may have enjoyed while walking in the mountains, the Lord expects us to find this one far greater than them all. Each of his references to *Israel*, to *Jacob*, to *Ephraim*[6], to *Samaria* and to *Ramah*[7] is meant to draw our breath in wonder at his grace towards the undeserving.[8] It is also meant to make us marvel at his wisdom in wielding the surgeon's scalpel. He really knows what he is doing. Even the hardened sinners of the northern kingdom will be saved!

The fifth viewing platform is 31:23–30. The Lord declares that he will be equally gracious to the southern tribe of Judah. At this point, Jeremiah wakes up and we discover that he received these visions in a dream. When he nods off again, it is to hear the Lord promise a new era in which it will not matter who our parents are. Regardless of whether they are Jews or Gentiles, devout or sinful, all that will matter is whether or not we place our own faith in Jesus the Messiah.

---

[6] Jacob chose Ephraim to be his firstborn heir, despite his being the second-born son of Joseph (Genesis 48:1–20). The Lord echoes that event in 31:9 and 20 to reassure Israel that he has loved them from of old (31:3).

[7] The great orator Cicero taught that there is no greater way to stir emotions than to resurrect from the dead one of the heroes of the past to personify the emotions of a nation. Jacob's wife Rachel had died whilst giving birth to Benjamin, so God makes her the embodiment of the grief of the ten northern tribes. *Ramah* was a town in the tribal territory of Benjamin, ten miles north of Bethlehem, so Matthew 2:18 quotes from 31:15 to describe the grief of Herod's slaughter. After all, Jesus is the *shepherd* prophesied in 31:10. The *"new thing"* described in 31:22, though unclear, appears to be the miraculous birth of Jesus to a virgin.

[8] For example, he calls the northern kingdom *"Virgin Israel"* in spite of her many adulteries (31:4 and 21).

The sixth viewing platform is the greatest of them all. Many readers regard 31:31–34 as "the great crescendo of Jeremiah". Certainly, these verses are the longest single passage to be quoted in its entirety in the New Testament. They are quoted in three different places because they form one of the greatest Old Testament summaries of what the coming of the Messiah has achieved.[9] It has brought about a *"new covenant"* that supersedes the Law of Moses, which repeatedly failed to bring about any long-term transformation of the hearts of the twelve tribes of Israel. It will be a new covenant of God's *Word*, since it inscribes his law on people's hearts, and a new covenant of God's *Spirit*, since it changes people from the inside out in a way that the Law of Moses never did.[10] It will bring forgiveness for sin and such infilling with the Holy Spirit that every believer, from the least to the greatest, will be able to enjoy a deep friendship with the Lord.[11]

The seventh and final viewing platform is 31:35–40. It offers us a place to sit in awed reflection on all that the coming of the Messiah has achieved for God's people. Jeremiah looked forward to it, predicting that this restored Israel would last forever. From our own perspective, centuries after the coming of Jesus, we can see much further than the borders of Israel. By bringing the Jewish exiles home to await their Messiah, the

---

[9] Romans 11:27, and Hebrews 8:8–12 and 10:16–17. This is the only Old Testament passage to use the phrase *"new covenant"*, so Hebrews quotes it to prove that the Law of Moses is now *obsolete*. The work of Jesus is described again as the *"new covenant"* in Luke 22:20, 1 Corinthians 11:25, 2 Corinthians 3:6, and Hebrews 9:15 and 12:24. It enables us to live out the marriage vow of 30:22 in a way the Law of Moses never could.

[10] Jeremiah had witnessed Josiah's short-lived revival, so he knew the limits of the Law. He knew we need the Lord to dwell inside us and to change us from the inside out (Ezekiel 36:26–27 and 2 Corinthians 3:1–6).

[11] Jeremiah 31:34 expresses the exact opposite of 14:10. Through the blood of Jesus, the Lord distinctly remembers having chosen not to recall any of our sins!

Lord restored his Kingdom such that even the gates of hell are powerless to overcome it.[12]

So don't rush on from these verses. Take some time to reflect on them. Enjoy the view.

---

[12] Nehemiah would rebuild the Tower of Hananel (Nehemiah 3:1), but only Jesus would extend the measuring line out over the Valley of Gehenna to plunder hell. That's why, even though Jerusalem would fall again in 70 AD, these verses predict something far greater (Galatians 4:25–26 and Revelation 21:2).

Promised Land
(Jeremiah 32:1–44)

*"I bought the field at Anathoth from my cousin
Hanamel."*

(Jeremiah 32:9)

On 24 May 1626, Peter Minuit purchased Manhattan Island for manufactured goods worth sixty Dutch guilders. There is debate today over how much those goods were worth – anything from $24 to $1,000 – but there is no debate that it represents one of the greatest real-estate bargains in history. The Native Americans looked at Manhattan and saw an island that was difficult to access and surplus to their needs. Peter Minuit looked at it and saw the natural harbour that would go on to become New York City. Recently, Manhattan Island was valued at $2 trillion.

Hold that thought, because this third chapter of Jeremiah's *Book of Comfort* is all about land prices being based on what we see. For generations, the Israelites had viewed the Promised Land of Canaan as essential to their national identity, but now their view was starting to change. House prices were tumbling. If Nebuchadnezzar was about to take their nation into exile, then the Promised Land wasn't worth very much at all.

In 32:1–5, we find the prophet Jeremiah in prison. We will learn much more about this period of his ministry in chapters 37–39, so for now all we need is a headline summary. It is 587 BC, midway through the two-and-a-half-year final siege of Jerusalem. Jeremiah has prophesied the imminent fall and destruction of the city, encouraging its defenders to surrender. King Zedekiah has therefore imprisoned him to silence him. There is enough talk in town to discourage the beleaguered citizens of Jerusalem already.

In 32:6–15, the Lord reveals to Jeremiah that he is about to receive a prison visitor. His cousin Hanamel is about to try to fleece him by selling him some of their family land. The last time we were told about Jeremiah's priestly family in Anathoth, they were attempting to murder him. This time they are merely out to rob him.[1] Hanamel's land has been overrun by the Babylonian army, so he hopes to offload it onto Jeremiah at a time when everybody wants to sell and nobody wants to buy.

When Hanamel arrives, Jeremiah sees his con-man cousin as a God-given way to prove to people that he truly believes what he is prophesying. Anathoth lay three miles northeast of the walls of Jerusalem so, even in prison, he knows that the fields he is being offered must have fallen into Babylonian hands. If he buys them, then word will quickly spread across Jerusalem that Jeremiah has been duped into the ancient equivalent of buying the Brooklyn Bridge. Everybody will be talking. He therefore buys the fields with meticulous precision and with a maximum of witnesses. He weighs out the exact sum of money on the scales and he signs a purchase deed that contains so much small print that it runs onto a second scroll. He then asks his secretary Baruch to seal up the purchase deed in a clay jar so that everyone can see that he is planning to preserve it for the return of the Jewish exiles, seventy years from now.[2] Hanamel is delighted with the sale, because he believes that foreign invasion has rendered the land worthless. But Jeremiah has the same foresight as Peter Minuit. He can see what will happen to the Promised Land in days to come. The joke is on his cousin, not on him.[3]

---

[1] Jeremiah 11:21 and 12:6. We know from 37:12 that one of Jeremiah's relatives had recently died, putting some of the family land up for sale, but the Babylonians were all over the land north of Jerusalem.

[2] This is the first mention of Baruch in the book of Jeremiah. His name means *Blessed* and he would play a key role in collating this book of prophecies. His appearance in the story at this point achieves the same effect as 30:1–3, emphasizing that the prophecies in this *Book of Comfort* are for many generations to come.

[3] Matthew 27:9–10 quotes from Zechariah 11:12–13, but Matthew also hints that he is also thinking about Jeremiah 19 and 32. Jeremiah's foolish-looking purchase has encouraged people for many centuries.

In 32:16–25, Jeremiah prays. He is in prison, so he cannot enjoy his new purchase. He is unmarried and childless, so neither will his grandchildren. He has bought this land solely as a way of testifying to the greatness of the Lord.[4] He has put his money where his mouth is in order to prove to the people of Jerusalem that he truly believes what he is prophesying – that Babylon will fall and that the Jewish exiles will come back home. Jeremiah therefore prays to God as the *"Sovereign Lord"*, the *"great and mighty God"* and the *"Lord Almighty"*. He trusts the one who brought the Israelites out of Egypt during the Exodus to bring the Jewish exiles out of Babylon through an even greater Exodus in days to come. He sees with eyes of faith as he prays, *"Nothing is too hard for you."*

In 32:26–40, the Lord answers Jeremiah's prayer. Note the deliberate echo between the prophet's prayer, *"Nothing is too hard for you"*, and the Lord's reply: *"Is anything too hard for me?"* The Lord is so delighted with Jeremiah's faith that he declares it a real-estate bargain to rank alongside that of Peter Minuit.[5] The city of Jerusalem is about to fall and be destroyed by the Babylonians. How could it not be, when its people have been sinning for centuries[6] and when every single sector of society has become contaminated with its sin?[7] How could it not be, when its people have set up idols in the Temple courtyards and started offering their children as human sacrifices to false gods

---

[4] Jeremiah recognizes in 32:20 that God's purpose in our lives is to reveal his greatness to the world. See also Exodus 9:16, 2 Samuel 7:23 and Isaiah 63:12. Jeremiah 32:21 is largely a quotation from Deuteronomy 26:8.

[5] 200 g of silver was not normally an exorbitant price for the land – but it was for land occupied by Babylon.

[6] The Lord mentions *Israel* as well as Judah in 32:30 to emphasize that their exiles would return home too.

[7] The Lord refers in 32:32 to *king*, *officials*, *priests*, *prophets* and *people*, as well as to both *Judah* and *Jerusalem*, in order to emphasize that there is no part of the southern kingdom that has not succumbed to sin.

in the Valley of Ben Hinnom?[8] But that will not be the end of the Jewish story.

The Lord declares that Jeremiah is wise to have put his purchase deeds in a clay jar to preserve them throughout one of the most turbulent periods in Jewish history. He has displayed the same far-sightedness as Peter Minuit, seeing the fields of Anathoth, not for what they are, but for what they will one day become. He has foreseen the day when the Lord will topple Babylon and bring the Jewish exiles back home to the Promised Land, renewing his marriage vows with Israel and establishing a new covenant with his people that will achieve for them what the covenant at Mount Sinai never did.[9] He will fill them with his Holy Spirit and empower them from the inside out to follow him.[10]

On that day, land will be bought and sold again in Judah. Fields will be farmed, not just in Judah but in the territory of Benjamin and of all the other northern tribes.[11] No longer will people attempt to offload land onto their unsuspecting relatives. They will prize it and, like Jeremiah, they will once more enjoy it as their precious Promised Land.

---

[8] The Canaanite idol Baal was different from the Ammonite idol Molek, but 19:5 and 32:35 suggest that the people of Judah had begun to conflate the two, sacrificing their children to Baal too.

[9] Jeremiah 32:38 echoes 30:22 and 31:33. Jeremiah 32:40 echoes 31:31. It is also possible that the Apostle Paul is quoting from 32:38 in 2 Corinthians 6:16.

[10] Although the Holy Spirit is not mentioned by name in 32:39, this verse is the Old Testament equivalent of Philippians 2:13.

[11] Jeremiah talks about *"the territory of Benjamin"* in 32:44 because Anathoth lay within its tribal lands.

Fenced-Off Things
(Jeremiah 33:1–26)

*"Call to me and I will answer you and tell you great
and unsearchable things you do not know."*

(Jeremiah 33:3)

Last year, I took my wife to Buckingham Palace. The royal family were away at one of their castles in the country, so its state rooms were open to the general public. The rooms we viewed were – well – palatial. There was nothing disappointing about what we saw. But it was pretty clear that we were only being permitted to view a fraction of the palace. "No entry" signs were everywhere. At one point, I entered a restricted area and found myself being shouted at by a policeman with a semi-automatic machine-gun.

That's why one of my all-time favourite verses in the book of Jeremiah is without doubt what God says to him at the beginning of this chapter. *"Call to me and I will answer you and tell you great and unsearchable things you do not know."* A more literal translation reminds me of the angry policeman at Buckingham Palace – *"Call on me and I will answer you and tell you great and **fenced-off things** you have not known."*[1] The Lord tells Jeremiah that most people are content to swim in the shallows of understanding God and his purposes, but that if we cry out for greater revelation he will not leave us in the state rooms of his palace. He will take down the no entry signs and grant us access to all areas.

---

[1] The Hebrew word *bātsar* in 33:3 means *fenced off*, *barricaded*, *fortified* and *inaccessible*. It describes cities under siege in 34:7, and the impregnable cities of Canaan in Deuteronomy 3:5 and Joshua 14:12.

The irony of this invitation is that Jeremiah is still being imprisoned by King Zedekiah. He cannot access any of the city of Jerusalem – he is not even free to go home – and yet the Lord insists that nobody can fence him off from accessing the things of God! The statement *"you have not known"* is plural in Hebrew, because ignorance of God is widespread. The promise *"I will answer you"* is singular in Hebrew, because God wants to reveal the great truths of the universe to any individual who is willing to seek him.[2]

In 33:1–5, the Lord reveals his character to Jeremiah. He helps the beleaguered prisoner grasp that he is praying to the *Creator*, *Shaper* and *Sustainer* of the universe, whose name is Yahweh – variously translated as *the Lord* or *the Eternal One* or *The One Who Really Is*. He is praying to the *God of Israel*, who is about to drive his surgeon's scalpel deep into Jerusalem in order to cut out his people's sin. These names of God are not exhaustive. They are merely meant to whet our appetites, because the first and greatest fenced-off area that God invites us to explore is that of his own character. *"Your thoughts of God are too human,"* Martin Luther warned his friend Erasmus.[3] The Christian writer J.I. Packer issues us the same warning too: *"People say they believe in God, but have no idea who it is that they believe in, or what difference believing in him may make."*[4] These verses are meant to stir our hearts to swim out from the shallows of quick-fix Christianity in order to dive into the deep waters of truly knowing God.

In 33:6–13, the Lord reveals his heart's desire to Jeremiah. He created the world as an expression of his glorious character,

---

[2] Daniel was already proving this at that very moment in Babylon. See Daniel 2:20–23 and 27–30.

[3] Quoted by A.W. Pink in *The Attributes of God* (1930). If you want to learn how to swim in the deep waters of God's character, then I highly recommend this book to you.

[4] J.I. Packer in his book *Knowing God* (1973). Once you have finished Pink, read this one too. God is speaking to us all the time, but we only grow in knowing him when we make room in our lives to listen (32:33).

so he longs first and foremost that his people should bring him *"renown, joy, praise and honour before all nations on earth"* (verse 9).[5] If we rebel against him and go our own way, while pretending to follow him, then we defame his name before the nations. His passion for his own name will then require him to discipline us and to humble us into repentance. He does not want to have to do this. These verses reveal his deeper desire to heal, bless, cleanse and forgive us so that we can give exuberant thanks to him before all nations for his goodness and his never-ending love.[6]

In 33:14–18, the Lord reveals his overarching plan to Jeremiah. If verses 15–16 seem familiar, it is because they repeat the promise God made to us at the top of the mountain, back in 23:5–6. From David's fallen dynasty, the Messiah would come to Judah as *Yahweh Tsidkênû* – that is, as *The Lord Who Makes Us Righteous*. We reflected at the top of the mountain on the difference that it makes for us to know that Jesus is not simply *The Righteous Lord*, in contrast to the sinful kings of Judah, but the one who confers God's righteousness on his sinful people. Now on our way back down the mountain, we catch a deeper insight into what this name means. The Lord changes his words as he quotes them 23:5–6. It is no longer the Messiah who bears the name *Yahweh Tsidkênû*, but the New Jerusalem. The Lord unveils his great strategy to save the nations of the world by filling his people so full of his Holy Spirit that they begin to bear the names of Jesus.[7] The true and better David and the Great High Priest, who is celebrated in verses 17–18, invites his people to be transformed into *"kings and priests"* who rule alongside him too.[8]

---

[5] This is the message of Ezekiel 20:9, 14, 22 and 44, and of Ezekiel 36:22–23 and 32.

[6] A literal translation of 33:6 is *"I will reveal to them the abundance of [my] peace and faithfulness."*

[7] Jeremiah has already stated this in 15:16. We see it in John 8:12 and Matthew 5:14. We also see it in Revelation 3:12, where Jesus deliberately refers to the Trinity as *Father, Son* and *Holy-Spirit-Filled Church*. I explain this more fully in *Straight to the Heart of Revelation.*

[8] Revelation 1:6 and 5:10. This is one of the big consequences of 31:34. We need no King or Priest other than Jesus, since we are all made kings and priests in Jesus. See also Romans 15:16.

I can hardly get over the splendour of this view. God wants to fill us so full of his Holy Spirit that people look at us and see Jesus![9]

In 33:19–26, the Lord reveals the certainty of all these things to Jeremiah. He does the same thing as he did in 31:35–37, underlining his faithfulness to his promises by pointing out that he is the one who ensures that the sun, moon and stars come out each day and each night. The whole of creation testifies that God is faithful to his Word, so we can put our trust in all of these great promises. The Lord underlines this further by reminding Jeremiah that he promised Abraham, Isaac and Jacob that he would make their descendants as countless as the stars in the sky and the sand on the seashore, and that he promised David that his son would reign forever on the throne of Judah.[10] Jeremiah must not therefore believe his neighbours when they tell him that God has finished with Israel and Judah. The reality is that the wisdom of God's plan is largely yet to be revealed.

These are just a few of the fenced-off things that God wants to reveal to us. We have reached the end of Jeremiah's *Book of Comfort*, but it feels as if we have barely scratched the surface together. So let's stop swimming in the shallows and let's respond to God today. Let's swim out into the deep waters of fathoming the purposes of the Lord.

"Call on me and I will answer you and tell you great and fenced-off things you have not known."

---

[9] The Apostle Paul says literally in Galatians 1:15–16 and 24 that *God was pleased to reveal his Son in me ... They glorified God in me*. He says in Colossians 1:27 that the gospel is *"Christ in you, the hope of glory."*

[10] Genesis 22:17, 26:4 and 32:12. Note that under the new covenant, the Lord makes these promises to *David* and the *Levites*. In other words, it's less about Jewish ethnicity and more about faith in the Jewish Messiah.

What God Can't Do
(Jeremiah 34:1–35:19)

"Hear the Lord's promise to you, Zedekiah king of Judah... I myself make this promise, declares the Lord."

(Jeremiah 34:4–5)

My children love riddles. Here is their current favourite: *What is stronger than God and more evil than the Devil? The rich want it, the poor have it, and if you eat it you die?*

If you are struggling with the answer, then you can find it in the footnotes.[1] But here's another, more serious riddle, which Jeremiah asks us through these two chapters: *What is the one thing that God cannot do?*

The reason most people find this riddle difficult to answer is that we tend to talk more about God's power than we do about his faithfulness. God is omnipotent, which most of us take to mean that he can do anything – but the Bible qualifies it to mean that he can do anything that is consistent with his character. God cannot deny himself, which is why Titus 1:2 describes him as the *"God who cannot lie."*[2] Lying is the Devil's native language, but if a word comes out of God's mouth then by definition it must be true.[3]

In 34:1–7, the action story begins again in earnest. Once more, it is an invitation for us to choose sides. Will we honour

---

[1] The answer to my children's riddle is: *Nothing*.

[2] American Standard Version. See also Numbers 23:19, 1 Samuel 15:29, 2 Timothy 2:13 and Hebrews 6:18.

[3] 2 Samuel 7:28, Psalms 31:5, 57:10, 119:151 and 119:160, Isaiah 65:16, and John 8:44 and 17:17.

God's utter truthfulness as something holy that we need to imitate? To help us make our choice, the Lord sends Jeremiah to King Zedekiah with a message. We can tell that this took place slightly earlier in the final siege of Jerusalem than the events described in chapters 32–33, because two of the other towns of Judah are still holding out against Nebuchadnezzar.[4] Furthermore, the Lord tells Jeremiah to *go to Zedekiah king of Judah*", which indicates that he has not yet been imprisoned by him.

The Lord's message to King Zedekiah is surprising. Jerusalem is about to fall, so we are bracing ourselves for a description of sin and a prediction of slaughter. Instead, the Lord promises King Zedekiah that he will die a natural death in Babylon and that it will be lamented by a crowd of loyal Jewish exiles.[5] Nebuchadnezzar had unceremoniously dumped King Jehoiakim's corpse on the main road outside one of the gateways of Jerusalem, so this promise addressed what must have been a very real fear for Zedekiah. Would he respond by honouring God's utter truthfulness through seeking to imitate it?

In 34:8–11, King Zedekiah makes his decision. He concludes that honesty is inconvenient in wartime. At the start of the siege, he had led the slave-owners of Judah in a public ceremony in which they freed all of their Hebrew slaves. The Law of Moses had required them to do this, but people had ignored that aspect of the Law for many years.[6] King Zedekiah's decision had not been religious, but pragmatic – they needed extra soldiers for the frontline and they could not afford to have disgruntled slaves

---

[4] *Lachish* was about fifteen miles southwest of Jerusalem. *Azekah* was halfway between the two. In a letter found in the ruins of Lachish, dating back to this time, a soldier in the countryside pleads despairingly: *"We are watching for the fire-signals of Lachish … for we can no longer see the signals of Azekah"* ('Lachish Letter IV').

[5] Jeremiah 34:5 is not a reference to cremation, but to the fires the Jews lit in honour of their dead kings.

[6] Jeremiah 34:14 says that they routinely ignored Exodus 21:2 and Deuteronomy 15:12–15.

at their backs while the enemy was at their walls. But there is a problem with pragmatism. When circumstances change, so do our principles.[7] Zedekiah didn't stop to ask if reneging on his promise would be the right thing to do before the Lord. It didn't occur to him that how he treated others would have any impact on how God treated him.[8]

In 34:12–22, the Lord sends Jeremiah back to King Zedekiah with a second message. He declares that he was pleased when the king led the wealthy men of Judah in a solemn covenant at his Temple to obey the Law of Moses in this matter.[9] He was pleased when they sacrificed a calf and cut it in two, walking in between the pieces as an ancient way of saying *"If I break my covenant then may God treat me like this calf"*.[10] He was appalled a short while later to see those same men despise his truthfulness by selling their honesty cheaply, breaking their word for the price of a few slaves. Jeremiah therefore pronounces the Lord's own "freedom" proclamation over King Zedekiah and the other slave-owners. He confers on them "freedom" to be slaughtered by the Babylonians![11]

In 35:1–19, Baruch records another episode from the life of Jeremiah that forms a contrast with this sin of Zedekiah. Baruch is more concerned with theme than with chronology, so the events of chapter 35 take place in around 600 BC, thirteen

---

[7] The reversal of their decision was probably linked to the arrival of an Egyptian army, which afforded a brief respite to the siege (37:5 and 11). The decision had been driven by desperation, not devotion to the Law.

[8] And yet it does. See Matthew 6:14–15, 7:2 and 18:21–35, 2 Corinthians 9:6 and James 2:13.

[9] We will discover in Ezekiel 9–11 that the Lord's presence had left the Temple in 592 BC. Even so in 34:15, God declares that whatever happened *"in the house that bears my Name"* still happened *"before me"*.

[10] The Bible describes one of these stomach-churning covenant-making ceremonies in Genesis 15:7–21.

[11] King Zedekiah would be blinded by Nebuchadnezzar but he would still die peacefully in Babylon (52:8–11). Even if we are unfaithful towards God in our promises, he remains faithful in his (2 Timothy 2:13).

years earlier than the events of chapter 34.[12] The Rekabites were foreign descendants of Jethro, the Midianite father-in-law of Moses.[13] They were nomads within Israel, famous for their refusal to drink any alcohol, so the Lord inspires Jeremiah to invite them to a party at the Temple at which he offers them some wine. Their shocked refusal shocks Jeremiah. How can these nomads care so deeply about a vow that one of their ancestors made more than two centuries ago?[14] Here at last are people who place a high value on God's truthfulness! They are "good figs" who stand in stark contrast to King Zedekiah and the many "bad figs" within Judah. The Lord will ensure that the Rekabites survive the coming slaughter.

Jeremiah's *Book of Comfort* is over. The action story has restarted, and it reminds us once more that God's radical surgery has begun. The Lord can neither tell a lie nor can he abide those who do. It is therefore time for us to choose sides in the spiritual battle. Will we be "good figs" or "bad figs" when it comes to keeping our promises?

Psalm 15 urges us to make our choice carefully: *"Lord, who may dwell in your sacred tent? Who may live on your holy mountain? The one whose way of life is blameless... who speaks the truth from their heart... who keeps an oath even when it hurts"*.

---

[12] We can tell from 35:11 that these events took place after the Babylonian and Aramean armies invaded Judah in response to King Jehoiakim's refusal to pay tribute in 601 BC.

[13] The Rekabites were Kenites, which was a clan of Midianites (1 Chronicles 2:55). Although the Rekabites were Midianites, they had separated themselves from the rest of Midian to be part of the people of God (Numbers 10:29, Judges 1:16, 4:11 and 4:17, and 1 Samuel 15:6).

[14] Jehonadab the Rekabite lived during the reign of King Jehu of Israel (841–814 BC). See 2 Kings 10:15 and 23.

First Edition
(Jeremiah 36:1–32)

*Even though Elnathan, Delaiah and Gemariah urged
the king not to burn the scroll, he would not listen to
them.*

(Jeremiah 36:25)

Rare book collectors are willing to spend eye-watering sums
of money to get their hands on an iconic first edition. I like
Geoffrey Chaucer's *Canterbury Tales*, but I can't quite fathom
how somebody was willing to pay £4,600,000 for a copy the last
time that a first edition went up for auction.[1]

Unlike me perhaps, Jeremiah was a man who knew the
value of a first edition. He was only five years into his prophetic
ministry when King Josiah's servants found an ancient copy of
the Law of Moses hidden in the Temple, in 622 BC. It had been
the rare book discovery of the century, so Jeremiah was almost
certainly involved. A secretary read the book to Josiah in his
palace and the king tore his clothes, thoroughly repenting of his
sin. The revival that ensued was too short-lived and superficial,
but Jeremiah cannot have forgotten the power that the Word of
God carries to transform a nation.[2]

That's what makes 36:1–4 very exciting. The Lord tells
Jeremiah that the time has come for him to create a first edition

---

[1] Sold by Christie's in London in 1998. In fairness, it was the first book ever
printed in England, produced by William Caxton in his workshop at Westminster
Abbey, in 1477.

[2] You can read all about this in 2 Kings 22:8–23:25.

of his own.[3] It is 605 BC, the year in which the Babylonian army will come and take the first group of Jewish exiles into captivity, so there is no time to lose in getting his prophecies out to a wider audience of readers. Jeremiah hires a scribe named Baruch, and together they start collating the book that you and I are reading together now. First editions don't get any more valuable than this one.[4]

In 36:5–10, Jeremiah sends Baruch out into the Temple courtyards to begin a first public reading of the book of Jeremiah.[5] The prophet is not referring to his imprisonment when he complains, *"I am restricted; I am not allowed to go to the Lord's temple."* He would not yet be imprisoned by King Zedekiah for the best part of twenty years. Nor can he be referring to a sickness, since he is not at all restricted from rushing into hiding later on in the chapter. Instead, it appears that he was briefly banned from entering the Temple courtyards after preaching his *Temple Sermon* there in the early days of King Jehoiakim. Baruch plans his own sermon carefully, making it coincide with a national day of prayer and fasting so that the crowds are at their fullest and their most contrite.[6] He finds a friendly official who owns a room that looks out onto the New Gate, where Jeremiah preached his *Temple Sermon*, and then he preaches from its balcony or from an open window so that he can be heard by the crowd without being lynched by them.[7]

---

[3] This was such a big moment for Jeremiah that he has already told us about it, in 30:1–2.

[4] Don't miss Jeremiah's own description of his book. He doesn't merely see it as a record of his own musings with God. He regards it as nothing less than *"the words of the Lord"*. See 2 Peter 1:20–21.

[5] We can tell from 36:1 and 9 that it took roughly a year for Jeremiah and Baruch to collate this first edition.

[6] It is likely that this was the Day of Atonement, in October 604 BC. See Leviticus 16:29–31 and Acts 27:9.

[7] Excavations of the ancient "House of Ahiel" in Jerusalem have yielded a clay seal from a letter, which is marked as having been sent by *"Gemariah son of Shaphan"*. Archaeology proves the historicity of Jeremiah.

In 36:11–19, the reading of the book of Jeremiah starts to reveal who are "good figs" and who are "bad figs" within Judah. The reading of God's Word always does, which is why the Devil will do almost anything to keep us from reading it. When Gemariah's son hears what Baruch is reading from his father's balcony or window, he is shocked and hurries down to the palace to call his father out of a meeting with the other royal officials. Is he actually aware of what the book of Jeremiah says? The officials quickly send for Baruch to come down and offer them a private reading at the palace. This is their moment of decision, when they will be revealed to be either "good figs" or "bad figs". Instead, they fudge it. They warn Baruch and Jeremiah that they had better go into hiding, but they keep hold of the first edition to pass the buck onto the king.

In 36:20–26, the reading of the Word of God reveals whether King Jehoiakim is a "good fig" or a "bad fig". This is his golden opportunity to behave like his father, and the text of this chapter makes a deliberate parallel between the reading of the book of Jeremiah in December 604 BC and the reading of the book of the Law back in 622 BC.[8] Sadly, King Jehoiakim is nothing like his father. After listening to each page, he cuts it out and throws it in the fire. He doesn't seem to realize that this is no way to treat a first edition of the book of Jeremiah.

Jehoiakim's arrogant disregard for the Word of God forces his royal officials to pick sides.[9] There can be no more hiding whether they are "good figs" or "bad figs", but what happens next is a bit of a surprise. We expect Gemariah to defend the prophet, because we know that his father was a leader in King Josiah's revival and that his brother saved the prophet's life back in 26:24. But we do not expect Elnathan, son of Akbor, to defend Jeremiah, since he helped execute the prophet Uriah

---

[8] Jeremiah 36:9 and 22. The time of year explains why there was a brazier in the palace.

[9] The officials are convicted of their sin in 36:16 but most of them are swayed back by the king's reaction in 36:24. Conviction of sin is of no benefit to us unless we actually do something about it.

back in 26:20–23. It turns out that spotting who are "good figs" and who are "bad figs" is a lot harder than it seems.

In 36:27–32, Jeremiah and Baruch are forced to make a clear choice of their own. It took them a year to collate their first edition of the book of Jeremiah. Now that it has been destroyed, it will take them another year to re-collate it. Rather than give up in despair, however, they roll up their sleeves and immediately start work on a second edition. We are told that as a result *"many similar words were added"*.[10] Because of their resolute decision to obey the Lord, the book of Jeremiah became the longest book in the Bible![11]

Jeremiah resolves not to kowtow to Jehoiakim. He risks his life to call God's judgment down upon the man who burned his precious first edition. He repeats what he prophesied in 22:13–19 – that King Jehoiakim and his children will be slaughtered by Nebuchadnezzar, and that his corpse will be thrown out onto the road outside the city.[12]

I don't know about you, but I feel challenged by this chapter. I still think that £4,600,000 is too much to pay for a first-edition Chaucer, but I have a new respect for the value of a first-edition book of Jeremiah. It revealed who were the "good figs" and the "bad figs" among the people. Whenever we preach from the book of Jeremiah, it still does.

[10] This is what happens whenever rulers try to ban, bin or burn the Bible. The Word of God actually increases!

[11] We are told in 36:2 that chapters 46–51 were already part of the first edition. Chapters like the one we are reading were later inserted midway through.

[12] Josephus Flavius confirms that this happened in his *Antiquities of the Jews* (10.6.3). By God's grace, his son Jehoiachin would survive the slaughter and go on to make Jehoiakim the ancestor of Jesus the Messiah.

Last-Chance Saloon
(Jeremiah 37:1–39:18)

Then he put out Zedekiah's eyes and bound him with bronze shackles to take him to Babylon.

(Jeremiah 39:7)

King Zedekiah had been drinking in the last-chance saloon for far too long. Time and time again, he had revealed himself to be a "bad fig". Unless he repented of his spiritual blindness, physical blindness would be inflicted brutally upon him.

Chapter 37 takes place during the two-and-a-half-year final siege of Jerusalem.[1] Zedekiah is still stubbornly drinking at the last-chance saloon. We are told that *"Neither he nor his attendants nor the people of the land paid any attention to the words the Lord had spoken through Jeremiah the prophet."* It may sound positive when he sends messengers to ask Jeremiah to pray for the leaders of Judah, but it isn't quite as positive as it seems. Zephaniah, son of Maaseiah, is the captain of the Temple guard, so his visit carries an implicit threat: *Sort out this siege, or I will finish what my predecessor Pashhur failed to do!*[2]

Jeremiah is not intimidated. He knows that Zedekiah has been emboldened to rebel against Nebuchadnezzar by a new pharaoh who came to the throne of Egypt in 589 BC. He knows that the news that an Egyptian army is marching to Jerusalem has engendered false hope that the city may yet be saved, so he

---

[1] We are told in 39:1–2 that the siege lasted from 15 January 588 BC to 18 July 586 BC.

[2] Jeremiah 20:1–6. Zephaniah had helped Jeremiah in the past (29:29), but now he reveals that his true loyalty is towards King Zedekiah. He would be captured and executed by Nebuchadnezzar in 52:24–27.

prophesies that any reprieve will not last long. Before Zedekiah knows it, his Egyptian ally will abandon him and flee. Let him be in no doubt about the fact that he is drinking in the last-chance saloon.[3]

King Zedekiah's officials are suspicious when they catch Jeremiah trying to leave the city. They don't buy his story that there has been a death in his family and that some of the family property over at Anathoth is going up for sale.[4] Thinking it far more likely that the prophet is a turncoat who is planning to go over to the enemy lines, they beat him up and imprison him. When King Zedekiah hears about it, he is granted another opportunity to switch sides. He asks the prophet privately, *"Is there any word from the Lord?"*, to which Jeremiah effectively replies: *"Yes, there is. Haven't you been listening? Get a copy of my book! You are about to be delivered into the hands of the king of Babylon."*[5] The prophet's courage here is astonishing, but instead of listening to him Zedekiah decides that moving the prophet to a nicer prison would be an easier option than repentance.[6]

In chapter 38, King Zedekiah carries on drinking in the last-chance saloon. Some of his officials complain to him that Jeremiah's message is discouraging the defenders of Jerusalem. They want the king's permission to execute him. This is another God-given call for him to switch sides, but instead he murmurs weakly: *"He is in your hands. The king can do nothing to oppose you"* (verse 5). The officials throw Jeremiah into one of the disused wells in the royal courtyard, fully expecting that he will die down there. But they are just extras in the story – the

RADICAL SURGERY HAS BEGUN

114

---

[3] Ezekiel also warned Zedekiah against trusting in Egypt in Ezekiel 17:11–21.

[4] We are told that Jeremiah's story is true in 37:12 and 32:8.

[5] Jeremiah sounds less respectful in 37:17 than he truly is. In 37:20, despite Zedekiah's sinfulness, Jeremiah still obeys the Lord's command in Exodus 22:28. He still addresses him as *"my lord the king"*.

[6] It was a much nicer prison. Jeremiah received a loaf of bread each day at a time when people elsewhere in the city were so hungry that they were devouring their own children (19:9, Lamentations 4:10).

spotlight is on Zedekiah.[7] Will this "bad fig" ever turn good?

While we await an answer, another player steps onto the stage. Ebed-Melek is not Jewish. He is a Cushite, a black man in a white man's world.[8] His name means *Servant Of The King*, and he is one of the palace courtiers. He plays the same part in the drama that the Rekabites did in chapter 35, as a "good fig" foreigner sent to shame the sinful people of Judah by being more devoted to the God of Israel than they are. When Ebed-Melek persuades Zedekiah to retrieve Jeremiah from the muddy well, it gives the king yet another opportunity to repent of his sins and to be saved. Instead, he chitter-chatters with Jeremiah over questions that the prophet has already answered many times before. In the end, an exasperated Jeremiah – still standing there with muddy feet from his time down in the well – declares that Zedekiah's own feet are sunk deep in the mud of failure. Even when confronted with such boldness, the king cannot bring himself to repent. He is more concerned about what his officials will think if they hear that he has spoken to Jeremiah than he is about what Jeremiah has spoken.[9]

Chapter 39 describes the moment when the last-chance saloon finally closes its doors on King Zedekiah. We will be given a much more detailed account of the fall of Jerusalem in chapter 52, so the one here is all about contrasting Zedekiah with Jeremiah. Sadly, the king remains a "bad fig" to the last. He refuses to listen to the prophet's warning in 34:3 and 38:23 that it is futile to attempt to flee the city. As a result, he is forced to watch as his sons and officials are murdered before his eyes, then he is blinded so that this becomes the last sight that he ever sees. He has been blind spiritually for so long that the

---

[7] Pashhur was one of the royal messengers in 21:1. Jehukal was one of the messengers in 37:3.

[8] Jeremiah asks literally in 13:23, *"Can a Cushite change his skin?"* The Hebrew word *sārīs* in 38:7 indicates that Ebed-Melek is a eunuch, which naturally makes us think of another Cushite eunuch in Acts 8:26–40.

[9] Jeremiah is not telling a lie in 38:24–27. He undoubtedly was pleading for this too (37:20).

loss of his eyesight is clearly a work of God's surgeon's scalpel. Zedekiah is taken to Babylon, where he will die a natural death in accordance with the promise that the Lord made to him in 34:1–5. The blind king cuts a tragic figure, as a "bad fig" who kept on drinking at the last-chance saloon when he should have been repenting on his knees.

As for Jeremiah, the disappointments of the past year prove to be the making of his future. Being in the royal prison kept him fed at a time when people were starving all across the city. Being in shackles earned him Nebuchadnezzar's favour, on the basis that his enemy's enemy must be his friend. Preaching that the city would fall and must surrender seemed such a deadly risk at the time, but now it transforms Jeremiah into a sought-after advisor to the Babylonians.[10] Because he was willing to throw his life away to obey the Lord, Jeremiah now finds life amidst his city's slaughter.

The last four verses turn the spotlight back onto Ebed-Melek, the foreigner who surprised us by turning out to be a "good fig" in the basket. The Lord inspires Jeremiah to prophesy that Ebed-Melek will make it through the tough days that lie ahead. *You ... will escape with your life, because you trust in me, declares the Lord.* In New Testament language, he declares that Ebed-Melek has been saved through his faith in the Lord.[11]

God's radical surgery has begun. Jerusalem has finally fallen. As the Lord calls time on Zedekiah's last-chance saloon, we are reminded that a far greater Judgment Day is coming, on which the "good figs" and the "bad figs" will finally be unmasked to everyone.

---

[10] Nebuchadnezzar tells his right-hand man to do whatever Jeremiah says in 39:12. In one leap, he is promoted from prisoner to chief adviser! When we say "yes" to being nothing, God can give us everything.

[11] Less explicit, but still in the text are two more prophecies about other Gentiles who would later be saved by faith. The Hebrew titles of the Babylonian officials in 39:3 and 13 mean literally *Chief of the Eunuchs* (*rab sārīs*) and *Chief of the Magi* (*rab māg*). One anticipates Acts 8:26–40 and the other Matthew 2:1–12.

After The Fall
(Jeremiah 40:1–44:30)

All the people disobeyed the Lord's command to stay in the land of Judah… they entered Egypt in disobedience to the Lord.

(Jeremiah 43:4, 7)

There is a persistent view in Christian circles that, if only God would judge the sin and compromise within his church, then swift revival would inevitably follow. Sadly, it simply isn't true.[1] Repentance and revival are the work of the Holy Spirit in a humble heart and, after the fall of Jerusalem, we discover that such humility is never automatic in the face of God's judgment. It often provokes sinful people to sin *even more*.[2]

In chapters 40 and 41, the scene is set for a great spiritual revival amongst the survivors of Judah. When Nebuzaradan, the commander of the Babylonian army, finds Jeremiah among his captives, he freely confesses that events have vindicated him to be a true prophet of the Lord.[3] Nebuzaradan sets Jeremiah free with a gift to reward him for his faithful prophesying, openly acknowledging that the Babylonian army did not conquer

117

---

[1] This should be obvious to us already from the fact that there were three Babylonian captivities – in 605 BC, 597 BC and 586 BC. The stubborn heart always finds ways to close its ears to what God is trying to say.

[2] The Ten Plagues hardened Pharaoh's heart instead of humbling him. The drought made King Ahab more determined to worship Baal rather than the Lord. See also Revelation 16:9, 11 and 21.

[3] Nebuzaradan means *Nebo [The Babylonian Idol] Has Given Me Offspring*, yet even this pagan idolater recognizes that the Lord has spoken truth through Jeremiah.

Jerusalem through its own skill, but because the Jewish nation sinned against the Lord.[4] He sends him back to his ruined homeland to lead the handful of Jewish survivors back to the Lord in repentance and revival.[5] When Jeremiah gets home, there is more good news. King Nebuchadnezzar has made Gedaliah son of Ahikam governor of the newly created province of Judah. Ahikam was a driving force behind King Josiah's short-lived revival and he saved Jeremiah from being executed in 26:24.[6] With Ahikam's son as the new governor and with even the leaders of Babylon recognizing God's scalpel at work in the fall of Jerusalem, the stage is set for a magnificent spiritual revival among the survivors of Judah. Gedaliah will surely finish what his father started.

Gedaliah urges the survivors to listen to what Jeremiah said in 27:17, embracing their new status as subjects of the Babylonian Empire.[7] He echoes the early days of Israel in the Promised Land when he urges the survivors to enjoy living in houses they have not built and harvesting crops they have not planted.[8] Many of the Jews who fled the land for fear of Babylon

[4] Jeremiah serves as a prophetic picture for us here. Our short-term suffering for the Lord will always lead to long-term reward when Jesus finally returns to vindicate the faithful preachers of his gospel.

[5] Nebuzaradan initially granted Jeremiah a choice between going home and going to Babylon, but the Hebrew word *shūb*, or *to turn back*, in 40:5 suggests that he revoked this choice before Jeremiah even had a chance to reply. Only 832 families were taken into captivity in the third wave of exiles in 586 BC (52:29). The vast majority were slaughtered, preserving only a tiny remnant of survivors to harvest the farmlands of Judah (39:10).

[6] 2 Kings 22:12–14 and 2 Chronicles 34:20. Ahikam's brother Gemariah had also taken Jeremiah's side in 36:10–25. Gedaliah therefore came from a family that represented the best of the "good figs" left in Judah.

[7] In 1932, archaeologists excavating Gedaliah's base at Mizpah found an onyx seal that bears the inscription: *"Belonging to Jaazaniah the servant of the king"*. We can trust the historicity of the book of Jeremiah.

[8] God granted the paupers of Judah the fields and houses of their oppressors, just as he had granted the Israelites the fields and houses of the Canaanites. See Deuteronomy 6:10–11 and Joshua 24:13.

now return to help bring in a bumper harvest.[9] Gedaliah is too busy planning revival to believe the rumours that people are plotting his assassination.

And yet they are. Ishmael son of Nethaniah is a minor member of the royal family who believes that the execution of King Zedekiah's children has given him a shot at the throne of Judah. Spurred on by promises of help from the king of the Ammonites, he murders Gedaliah, his officials and his Babylonian bodyguard.[10] The arrival of eighty pilgrims from the northern tribal lands of Israel, on their way to offer sacrifices to the Lord amidst the blackened ruins of his Temple, ought to have convicted Ishmael of his own need to repent alongside them. Instead, he adds to his sins by slaughtering the pilgrims too. Although he fails in his attempt to enslave the Jewish survivors and to force them to crown him king, he succeeds in robbing them of their revival. They are now too afraid of reprisals from Babylon to remain in the Promised Land. In a tragic reversal of the Exodus, they decide to flee back to the land of their former slavery.

Even now, all is not yet lost. In chapters 42 and 43, the Lord grants the Jewish survivors a second shot at repentance and revival. Jeremiah reassures them that Nebuchadnezzar will not blame them for Ishmael's rebellion, but he also warns them that if they leave the Promised Land then they will repeat the sin that caused the destruction of Judah – they will be relying on Pharaoh instead of on the Lord. They can still enjoy God's blessings in the Promised Land, but if they flee to Egypt then all of them will die there.[11] Sadly, the Jewish survivors still refuse

---

[9] Gedaliah ruled from August to October 586 BC – the time of the grape, fig and olive harvests in Israel. The *seventh month* in 41:1 refers to the seventh month of the Jewish year, not the seventh month of Gedaliah's governorship, so the eighty pilgrims are going up to the Temple ruins for the Feast of Tabernacles.

[10] Jeremiah 41:10 and 15. Ishmael is a picture of pragmatism within the church, attempting to resolve its issues through human strength and self-promotion instead of through repentance and obedience to the Lord.

[11] The Lord calls Nebuchadnezzar *"my servant"* in 43:10, just as he did in 25:9 and 27:6. Even now, if the Jewish survivors will only trust the Lord, he is more than able to save them from the Babylonians.

to listen. They accuse Jeremiah and Baruch of being in cahoots with the Babylonians, speaking lies to enslave God's people instead of truth to set them free.[12] Even when Jeremiah shows them the very paving stones in the Egyptian border town of Tahpanhes where Nebuchadnezzar will set up his throne after invading Egypt, they still refuse to submit to God's Word.[13] They choose the path of rebellion instead of the path of repentance, of restoration and of revival.

These chapters are very relevant to our own day. They expose the lie that divine judgment inevitably leads God's people towards repentance and revival. In the days after the destruction of the Twin Towers of the World Trade Center in New York on 11 September 2001, many Christians predicted a spiritual sea change for the Western world. It was widely described as a "day that changed the world". Sure enough, according to a 2006 study conducted by Barna Group, many church congregations across America doubled in size the following Sunday – but within four months church attendance was back down to pre-attack levels. The director of the 2006 study, David Kinnaman, came to the difficult conclusion that *"Five years removed from that fateful day, spiritually speaking, it's as if nothing significant ever happened."*[14]

The truth is that repentance and revival are not primarily the fruit of God's judgment, but the work of God's Spirit in

---

[12] They pretend to have changed in 42:1–6, but sounding repentant is easy. The reality of our repentance is revealed whenever God gives a different answer to the one we want to hear (Matthew 3:8 and Acts 26:20).

[13] An important border town like Tahpanhes would receive regular visits from Pharaoh. Archaeologists have discovered the ruins of a royal border-palace at Elephantine, a town on Egypt's southern border.

[14] This was the conclusion of David Kinnaman, the director of a study by the Barna Group in August 2006. He observed that *"People used faith like a giant band-aid ... and it was discarded after a brief period of use."* (Quoted on the Barna Group website).

those who are humble enough to surrender to God's Word.[15] Jeremiah underlines this through a prophecy in 44:1–30 that reveals that God's judgment provoked Jewish survivors to sin *even more*. Rather than repenting, they convinced themselves that their nation's misfortune was the result of its neglect of idols during the days of King Josiah. They started worshipping false gods in Egypt with even greater gusto than they had in the land of Judah. Four times in these verses, Jeremiah calls them back to *"the Lord Almighty, the God of Israel"*, because rejecting their own God flies in the face of all common sense.[16] It is an act of spiritual self-harm. Jeremiah 44:7 asks literally, *"Why are you doing such great evil to your own souls?"*

A few years ago, my route to work was flooded and my office was cut off from where I live. I spent hours in traffic trying to find a route around the flooding. It was only when I finally gave up that I noticed that my phone was switched off. As soon as I turned it on, I received a message warning me not to come into work because the office was not open. Had I turned my phone on earlier, I could have saved hours of wasted effort.

That's the message of these chapters. Trouble makes the ringtone sound more loudly for God's messages to us, but we need to ask the Holy Spirit to switch on our hearts to hear messages from God, because repentance and revival are never automatic. Even after the fall of Jerusalem, the Jewish survivors kept on sinning. None of those who went to Egypt would ever make it home.[17]

---

[15] Jeremiah puts his finger on the root problem in 43:2 by using the Hebrew word *zēd*, which means *arrogant* or *proud* or *insolent* or *presumptuous*. The Lord calls the survivors to show some humility in 44:10.

[16] Jeremiah 44:2, 7, 11 and 25. God continues to show mercy by forcing these survivors to reflect on their actions for ten long days while they wait for Jeremiah in 42:7. He also preserved Pharaoh Hophra from his enemies until 570 BC, and Egypt from Babylonian invasion until 567 BC.

[17] They feared the giants in the Promised Land, so the Lord put their generation to death and rescued only a handful of their children (42:17, 44:14 and 44:28).

God's World Tour (Jeremiah 45:1–49:39)

"I will overthrow what I have built and uproot what I have planted, throughout the earth… For I will bring disaster on all people, declares the Lord."

(Jeremiah 45:4–5)

But Dad, that's not fair! My youngest son accepts most punishments if he can see that his older siblings are being punished too. What he can't abide is a sense that he is being singled out for punishment while his older siblings do the same things and get off scot free. That's how the Jewish readers of the book of Jeremiah must have felt during their exile in Babylon. How could it be fair for the Lord to have come down so hard on the sins of Israel and Judah, while their pagan neighbours were every bit as sinful too?

The Lord has anticipated this question. He has held back several prophecies that Jeremiah spoke in his early days of ministry so that he can place them here as a vindication of his fairness towards Judah. He inspired Baruch to end the book of Jeremiah with chapters that take us on a whirlwind world tour of God's judgment.

In chapter 45, Baruch shares five verses of personal prophecy that he received from Jeremiah when he complained about how much it cost him to serve as the prophet's secretary. This is the shortest chapter in the book, dating back to the months between 36:8 and 36:9. Baruch places it here because the rebuke he received from the Lord spoke about God's plan to pour out his judgment *on all flesh throughout the earth.*[1] It therefore serves as an introduction to this world tour of judgment, reassuring us that whatever God meted out against the sins of his people, he would mete out to their pagan neighbours too.[2]

In chapter 46, God begins his world tour in Egypt, since this is where we left Jeremiah and Baruch at the end of chapter 44. The first twelve verses of this prophecy came before the Battle of Carchemish in 605 BC, predicting the fall of Egypt long before the Jewish survivors foolishly fled there. Egypt was feared for its chariots, its spearmen and its bowmen, but the Lord predicts their humiliation by the Babylonians on the battlefield. The final sixteen verses of this chapter were prophesied after the battle, predicting that Egypt would never recover and regain its status as a superpower: *"Pharaoh king of Egypt is only a loud noise; he has missed his opportunity"* (verse 17).[3] It would fend off the Babylonians until 567 BC, but then it would fall to Nebuchadnezzar as proof to the whole world that the puffed-up idols of Egypt are powerless to save anyone. This would prepare them to witness the Lord bringing his Jewish exiles safely home from Babylon.[4]

In chapter 47, God takes his world tour eastwards into the land of the Philistines.[5] This prophecy dates back to before

---

[1] The Hebrew phrase *al kol bāsār* in 45:5 means *"on all flesh"* or *"on all of humankind"*.

[2] This is the last mention of Baruch in the Bible. There is a *Book of Baruch* in the Apocrypha, but it was written by someone else in his name after 75 AD in order to urge the Jews to submit to the Roman Empire.

[3] Jeremiah 46:26 echoes God's promise in Isaiah 19:18–25 to preserve a remnant of Egyptians to worship him. The Babylonians would kill, steal and leave in 567 BC (43:12), allowing the Egyptians to limp on until the Persians came in 525 BC. Jeremiah 46:27–28 is reassurance for the repentant Jewish exiles in Babylon, not for the rebellious Jewish fugitives in Egypt.

[4] The Lord declares in 46:25 that his battle against Egypt is primarily against its gods, just as it was in the days of Moses (Exodus 9:14 and 12:12, and Numbers 33:4).

[5] The Philistines were descended from the Sea Peoples of *Caphtor*, an ancient name for Crete. Their end would be so terrible that Philistine fathers would even abandon their children in their eagerness to flee (47:3).

the Battle of Carchemish, predicting that the Egyptian army would destroy Gaza on its way to the battle and that the Babylonian army would destroy Ashkelon on its way back from it. The Philistines had been the arch-enemies of Judah since the days of the Judges, but none of them would survive this slaughter.[6]

In chapter 48, God's world tour continues eastwards to the land of Moab, across the Dead Sea from the land of Judah, where the Lord expresses the totality of his judgment by mentioning over twenty Moabite towns by name.[7] He stays in the area to speak similar judgment over Ammon in 49:1–6, since the Moabites and Ammonites were both descended from Lot's drunken incest with his two daughters in Genesis 19:30–38 and therefore operated as close allies.[8] Nebuchadnezzar would destroy both Moab and Ammon in 582 BC, but the Lord declares that it will be his own doing (48:10) in order to prove that the Moabite national god Chemosh and the Ammonite national god Molek are imposter idols with no power to save anyone.[9]

Moab and Ammon were such inveterate enemies of Israel that they were banned from worship services at the Tabernacle.[10] They had taken advantage of the destruction of Israel by occupying the tribal lands of Gad on the eastern side

---

[6] The total annihilation of the Philistines is also predicted in Isaiah 14:28–32, Ezekiel 25:15–17, Amos 1:6–8 and Zephaniah 2:4–7. Their Phoenician allies in Tyre and Sidon would be next on the Babylonian shopping list.

[7] Many of these towns were allocated to the tribe of Reuben in Numbers 32 and Joshua 13. The town named *Madmen* has nothing to do with crazy males, but comes from a Moabite word for *Dunghill*. Note that 48:45–46 echoes Israel's victory song over Sihon, an ancient ruler of the area, in Numbers 21:27–29.

[8] *Rabbah* was the capital city of Ammon, a fact reflected by its modern name *Amman*, the capital of Jordan.

[9] See 48:7, 13, 35 and 46, and 49:1 and 3. The Hebrew word *malkām* in 49:1 and 3 could either mean *their king* or *their Molek*. In the context of 48:7 and 13, however, it is almost certainly a reference to Ammon's national god. See 1 Kings 11:33.

[10] Deuteronomy 23:3–4. The Moabites and Ammonites had attacked Israel many times without reason. See Numbers 25:1, Judges 11:12–13, 1 Samuel 11:2, 2 Samuel 10:1–19, 2 Kings 13:20 and 24:2, Nehemiah 4:7, Jeremiah 40:14, Ezekiel 25:1–11, Amos 1:13–2:3 and Zephaniah 2:8–11.

of the River Jordan. Nevertheless, for the sake of their ancestor Lot, the Lord ends these two prophecies with a promise that he will preserve a remnant of Moabites and Ammonites to worship him.

In 49:7–22, God's world tour arrives in the land of Edom. As descendants of Isaac's son Esau, the Edomites were natural allies for Israel and Judah. Instead they were persistently hostile towards God's people, so the Lord declares that their famous mountaintop fortresses will be powerless to save them from the Babylonians in 583 BC.[11] Unlike Egypt, Moab and Ammon, no remnant of Edom would survive its destruction.[12]

In 49:23–27, God's world tour moves north to Damascus, where the Lord predicts the Babylonian conquest of the Arameans. In 49:28–33, it encompasses the Arab nomads and the Arab settlers. In 49:34–39, it reaches the kingdom of Elam, in modern-day Iran. Although Elam was famous for its archers, Jeremiah predicts in around 596 BC that it will soon fall to the Babylonians alongside all these other pagan nations.[13]

Baruch has taken us on a tour of over a thousand miles in these five chapters in order to give a comprehensive answer to the complaint of the Jewish exiles in Babylon: *But God, that's not fair!* God's world tour predicts the avalanche of judgment that would soon fall on Judah's pagan neighbours. It reminds us that he is far more than just the Judge of Israel. He is the Judge of every nation of the world.[14]

---

[11] Numbers 20:18–20, Deuteronomy 2:1–6, 1 Samuel 14:47, 1 Kings 11:14, Psalm 137:7, Isaiah 34:5 and 63:1–6, Lamentations 4:21, Ezekiel 25:12–14 and 35:1–15, Joel 3:19, Amos 1:11–12, Obadiah 1–21 and Malachi 1:2–5.

[12] *Teman* was a city named after the grandson of Edom (Genesis 36:8–11). Jeremiah's prophecy against Edom has many parallels to the one delivered by another of his contemporaries in the book of Obadiah.

[13] The Lord promises in 49:39 to preserve a remnant of Elamites to serve him. Sure enough, we discover that Elamite converts to Judaism were among those saved on the Day of Pentecost in Acts 2:9.

[14] Malachi 1:5 explains that this is the lesson we are meant to draw from chapters such as these. The Lord also reveals himself to be the God of all nations in Jeremiah 5:15, 18:7–10, 23:24, 25:17–29 and 32:27.

The Big One
(Jeremiah 50:1–51:64)

*"Babylon will be captured; Bel will be put to shame,
Marduk filled with terror."*

(Jeremiah 50:2)

You don't have to know much about computer games to know
that the final level of a game is always the big one. You have to
fight a lot of enemies to get there, but it's on the final level that
you are confronted with the biggest enemy of them all. That's
also how it is with God's world tour of judgment. The two final
chapters are all about Babylon.

When Jeremiah prophesied these words in 593 BC,
Babylon appeared invincible.[1] After the Battle of Carchemish, it
had swooped on so many of the nations of the Middle East that
Jeremiah likens it to an *"eagle"* in 48:40 and 49:22.[2] Its army
looked as unstoppable as its city walls looked unscalable – yet
Jeremiah prophesies that God's world tour of judgment will
play there too. Babylon, the big one, will be destroyed.

Jeremiah hints at the specifics of the fall of Babylon in
49:39, where he predicts that the Elamites would recover from
their defeat at the hands of King Nebuchadnezzar. The Persians
(described in 50:3 as *"a nation from the north"*) would persuade
the Medes and Elamites to march with them against Babylon
in 539 BC (described in 50:9 as *"an alliance of great nations
from the land of the north"*). Even to the commander of this

---

[1] We are told in 51:59 that Jeremiah sent these words to Babylon in 593 BC.

[2] Ezekiel is about to take the prophetic baton from Jeremiah's hand, so he also
describes Babylon as an eagle in Ezekiel 17:3. Other major prophecies against
Babylon can be found in Isaiah 21:1–10 and Habakkuk 1–2.

grand coalition, capturing Babylon appeared impossible. After examining its massive walls and mighty gates, King Cyrus of Persia admitted frankly that *"I am unable to see how any enemy can take walls of such strength and height by assault."*[3]

That's why Jeremiah insists over twenty-five times in these two chapters that the fall of Babylon will come as a result of the judgment of God, not the genius of Cyrus. By choosing the Babylonians as his tool to judge the nations, the Lord had granted them front row seats at each venue of his world tour.[4] Yet instead of repenting, they outdid the sins of those they conquered. God therefore summons the nations of the north to become new tools in his hand in order to work his judgment upon Babylon.

Six times the Lord attributes his judgment to the *idolatry* of Babylon.[5] The city's patron deity was known by two names – *Bel* and *Marduk* – and he was normally depicted walking with a dragon. You don't need to have read the book of Revelation to spot that this portrayed the demon that was at work behind the idol. Since the military successes of Babylon had made the nations of the world conclude that its god must be the driving force behind world history, Jeremiah predicts that the Lord will bring Babylon back down to earth with a bump to prove that he is the true God of all nations.[6]

Ten times the Lord attributes his judgment to *his continued love for Israel and Judah.*[7] The fall of Babylon would do more

---

[3] The Greek historian Xenophon quotes King Cyrus in his *Cyropaedia* (8.5.7).

[4] Jeremiah 25:9, 27:6, 43:10, 50:23, 51:7 and 51:20–23.

[5] Jeremiah 50:2, 50:38, 51:17–19, 51:44, 51:47 and 51:52 all echo 46:25, 48:7, 13, 35 and 46, and 49:1–3.

[6] Babylon began its history as *Babel*, the city that tried to build a tower to heaven in Genesis 11. Jeremiah 51:53 therefore likens its fall to the failure of the builders of the Tower of Babel.

[7] Jeremiah 50:4–8, 50:17–20, 50:28, 50:33–34, 51:5, 51:10, 51:11, 51:24, 51:35–36 and 51:49–51. We are meant to spot that the fate of Babylon in 50:41–43 echoes the fate of Jerusalem in 6:22–24, because what goes around comes around. Items stolen from the Temple in Jerusalem precipitate the downfall of Babylon in Daniel 5.

than simply punish the sins of its citizens. It would precipitate the return of the Jewish exiles to their homeland, which would embolden the survivors of the northern tribes of Israel to return too. Israel and Judah would be reunited as a single nation under God, humbled into repentance through their many years of exile, and having received complete forgiveness for all their sins.[8] Jeremiah reassures the Jewish exiles that the Lord has not been unfair towards their nation. The world tour of his judgment will end with the total restoration of God's people.

Jeremiah is cryptic at times in his predictions about the fall of Babylon.[9] But what strikes us most is how specific he is about the detail of what actually happened in October 539 BC. He tells us that the city will be captured *"from the north"* (50:9) through a cunning stratagem (50:24), which will involve the waters of its river running dry (50:38 and 51:36). It will fall suddenly (51:8) to the Medes (51:11 and 28) while its rulers are drunk and drowsy (51:39 and 57). Perhaps as astonishing as the fall of Babylon itself is the prediction that, despite the city's prime position on the River Euphrates, it will never be rebuilt. Sure enough, its ruins still remain a wasteland (50:39–40, 51:30 and 51:37).

All of these predictions must have sounded like nonsense to Seraiah, son of Neriah, when Jeremiah asked him to read out these two chapters in the streets of Babylon in 593 BC. The brother of Baruch served as King Zedekiah's chamberlain, so he accompanied his master on his journey to swear a solemn

---

[8] *Carmel* and *Ephraim* were on the west side of the River Jordan; *Bashan* and *Gilead* were on the east side. The Lord therefore promises to restore the whole of the Promised Land to Israel. Note the echo of 31:34 in 50:20.

[9] *Leb Kamai* and *Sheshak* in 51:1 and 41 are codenames for Babylonia and for Babylon. Using the Hebrew alphabet, they do the equivalent of our swapping A for Z, B for Y, C for X, and so on. See also 25:26.

oath of allegiance to King Nebuchadnezzar.[10] Jeremiah told Seraiah to read these two chapters aloud to the people of Babylon, as a final call to repentance, before tying a rock to the scroll and tossing it into the city's great river, which was to prove so pivotal to its sudden downfall. The Lord warned the Babylonians that he had set a date for his world tour to arrive at their wicked city. After judging many other sinful nations, he would finally pass judgment on the big one too.[11]

Against all odds, this is actually what happened to the city of Babylon in October 539 BC. The Greek historian Herodotus is exaggerating when he tells us that the walls of Babylon were 25 m thick and 100 m high (as wide as a basketball court and fifteen times taller than the Great Wall of China!) but King Cyrus of Persia knew he could not scale them.[12] Instead, he noticed that the River Euphrates passed under the walls of Babylon, so he told his men to dam the river upstream to the north of the city. While Belshazzar of Babylon partied in his palace with his noblemen and generals, the Persian soldiers watched in wonder as the riverbed emptied to expose a broad and undefended passageway under the wall. By the time Belshazzar and his drunken generals even realized that their walls had been breached, it was too late for them to fight back. The Greek historian Xenophon tells us that the Persian soldiers *"fell upon them as they were drinking by a blazing fire, and without waiting they dealt with them as with foes."*[13]

---

[10] 2 Chronicles 36:13. Archaeologists have found a seal in the ancient ruins of Jerusalem that reads *"Belonging to Seraiah son of Neriah"*. We can be confident about the historicity of the book of Jeremiah.

[11] Revelation 17–18 uses Jeremiah 50–51 as a prophetic picture of the sudden Day of Judgment on which Jesus will judge humanity as a whole. Note the clear echo of 51:6, 45 and 63 in Revelation 18:4 and 21.

[12] Herodotus in his *Histories* (1.178). He goes on to describe the fall of Babylon in 1.191.

[13] Xenophon in his *Cyropaedia* (7.5.1–32). You can also read about Belshazzar's final party in Daniel 5.

Babylon, the big one, the largest and strongest city in the world, had been conquered.[14] In the aftermath of victory, just as Jeremiah predicted, King Cyrus of Persia informed the Jewish exiles in Babylon that he had decided to send them back home.

---

[14] The Persians did not destroy Babylon completely in 539 BC. God gave the city a few more years of grace in which to repent, before the Persians finally razed it in about 520 BC. Even today, its site remains a wasteland.

A New Hope
(Jeremiah 52:1–34)

*So Jehoiachin put aside his prison clothes and for the
rest of his life ate regularly at the king's table.*

(Jeremiah 52:33)

In her classic Christian memoir, *The Hiding Place*, Corrie ten
Boom recalls a message she received in prison after being
arrested by the Nazis for hiding Jews in her Dutch home during
World War Two: *"All the watches in your closet are safe."* To her
captors, the message would seem quite commonplace, but
when Corrie read it she sobbed great tears of joy. It revealed
that all of the Jews in the secret room at her home had escaped
from the Nazis as a result of her refusal to talk on the night she
was arrested.[15]

That's how we are meant to see the final chapter of the
book of Jeremiah. It is much more than an account of the fall of
Jerusalem, since the prophet has already given us that in chapter
39. Nor is it a final prophecy to finish off Baruch's collection,
since he expressly tells us that the words of Jeremiah end in
51:64. It is like Corrie ten Boom's secret message in *The Hiding
Place* – a coded message that was given to the Jewish exiles
while they were still living in captivity in Babylon. It reassured
them, in language that would be lost on their captors, that a new
hope was arising for their nation.

The early verses of this final chapter seem pretty hopeless.
King Zedekiah refuses to accept that only radical surgery can
save his nation. Instead, he adds a new sin to the catalogue of

---

[15] Corrie ten Boom in her book, *The Hiding Place* (Hodder & Stoughton, 1971).

his rebellion against the Lord by reneging on the solemn oath of allegiance that he swore to King Nebuchadnezzar in the name of Yahweh when he visited Babylon with Baruch's brother in 593 BC.[16] This act of rebellion provokes the final siege of Jerusalem, which lasts from 15 January 588 BC to 18 July 586 BC.[17] When the city walls are finally breached, King Zedekiah tries to flee but he is captured and hauled before the king of Babylon.[18] Nebuchadnezzar has Zedekiah's sons slaughtered before his eyes, then gouges out his eyes so that their deaths become the final image that is embedded in his mind. Zedekiah would live out his days as a blind and broken prisoner in Babylon.[19]

Meanwhile, on 14 August 586 BC, the Babylonian army burns down the Temple, the royal palace and every other important building in Jerusalem. They demolish its city walls and carry off the sacred furnishings of its Temple as spoils of war.[20] They slaughter the high priest, the captain of the Temple guard and every other senior official of Judah. Only 832 Jewish families survive the slaughter to be taken as captives to Babylon, including all those who heeded Jeremiah's call in 21:1–10 to surrender to the Babylonians. A few of the poorest Jews are also spared to till the ruined fields of Judah, but only 745 families dare to stay on after the assassination of Gedaliah

[16] 2 Chronicles 36:13 and Ezekiel 17:13–19 tell us that breaking this oath was not just foolish – it was sinful. By despising his oath, King Zedekiah showed that he despised the God in whose name he had sworn it.

[17] King Zedekiah was emboldened by a promise of help from Egypt, despite God's warning that Pharaoh was a false friend (37:5–10 and Ezekiel 17:11–21). Pointedly, Pharaoh plays no role in this chapter.

[18] Jeremiah warned Zedekiah not to try to flee in 34:1–3. This was therefore an act of rebellion as well as of stupidity. The Hebrew text of 52:7 describes his soldiers as *men of war*, but they surrender without a fight.

[19] The Hebrew story begins in Genesis 11 when Abraham sets out in faith from Ur, in Chaldea. Now it appears to come to an end when the unbelieving Zedekiah is hauled back to Babylon, also in Chaldea.

[20] The comprehensive list of articles in 52:17–23 is meant to make our hearts grieve for the Lord's Temple. The Hebrew words for *pure gold or silver* in 52:19 are literally *gold gold* and *silver silver*, helping us to understand what the Lord intends to convey by revealing himself in Isaiah 6:3 as *holy holy holy*.

and are eventually deported to Babylon to join the other Jewish exiles.[21] All of the others die in Egypt.

If you find these verses even more depressing than the account of the fall of Jerusalem in chapter 39, then take heart – you are meant to! The key to understanding this chapter lies in spotting that it is an almost word-for-word repetition of 2 Kings 24:18–25:30. Jewish tradition claims that Jeremiah wrote 1 and 2 Kings during his final years in Egypt, as a prophetic explanation of why the Lord had sent the people of Judah into exile. This would account for why the vocabulary and writing style of 1 and 2 Kings is quite similar to the book of Jeremiah, and it would also explain why those two books fail to mention Jeremiah even once – surely unthinkable for such a giant of a prophet unless it was a result of the author's own humility.[22] The final four verses of 2 Kings 25 and Jeremiah 52 describe an event that took place on 22 March 561 BC, which either makes Jeremiah very old or the event must have been added to both books by Baruch or by another scribe after the prophet died. They are what this chapter is really all about. Like Corrie ten Boom's cryptic message in a Dutch prison that evaded the prying eyes of her Nazi jailers, these verses express a new hope for Judah, even in the heart of Babylon.

Most readers have forgotten King Jehoiachin by the time they reach the end of Jeremiah. Some have confused him with his father Jehoiakim and think that Nebuchadnezzar killed him and threw his body outside the gate of Jerusalem to rot in the road. Since he only reigned for three months before Nebuchadnezzar took him into captivity, other readers have forgotten him altogether. They assume that the royal dynasty of David was wiped out when Nebuchadnezzar executed Zedekiah's children.

---

[21] Only 3,023 men were taken into captivity in 597 BC, in addition to their wives and children. They were joined by just 1,577 more men in 586 and 581 BC, adding a total of 4,600 families to the 7,000 who had been taken into exile in 605 BC. From this tiny remnant, the Lord would rebuild the entire nation of Judah.

[22] By way of contrast, Jeremiah is mentioned four times by name in 2 Chronicles 35–36 alone.

That's why these final verses are such good news and why their message needed to be delivered cryptically in order to evade the attention of the Babylonians.

The former King Jehoiachin is still very much alive. After thirty-seven years of imprisonment in Babylon, he is suddenly set free and granted a place of honour at the royal table in the palace of Babylon.[23] Jehoiachin means *The Lord Establishes*, and there is no other reason why he should have been remembered and promoted in this way. The Babylonians blinded and castrated their defeated kings. They didn't wine and dine them! Perhaps he had repented as a result of Ezekiel's preaching. We cannot know for sure. All we know is that the final verses of the book of Jeremiah treat his sudden elevation as a prophetic picture for the Jewish exiles. A new hope is arising for their nation.

Only radical surgery could save Judah, so God didn't shrink back from wielding his surgeon's scalpel. But as a result of his fierce judgment, there is now a new hope for the survivors of Judah. Babylon will not represent the end of their national story. It will merely serve as a pit stop on the death-and-resurrection pathway on which God's people need to travel from repentance to restoration and revival.[24]

We began this second section of the book of Jeremiah by recognizing that the patient's wounds are beginning to heal. By God's grace, a new hope is dawning for the exiled survivors of Israel and Judah.

---

[23] Amel-Marduk was the son of Nebuchadnezzar. His name meant *Labourer of Marduk*, but those who disapproved of him gave him the nickname *Awel-Marduk* instead, meaning *Fool of Marduk*.

[24] Judah was saved through its "death and burial" in exile because these served as a prophetic picture of the death-and-resurrection pathway that we must all travel with Christ in order to be saved. We discover in Matthew 1:1–17 that Jehoiachin was the grandfather of Zerubbabel and the ancestor of Jesus. We discover in 1 Chronicles 6:14–15 and Haggai 1:1 that, although the high priest Seraiah was executed in 52:24–27, God preserved his grandson Joshua to become the new high priest after the Jewish return from exile.

Face the Facts
(Lamentations 1:1–22)

Lamentations:

Responding to Surgery

Face the Facts
(Lamentations 1:1–22)

"Look around and see. Is any suffering like my suffering that was inflicted on me, that the Lord brought on me in the day of his fierce anger?"

(Lamentations 1:12)

The prophet Jeremiah was a prolific writer. Not only is the book that bears his name the longest book in the Bible, but Jewish tradition informs us that he wrote 1 and 2 Kings too. There are also some compelling reasons to believe he wrote the book of Lamentations.

For a start, we are told in 2 Chronicles 35:25 that *"Jeremiah composed laments for Josiah, and to this day all the male and female singers commemorate Josiah in the laments. These became a tradition in Israel and are written in the Laments."* Jeremiah was a celebrated writer of laments, which makes him the most obvious author of the five anonymous poems in Lamentations that express his nation's grief after the fall of Jerusalem. Add to this some similarities in vocabulary and writing style, plus the fact that both Jewish and Christian traditions attribute authorship to Jeremiah, and we can see why Jerome, the great translator of the Bible into Latin, states so categorically in his Vulgate translation of the Bible into Latin that these are *"the Lamentations of Jeremiah"* who *"lamented the ruins of his city in a fourfold alphabet."*[1]

Jerome is referring to the remarkable layout of the book of Lamentations. Its five chapters record five separate poems of lament that are linked together by a common sophisticated

---

[1] Jerome says this in the Vulgate, in his prologues to 1 and 2 Kings and to Jeremiah.

structure. Chapters one, two and four are "alphabet acrostic" poems – that is to say, each of their twenty-two verses begin with successive letters of the Hebrew alphabet. If they were written in English, they would consist of twenty-six verses, the first beginning with A and the last beginning with Z. Since there are only twenty-two letters in the Hebrew alphabet, the poems are slightly shorter and run from *Aleph* down to *Taw*.[2] Chapter three consists of sixty-six verses, the first three beginning with *Aleph*, the next three beginning with *Beth*, and so on all the way down to the last three that begin with *Taw*. Chapter five is not an "alphabet acrostic", but it is twenty-two verses long in order to fit snugly with the other four poems in the collection. Together, they represent some of the most sophisticated writing in the ancient world.[3]

The first of the five poems presents the fallen city of Jerusalem as a lonely lady, a weeping widow, overwhelmed by the catastrophe that has befallen her. The Hebrew text uses female pronouns to indicate that Jerusalem herself is doing the talking at the end of verses 9 and 11, and throughout verses 12–22. *"Virgin Daughter Judah"* (verse 15) confesses that she has sinned against the Lord and that he was justified in judging her, but she also laments how much his radical surgery has hurt her. Her people are dead or in exile, her Temple ransacked by foreigners.[4] She has been left drowning in grief and confusion.

---

[2] Other "alphabet acrostics" can be found in Psalms 34, 111, 112, 119 and 145, and in Proverbs 31:10–31.

[3] Other poems of lament have survived from the ancient world, most notably 2 Samuel 1:17–27, Job 3, Psalms 102 and 137, and the Sumerian *Lament over the Destruction of Ur* at the hands of the Elamites in about 1940 BC. But none of those ancient poems of lament are anywhere near as complex as these five by Jeremiah.

[4] Gentiles were not permitted to enter the inner courtyard of the Temple, let alone its inner sanctuary. Jerusalem therefore shudders with horror in 1:10 over what the Babylonians have done to her Temple.

Many modern readers find ancient poems of lament difficult to read. They dismiss the book of Lamentations as a bit depressing and irrelevant to their own lives. In reality, nothing could be further from the truth. The New Testament may not quote directly from Lamentations, but Handel's *Messiah* is right to put the words of 1:12 in the mouth of Jesus to express the horror that he felt during his crucifixion. We are also right whenever we put these words in our own mouths to express our horror at the decimation of the Western church in our own generation. We don't like to talk about the fact that the number of British people who identify as Christian has almost halved in the past thirty-five years.[5] We would rather not dwell on the fact that the average Church of England congregation now consists of only twenty-seven people.[6] But the book of Lamentations urges us to face the facts and to cry out to God in anguished pain over what we see. When we close our eyes to the disaster that has befallen our churches, we are more like the stubborn Jewish survivors who rejected Jeremiah's warnings in Egypt than we are like the prophet Jeremiah. It isn't right that we live at a time when the European population is at its largest and European church attendance is at its lowest. We need to face up to such facts and we need to call on the Lord to face up to them too.[7]

Roger Harding, who conducts the *British Social Attitudes* survey, does not mince his words with us.

Our figures show an unrelenting decline in Church of England and Church of Scotland numbers. This is especially true for young people where less than one in twenty now belong to their established church. While the

[5] In 1983, 66% identified as Christian, but only 38% did so in 2018 (*British Social Attitudes* survey, 2019).
[6] Taken from the Church of England's *Usual Sunday Attendance* report in 2019.
[7] Churches are empty, even at Christmas and Easter (1:1 and 4). There are many more single Christian women than single Christian men (1:4 and 15), and many more old people than teenagers and twenties (1:5 and 18). Such disaster ought to drive every remaining believer to their knees in anguished prayer.

The writer of Lamentations teaches us what to do with such statistics. Rather than ignoring them, we are to bring them to the Lord in anguished prayer. God had promised to be the Helper of Israel (Deuteronomy 33:29), so Jerusalem confronts him with the fact that she feels she has no helper (1:7). God had promised to be the Comforter of Israel (Isaiah 51:3), so Jerusalem confronts him with the fact that she feels she has no comforter (1:2, 9, 16, 17 and 21). Wherever we see a gulf between God's promises and our present experience, that is the place where God would have us offer prayers of lament to him. We are not to hide our feelings beneath the unreality of Christian jargon and of happy-clappy worship songs. We are to face the facts, and then we are to confront God with them.

This first poem teaches us that it's the key to obtaining spiritual revival. It is only as Jerusalem voices her grief to the Lord that she realizes that her citizens can never feel at home in Babylon.[9] It is only as she laments her destruction that she acknowledges that God was right to drive his scalpel into her sin-ridden body.[10] It is only as she admits that the Lord was faithful to his promises in destroying her that she begins to trust him to be faithful to his promise to deliver her from the

---

[8] Quoted in a report © *The Independent* newspaper on 7 September 2018 entitled *Church of England Staring at Oblivion*, which revealed that 78% fewer 18–24-year-olds claimed to be Anglican than just 16 years earlier.

[9] The Hebrew word for *resting place* in 1:3 is *mānōah*, the same word that God uses in his curse on sinful Israel in Deuteronomy 28:65. Even as she voices her grief, Jerusalem realizes that repentance can reverse it.

[10] The Hebrew word for Jerusalem's *destruction* in 1:7 is linked to the word *Sabbath*. This is appropriate, given that 2 Chronicles 36:21 lists one of the reasons for its destruction as its failure to observe the Sabbath. Seventy years of exile would allow the land of Judah to catch up on all of its unobserved Sabbaths.

pagan nations that are gloating over her,[11] and to send a Messiah who will deliver her from the heavy burden of her sin.[12]

Jeremiah wrote Lamentations to teach the Jewish survivors how to pray during their exile in Babylon, because how we respond to God's surgery is crucial if we want to experience restoration and revival. The Lord has preserved these five poems for us to teach us how we are to pray to him about the church's problems in our own generation.

[11] As Jerusalem confesses that God is the one who has struck her, she expresses her belief in *"the day you have announced"* (verse 21) for judging the pagan nations. She trusts that God has set a day to bring the Jewish exiles home.

[12] Jerusalem's reference to the "*yoke*" of her sins in 1:14 echoes the messianic promises of Jeremiah 23:3–6, 30:8 and 31:31–34, and of Isaiah 9:4, 10:27 and 53:6. Jesus would come to bear the yoke of our sins for us, and he echoes this verse from Lamentations when he speaks his famous words in Matthew 11:28–30.

Who Hit You?
(Lamentations 2:1–22)

The Lord has done what he planned; he has fulfilled his word, which he decreed long ago.

(Lamentations 2:17)

The soldiers played a game with Jesus before they crucified him. They blindfolded him, hit him and taunted him repeatedly: *"Prophesy! Who hit you?"*[1]

The Devil still plays that same game with you and me. He doesn't just enjoy watching us suffer. He loves to twist the scalpel in us by deceiving us as to whose hand is at work in our suffering. That's the main theme of the second of the five poems in Lamentations. It aims to take the blindfold from our eyes and to answer the Devil's question: *Who hit you?*

When most people look at the disaster that has befallen the Western church in our generation, they attribute it to *purely natural causes*. They point out that people are far busier and far more self-sufficient that in previous generations. It only stands to reason that in a modern, scientific age, very few people exhibit much interest in ancient religion. But attributing church decline to market forces makes God out to be a powerless spectator, rather than the orchestrator of our sufferings and our only Saviour from them.

Other people look at the struggling Western church and see *the hand of the Devil*. They talk a lot about spiritual warfare, but they don't appear to grasp that we are fighting a battle that has already been won. Whenever we attribute church decline to

---

[1] Matthew 26:68, Mark 14:65 and Luke 22:64.

the work of evil spirits in the world, we credit the Devil with far too much power and the Lord with far too little. Is it really any wonder that so many Christians end up in despair, when we act as if the Devil and his demons wield enough power to thwart the promises of God?[2]

The glory of the second poem in the book of Lamentations is that it squarely and firmly attributes our spiritual disasters to *the hand of the Lord*. It is another "alphabet acrostic". Its twenty-two verses each begin with successive letters of the Hebrew alphabet, from *aleph* down to *taw*, which indicates that Jeremiah chose his words very carefully. This poem gives us an A-to-Z anatomy, not just of grief itself, but of whose hand we are to see behind the griefs that we bear. It firmly underlines the sovereignty of God. The dominant pronoun in the first poem is *she* – Jerusalem – as she wept like a widow. The dominant pronoun in this second poem is *he* – the Lord – as the prophet calls Jerusalem to recognize that the Lord himself is at work amidst her sufferings.

In 2:1–12, Jeremiah repeats twenty-four times that it was the Lord who destroyed Jerusalem. The city would still be standing had its people listened to his prophecies.[3] This does not lessen the prophet's horror at what took place in 586 BC. He uses eight different words and phrases to describe the destruction of the Temple.[4] He uses five different words to lament the destruction of the city walls.[5] He uses nine different words to remember the slaughter of the leaders of Judah.[6] He still weeps over the children who have died and who are

---

[2] The only person who ever shuts down a church in the Bible isn't the Devil. It is Jesus (Revelation 2:5).

[3] Lamentations 2:9 echoes Amos 8:11. When people repeatedly refuse to listen to God's Word, he responds by refraining from speaking altogether, until people long for this famine of the Word of God to end.

[4] Footstool, tent, dwelling, place of meeting, festivals and sabbaths, altar, sanctuary and house of the Lord.

[5] Strongholds, walls, ramparts, gates and bars.

[6] Kingdom, princes, horn, palaces, king, priest, law, prophets and elders.

still dying in their mothers' arms amidst the blackened ruins. Seeing God's hand behind the fall of Jerusalem does not lessen Jeremiah's pain, but it helps him to trust that its destruction must serve a vital purpose in God's perfect plan.[7]

Six times in these twelve verses, Jeremiah refers to the *anger* or *wrath* of the Lord.[8] Unlike human anger, which tends to be hasty and volatile, the prophet emphasizes in verse 8 that the Lord's anger is always determined and perfectly measured. Since Jerusalem was proud like Satan, it was right for God to hurl her splendour down from heaven. He has humbled her just enough for her survivors to weep before him in sackcloth and ashes, but not so much that her name has been erased from the earth, never to rise again.[9]

In 2:13–19, Jeremiah repeats the imagery of his first poem by urging Daughter Jerusalem to reflect on what it means for the Lord's hand to have wielded the surgeon's scalpel. *"Your wound is as deep as the sea. Who can heal you?"* Certainly not the caricature of God that her false prophets peddled to her when they promised her *"peace, peace"* in the face of his judgment.[10] The destruction of Jerusalem has proved beyond all doubt that such a sentimental view of God is always dangerously misleading. Nor will Jerusalem find healing in a fresh alliance with foreign nations, since they have revealed their hatred of her by their delight in her sudden destruction.[11] The only person who can heal Jerusalem is the very one who hurt her. *"The Lord has done what he planned;*

---

[7] Lamentations 2:15 encourages us that the Lord wants far more from our suffering than a return to our former comfort – he wants to transform the church into *"the perfection of beauty, the joy of the whole earth"*.

[8] Verses 1 (twice), 2, 3, 4 and 6.

[9] Compare 2:1 with Isaiah 14:12 and Luke 10:18. Unlike Satan, the survivors of Jerusalem repent in 2:10.

[10] Jeremiah 6:14, 8:11, 14:13, 23:17 and 28:9, and Ezekiel 13:10 and 16.

[11] This is a vital lesson for the Western church today. If the Lord has caused the demise of his church due to its sin and compromise, then it can never be reversed through a paperback or a conference or a gifted leader.

he has fulfilled his word, which he decreed long ago."[12] Jeremiah therefore urges Jerusalem to weep night and day before the Lord. If she repents, God promises to restore and revive her.[13]

In 2:20–22, Jerusalem begins to do as the prophet urges. For the first time in the books of Jeremiah and Lamentations, she gets down on her knees and begs the Lord to show pity towards her. Has he not seen her women eating their own children under siege?[14] Has he not witnessed her priests and prophets being slaughtered at the altar of his Temple? Has he not noticed the corpses of her men and women, both young and old, being piled high in her streets? Of course he has. He was the leading architect of Jerusalem's destruction. This may not be the most eloquent prayer of repentance, but it marks a major milestone in Jewish history. As soon as Jerusalem recognises whose hand wielded the scalpel, she starts out on a journey that will lead to restoration and revival.[15]

The same is true for us today. It is only when we recognize that the Lord has judged his church that we will witness its revival. A high view of God's sovereignty lifts us out of a place of *defeat* (the Devil did this to us!) and out of a place of *despair* (God's promises have failed!), and brings us into a place of *deliverance* (God knows what he is doing!). The moment we confess it is the hand of God that has struck us, we quickly discover that the same hand of God is more willing to bring healing to us.

---

[12] Verse 17. The Lord waited centuries before enacting the full weight of his curses on sinful Israel in Leviticus 26 and Deuteronomy 27–28. He is *"slow to anger"* (Exodus 34:6, Psalm 103:8 and Jonah 4:2).

[13] These verses are one of the reasons why Jews still read the book of Lamentations on the anniversary of the destruction of the Temple, and why it is still a favourite at the Western Wall in Jerusalem.

[14] Ezekiel 5:10 tells us that the men of Jerusalem also ate their own children, plus their own fathers too.

[15] No longer does Jerusalem feel entitled to God's help simply because she is home to his Temple. Responding to the *Temple Sermon* in Jeremiah 7–10, she places her hope in God's loving grace towards her.

Difficult to Say
(Lamentations 3:1–66)

Because of the Lord's great love we are not
consumed, for his compassions never fail.
They are new every morning.

(Lamentations 3:22–23)

Anybody who
Believes that alphabet acrostics are easy
Clearly hasn't written one. They
Don't realize how difficult it is to
Express yourself this way.

If you want to grasp how difficult it must have been for the prophet Jeremiah to express his grief over the fall of Jerusalem in the form of an "alphabet acrostic" poem, then have a go yourself. Start the first line with A and the second line with B, all the way down to Z. It won't take you long to see why I gave up on my poem after the letter E.

Jeremiah, on the other hand, was determined to persevere. It wasn't just that the ancient Hebrews viewed acrostics as their most beautiful form of poetry. It was that he knew the Lord had called him to teach the Jewish survivors to pray things that are difficult to say. The well-ordered structure of his poems was meant to help them bring order to the chaotic feelings of their hearts. As if to emphasize this, he makes the structure of his third poem even more exacting than the first two. It is the same length as the others, but modern Bibles divide it into sixty-six verses because he doesn't merely start each of its twenty-two stanzas with successive letters of the Hebrew alphabet. He begins each of the three statements in each stanza with that letter. Verses 1–3 all begin with *aleph*, verses 4–6 all begin with *beth*, verses 7–9 all begin with *gimel*, and so on.[1]

Perhaps Jeremiah adopts an even more exacting structure for this third poem because its words come harder than his previous poems. Chapter 1 expressed the agony of Jerusalem and chapter 2 responded with truth about God's sovereignty, but chapter 3 is the most personal of his five poems. The dominant pronoun in chapter 3 is neither *she* nor *he*, but *I*, as the prophet voices his own private grief at the destruction of Jerusalem.

In 3:1–18, Jeremiah laments the fact that he has ended up in Egypt. *"I am the man who has seen affliction by the rod of the Lord's wrath."* He was faithful to the Lord, yet he has become collateral damage in the city's downfall. In verse 8, is he recalling the three occasions when the Lord forbade him from praying for his city? In verse 18, is he wishing that he had said "yes" to Nebuzaradan's tantalizing offer to make him an honoured dignitary in Babylon, instead of a mistreated fugitive in Egypt? We cannot know for sure, but such regrets would fit well with what we know about the prophet's final years.[2]

We can tell that Jeremiah found these words difficult to say from the fact that some of what he says is lifted from other books of the Old Testament. Verse 6 quotes from David's words as a fugitive from King Saul in Psalm 143:3. Verse 12 borrows a metaphor from Job 7:20 and 16:12. When Jeremiah likens his suffering in Egypt to *bitter herbs* and *gall* in verse 15, he is using imagery from the Passover meal in Exodus 12:8. None of this is plagiarism. It is part of the prophet's lesson. We are meant to draw on the prayers that are recorded in Scripture whenever we need help to pray things that are difficult to say.[3]

---

[1] This is important for the structure and meaning of this third poem. We are not to read it as if it were three stanzas of twenty-two verses each. We are to read it as twenty-two stanzas of three verses each.

[2] Jeremiah 7:16, 11:14, 14:11 and 40:1–4.

[3] Jonah's prayer in the belly of the fish also borrows many stock phrases from the Psalms. Jesus drew strength from Lamentations 3:15 and from the Psalms when he was taunted with bitter drink while dying on the cross. See Psalms 22:1, 22:31 and 31:5, Matthew 27:46–50, Luke 23:46 and John 19:28–30.

As Jeremiah perseveres in prayer, he sees a breakthrough in 3:19–24. Having found words to express the dark depression of his soul, he finds the strength to fix his mind on truth about God's character instead.[4] *"This I call to mind and therefore I have hope: Because of the Lord's great love we are not consumed, for his compassions never fail. They are new every morning; great is your faithfulness."* As Jeremiah lifts his gaze from earth to heaven, he grasps that the existence of survivors from Jerusalem is proof of God's continued love and faithfulness towards Israel.[5] The fact that his nation has not been completely consumed by the sword proves that there will yet be a sequel to its story.

In 3:25–66, Jeremiah shows us why it is worth persevering in prayer, even when we find things difficult to say. The final two thirds of the poem are as full of hope as the first third was full of despair.[6] I find the three words *"I will wait"* some of the hardest words to say to God, but Jeremiah rejoices that Lord's timing is always perfect. He is an old man, so we ought to understand his observation that *"It is good to wait quietly for the salvation of the Lord. It is good for a man to bear the yoke while he is young"* as a promise that God has barely started with his plans for the Jewish nation.[7] It may look like it is game-over for Israel, but the Messiah is on his way.[8] Israel is but a child in the Lord's purposes.

---

[4] Faith does not ignore the earthly facts about our situation. Jeremiah *well remembers* the facts, but he chooses to allow heavenly facts to trump them (2 Corinthians 4:18, Colossians 3:1–2, and Hebrews 3:1 and 12:2).

[5] The Hebrew word *hēsēd* appears in its unusual plural form in 3:22, referring literally to the *loving kindnesses* of the Lord. Jeremiah's hope in God's *daily mercies* in 3:22–23 is echoed in Matthew 6:11.

[6] The Hebrew word *hēleq*, or *"portion"*, in 3:24 is used throughout the Old Testament to refer to parcels of the Promised Land. Since Jeremiah was a priest, his portion was always meant to be the Lord (Numbers 18:20). He therefore rejoices in Egypt that the Babylonians can never take his Promised Land away from him.

[7] This is also a general principle for young Christians today. See Hebrews 12:7 and 1 Peter 5:5–6.

[8] We can catch a glimpse of the Messiah's sufferings in 3:30. See Luke 22:63–65 and John 19:1–3.

As Jeremiah continues to meditate more on the character of God than on his own sufferings, he becomes even more excited. Since the Lord *"does not willingly bring affliction or grief to anyone"*, this must mean that *"No one is cast off by the Lord for ever."* Since he only ever uses his scalpel reluctantly, when he sees that only radical surgery can save a patient, his true desire must therefore be to show compassion towards people.[9] If the Lord is sovereign over the sufferings of Jerusalem – *"Who can speak and have it happen if the Lord has not decreed it? Is it not from the mouth of the Most High that both calamities and good things come?"* (verses 37–38) – then it stands to reason that he will be sovereign over her restoration, the moment she starts weeping over her sins.[10] If God is powerful enough to protect Jeremiah from his enemies in Egypt, then he is also powerful enough to bring the Jewish survivors safely back home from their exile in Babylon.

The dominant pronoun throughout this third poem is *I*, so don't miss the way that Jeremiah uses the pronouns *we, us* and *our* thirteen times in these final verses. He is inviting the Jewish exiles to join him in praying words that are difficult to say.[11] He is inviting us to pray these words too, as we weep for the church in our own generation. He is encouraging us to believe that God will answer our prayers of repentance, even if we find them difficult to say.[12]

---

[9] The Hebrew text of 3:33 tells us literally that God never brings sorrow on people *"from his heart"*. He does so out of necessity, rather than desire. See Ezekiel 18:23, 18:32 and 33:11, and 2 Peter 3:9.

[10] Lamentations 3:44 stands alongside Isaiah 59:1–2 as a clear warning that sin separates people from God until they lay hold of the blood sacrifice that he has provided for their sins through the gospel.

[11] The New Testament never quotes directly from Lamentations, but Paul surely has 3:45 in mind when he faces up to the fact that people treat him as *"the scum of the earth, the garbage of the world"* (1 Corinthians 4:13).

[12] Lamentations 3:48–50 stands alongside 2:18, Isaiah 62:6–7 and Nehemiah 1:1–4 in urging us to give the Lord no rest in prayer until he revives the church in our land.

Say How You Really Feel
(Lamentations 4:1–5:22)

Remember, Lord, what has happened to us.

(Lamentations 5:1)

When the Mughal emperor Shah Jahan built the Taj Mahal as a mausoleum for his wife, he followed the ancient practice of creating beauty through absolute symmetry. He made sure that its main marble building and its dome were symmetrical. He insisted that its four smaller domes and its four minarets were perfectly symmetrical too. He placed his wife's sarcophagus in the exact centre of the mausoleum so that nothing should detract from its perfect symmetry. Sadly for Shah Jahan, his servants were a lot less careful. When he died, they placed his sarcophagus next to hers, meaning that the perfect symmetry of the Taj Mahal is undermined by Shah Jahan's own body.

Jeremiah is as meticulous as Shah Jahan in the first three poems in the book of Lamentations. The first two poems are twenty-two verse "alphabet acrostics". Both begin with the Hebrew word *ēkāh*, which means *How?!* and expresses the horror and confusion that surrounded the destruction of Jerusalem.[1] The third poem acts as a centrepiece to the collection – a sixty-six verse "alphabet acrostic" that scales the mountain of God's character and leaves us breathless with its magnificent view of his love, compassion and faithfulness towards his people.

---

[1] *Ekah* is the Hebrew name for Lamentations, meaning that modern Jews still refer to it as the book of *How?!* They group it among the *Writings* rather than the *Prophets* – that is, alongside Job and Psalms rather than alongside Jeremiah and Ezekiel.

You don't have to be Shah Jahan to expect poems four and five to be twenty-two verse "alphabet acrostics" that begin with the word *ēkāh* and that lead us down the other side of the mountain in the same way that the first two poems led us up it. That's why it's so surprising that the prophet Jeremiah takes a hammer to the perfect symmetry of Lamentations in its final chapters. Unlike Shah Jahan, the prophet knows what he is doing. He wants to reinforce to us that praying the perfect prayer of repentance matters a lot less to God than telling him how we genuinely feel.

Chapter 4 is a twenty-two verse "alphabet acrostic" that begins with the word *ēkāh*. So far so good, but that's where the symmetry ends. Instead of carrying on from the mountaintop delights of poem three, Jeremiah drags us straight back into the darkness of his own despair. This fourth poem laments the great gulf that still exists between Jerusalem's glorious past and her inglorious present.[2] Children used to play happily in her streets, but now they beg hungrily for food.[3] Noblemen used to entertain one another with lavish feasts, but now they hunt for scraps of food amid the rubbish heaps.[4] Mighty men used to flash their muscles across the city, but now their arms are skinny and their faces unrecognisable. The king of Judah has been blinded and taken into exile.[5] Those who were slaughtered

---

[2] The twelve tribes of Israel were represented as *sacred gems* in Exodus 28:21. Jeremiah laments that their survivors have become nobodies, more akin to common pottery than to the crown jewels of heaven's King.

[3] Even the most heartless of animals care for their young, but not the survivors of Jerusalem. Their desperate self-centredness (4:3–4) reminds Jeremiah of what happened during the siege of Jerusalem, when starving mothers cooked and ate their own children (4:10).

[4] 1 Samuel 2:7–8. The Lord had called the Jews to separate themselves from the sins of the world so as not to be defiled, yet now it is the pagan nations who reject the grubby Jewish survivors as unclean.

[5] The lament in 4:20 is for King Zedekiah. Few people remembered King Jehoiachin after the fall of Babylon, much less imagined that the Lord planned to raise up a new and better King of Judah through him.

are the lucky ones, spared the sight of such dark days.[6]

Nobody prays in this poem. There is precious little to encourage us, save the thought that if *"the Lord has given full vent to his wrath"* (4:11) then there must be no more judgment yet to fall on Judah. The poem's gloomy tone stands in deliberate contrast to the upward arc of hope that ran throughout the first three poems, because that's how it often is with grief. We have good days and we have bad days. One moment we see God in the midst of our sufferings, and the next we plunge back down into the pit of our despair. Jeremiah undermines the symmetry of this collection of poems to teach us that God prizes perfect poetry a lot less than honest prayers. We are to say how we really feel.

Chapter 5 is even more surprising. It is twenty-two verses long, but it is not an "alphabet acrostic" and nor does it begin with the word *ēkāh*. It is a prayer for the Jewish survivors to pray to God together, and it feels almost as if Jeremiah runs out of strength to hold himself together. His perfect rules of poetry go out of the window. The verses become shorter and more anguished. Who can marshal their thoughts properly when the Jewish homeland has become a province of pagan Babylon, when its women have been raped by foreign soldiers, and when the corpses of its rulers have been subjected to shame?[7] Who cares about symmetry, when the handful of Jewish young men who escaped the slaughter are now the slaves of foreigners,[8] and when Mount Zion and its Temple have been reduced to a

---

[6] We are told in the book of Obadiah that, during the Babylonian sack of Jerusalem, the Edomites robbed and killed any Jewish survivors who fell into their hands. This explains the curses in 4:21–22.

[7] The Hebrew word *tālāh* in 5:12 means *to hang* or *to impale*. The same word is used in Esther 9:13–14.

[8] The Lord had planned for foreigners to fetch and carry wood for his obedient people (Deuteronomy 29:11). Now that blessing is reversed as a result of his people's sin.

deserted pile of rubble?[9] We mustn't try to hide our true feelings from God behind the veneer of perfect poetry or of Christian jargon. *Say how you really feel.*

Jeremiah therefore ends the book of Lamentations with two paradoxes that are meant to stir us to write many more prayers of lament of our own. How can we fail to do so, when the Lord reigns as the eternal King of kings (5:19) but his people look like down-and-outs, forgotten and forsaken by him? (5:20) How can we fail to do so, when the Lord promises to restore and revive his repentant people (5:21) but their prayers as yet appear to have been rejected and ignored (5:22)?[10]

Jeremiah leaves these questions hanging in mid-air, because he wants these paradoxes to stir us to seek out answers in the place of prayer. The aim of his first three poems was to teach us principles that give us hope in the midst of our suffering. The aim of his fourth and fifth poems is to convince us that we can pray prayers of lament just as easily as he can. Through these last two poems, he encourages us to *say how you really feel.*

So let's do it. Let's face up to the facts about the church's struggles in our generation and let's respond to God's surgeon's scalpel, even if we find the words difficult to say. Let's confess that the Lord is behind the church's devastation, determined to cut out its sin and compromise. Let's confess to him that he is the only one who can heal its gaping wound. Let's take the time to stand before him, as we were taught in chapter 3:

"I will wait for him. The Lord is good to those whose hope is in him, to the one who seeks him" (3:24–25).

---

[9] In David's song of dedication for the Temple, he rejoiced that *"You turned my wailing into dancing; you removed my sackcloth and clothed me with joy"* (Psalm 30:11). Lamentations 5:15 reverses David's song.

[10] The Hebrew word *shūb* in 5:21 means either to *restore* or to *return.* Alongside Jeremiah 31:18, this verse reminds us that revival is a work of God, not of men and women. Our greatest calling is therefore to pray.

Ezekiel 1–32:

Further Surgery is Needed

God on the Move
(Ezekiel 1:1–28)

The word of the Lord came to Ezekiel the priest, the son of Buzi, by the Kebar River in the land of the Babylonians.

(Ezekiel 1:3)

Jeremiah and Ezekiel are like twins. They have a lot in common. Each of them wrote one of the longest books in the Bible, each of which is much neglected by modern readers. Both books are dismissed by many as too gloomy, or as too difficult, or as irrelevant for our own day – and in both cases, nothing could be more short-sighted. The book of Ezekiel makes vital reading for our generation, since it picks up where Jeremiah leaves off in order to explain that there is more work for God to do before the Jewish exiles can return home. The first section of Ezekiel completes the message of Jeremiah and Lamentations to God's people. Ezekiel 1–32 warns that, often, further surgery is needed.

Like Jeremiah, the prophet Ezekiel was a priest. Like Jeremiah, he was excluded from serving at the Temple – not by his birth at Anathoth, but by captivity in Babylon. Ezekiel was only twenty-five years old in 597 BC, when King Nebuchadnezzar carried off three thousand Jewish men into exile. He was among them, and we can only imagine how he must have felt when his hope of serving the Lord as a priest in Jerusalem was dashed. Perhaps he wrote a few confused and angry lamentations, like Jeremiah.[1]

---

[1] Jeremiah 52:28. Lamentations 2:20 gives us the sequel: had Ezekiel remained in Jerusalem, he would almost certainly have been slaughtered in 586 BC. The Lord knows what he is doing, and the commissioning of Ezekiel aged thirty is meant to demonstrate the glorious principle of Romans 8:28.

Nevertheless, we discover in 1:1–3, that God has better plans for Ezekiel. The book begins on 31 July 593 BC, so he has just turned thirty, the very age at which he would have been commissioned as a priest had he remained in Jerusalem.[2] Instead, we find him at the town of Tel Aviv, *"by the Kebar River in the land of the Babylonians"*, a manmade waterway that connected the River Euphrates to the region of Nippur, to the southeast of Babylon.[3] Ezekiel's life seems to have taken a wrong turn, but there are several hints in these verses that he still believes the Lord is his true Master. First, his name means *God Is My Strength*. Second, he is by the riverbank, where ancient Jews established a place of prayer whenever they were living in a pagan city.[4] Third, we are told that *"the hand of the Lord was on him"* – that he still walked with the Holy Spirit.[5] The Babylonians had dragged him out of the Temple, but they had not dragged the Temple out of him.

In 1:4–28, Ezekiel looks up from his prayers and sees a mysterious object coming towards him from the direction of Babylon, to the north of Tel Aviv. He can only describe it as a *violent storm*, as an *immense cloud*, and as *lightning* and *fire* – all of which are signs of God's presence throughout the Old Testament.[6] But Ezekiel knows better than to expect to find God's presence in Babylonia. You didn't have to be a priest to know God's presence dwelt above a gold box within the inner sanctuary of the Temple in Jerusalem.

As it gets nearer, Ezekiel makes out the shape of four mysterious creatures within the cloud and fire. Each of the

---

[2] Numbers 4:3. Ezekiel dates events in his book from the year of his own exile (33:21 and 40:1). The mention of King Jehoiachin in 1:2 helps us to link the opening verses of Ezekiel to the closing verses of Jeremiah.

[3] Ezekiel was in Babylonia, rather than in Babylon. A modern Israeli city is named after the town in 3:15.

[4] Psalm 137:1 and Acts 16:13. We are most likely to encounter God when we actively seek him.

[5] This same phrase is used in 3:14, 3:22, 8:1, 33:22, 37:1 and 40:1, as well as in Ezra 7:6 and Nehemiah 2:8.

[6] Exodus 3:2, 13:21, 19:18, 20:18 and 40:34–38, 2 Kings 2:11, Job 40:6, Isaiah 4:5 and 30:30, and Daniel 7:9.

creatures has four faces, four wings and four hands. The faces of a *man*, *lion*, *ox* and *eagle* express their power – the mind of the most intelligent creature combined with the strength of the strongest wild animal, farm animal and wild bird. As the windstorm moves closer, Ezekiel spots intersected wheels beside each of the four creatures, which enable them to travel in any direction.[7] Despite the blur of constant movement, as the creatures dash back and forth like lightning, he can see that the wheel-rims are covered with eyes, expressing a great knowledge that accompanies their great power. Some of this detail reminds us of the Lord's appearance to Isaiah in the Temple courtyard, but of course it can't be.[8] That was Jerusalem, this is Babylonia.

As Ezekiel gazes more intently into the windstorm of cloud and fire, he sees that the wings of the four creatures are supporting a dazzling platform above their heads. On the platform is a giant throne that looks like a dazzling giant jewel. On the throne is someone like a man whose body is surrounded by a bright, fiery beauty that hurts the eyes, like looking directly at a rainbow when the sun bursts through the clouds on a dark and rainy day. Suddenly, it dawns on Ezekiel what he is seeing. He doesn't dare to gaze intently at the figure on the throne, much less describe it for us. He simply states in breathless wonder that *"This was the appearance of the likeness of the glory of the Lord."*[9]

---

[7] If you find the details of this vision confusing, then don't be discouraged. You are in good company! Even John Calvin says in his commentary on these verses, *"I confess its obscurity, and that I can barely understand it"*! The detail of the vision matters a lot less than the message behind the vision. God is on the move!

[8] *Seraphim* in Isaiah 6:1–13 means *Fiery Angel*. In both visions, the angels cover their bodies with their wings in order to emphasize that, despite their brilliance, the Lord himself is far holier than they are.

[9] Verse 28. Ezekiel does not describe the Lord. He does not even describe the glory of the Lord or the likeness of the glory of the Lord. He only dares to describe *"the appearance of the likeness of the glory of the Lord."*

Ezekiel knew a lot about the Temple in Jerusalem. He knew that four golden cherubim angels stood in its inner sanctuary: two on the lid of the ark of the covenant and two more providing a protective canopy over it. He also knew that the presence of the Lord dwelt in the space between those four cherubim angels.[10] He therefore recognizes these four mysterious creatures as the real cherubim angels that were merely depicted in the inner sanctuary of the Temple. They are carrying God's presence deep into Babylonia.

Much has been written about the Hebrew word *kābōd* or *"glory"* in verse 28. It literally means *weight* or *heaviness*, and it is used throughout the Old Testament to describe the *manifest glory* of God, the sweet reality of his presence, especially when made visible through cloud or fire. A lot less has been written about the little Hebrew word *shām* in verse 3, but it is every bit as full of wonder. *Shām* means *there*, and it expresses something of Ezekiel's amazement that the presence of God that dwelt within the inner sanctuary of the Temple in Jerusalem should suddenly appear in the land of the Babylonians.[11]

Ezekiel falls face down in fear. He is all ears, just as the wheels he sees are full of eyes. He does not speak a single word while God commissions him in these chapters, and then he spends a further seven days in silence contemplating what this vision means. Ezekiel had been brought up to believe that the God of Israel dwelt within his Temple in Jerusalem, and nowhere else, so this vision marked a major revolution in his thinking.[12]

---

[10] Exodus 25:10–22, Numbers 7:89 and 2 Chronicles 3:10–13. Those cherubim angels reflected a greater reality in heaven (Hebrews 8:5), which is why John meets them again in his vision of heaven in Revelation 4:1–11.

[11] Not just his presence, but also his *throne*. Every flap of the wings of his cherubim angels sounds like the boot steps of a marching army because the Kingdom of God is invading Babylon!

[12] At the dedication of his Temple in 1 Kings 8, King Solomon declared nine times that the Lord was far greater than the Temple. However, Psalm 137:1–4 reveals that the Jewish exiles had forgotten this in Babylon.

It meant that God's glorious presence was not restricted to the back room of any building. Even here, deep in the pagan heartland of brutal Babylonia, God was on the move!

Our Man in Babylon
(Ezekiel 2:1–3:27)

"Son of man, I have made you a watchman for the people of Israel."

(Ezekiel 3:17)

The Lord had a man in Jerusalem. At the start of Jeremiah, we are told that he began his public ministry in 627 BC and continued prophesying until after the fall of Jerusalem in 586 BC. He was there when King Josiah launched his short-lived revival in 622 BC. He was there when Daniel and the first wave of exiles were taken away to Babylon in 605 BC. He was there when Ezekiel and the second wave of exiles were dragged off to join them in 597 BC. But Jeremiah could not be in two places at once. He could send letters to Babylon, but the Lord wanted to have a man on the ground in Babylonia who could warn the Jewish exiles that further surgery was needed.

That's why the Lord appeared to Ezekiel by the banks of the River Kebar. After the initial vision of his glory came a mighty moment of commissioning. These two chapters record the calling of a new prophet and his appointment to serve as the Lord's man in Babylon.

In 2:1–8, the Lord does all the talking. He addresses Ezekiel as *"Son of man"*, a name he uses ninety-three times throughout this book to emphasize that Ezekiel is the human mouthpiece in Babylon for the divine Majesty in heaven.[1] To empower him for this new role, the Lord fills him with his Holy

---

[1] Jesus calls himself the *Son of Man* throughout the gospels to emphasize that his incarnation makes him the true and better Ezekiel. It also echoes Daniel 7:13, where a human Messiah stands before the throne of God.

Spirit and tells him to stand up. Falling face down in worship is a great start to serving God but it makes for a lousy ending. Our private experiences of God's glory are meant to empower us to take a stand for him in public ministry.[2] The Lord informs Ezekiel that he has chosen him to be his prophet *"to the Israelites, to a rebellious nation"* – that is, to the Jewish exiles and to those survivors of the ten northern tribes who are willing to gravitate towards them.[3] Note the deliberate echo of Jeremiah's commissioning when the Lord warns Ezekiel that many of the Jews will refuse to listen to him and will attack him, but that he can trust the Lord to defend him.[4] Just as Jeremiah is God's man in Jerusalem, so Ezekiel must be God's man in Babylon.

In 2:9–3:3, the Lord makes Ezekiel eat a scroll. Ancient scribes only wrote on one side of a scroll, so the fact that *"on both sides of it were written words of lament and mourning and woe"* is meant to signify that Ezekiel's message will be jampacked with confrontation. He will unsheathe the surgeon's scalpel of the Lord. Ezekiel needs to eat the scroll because he can only become God's man in Babylon if he takes God's Word to heart, resolving to find sweet what many of his listeners will find bitter.[5] He must not lose his clarity of mission when he finds that many people find his preaching intolerant and offensive.[6]

---

[2] God wants to do more than simply rid us of our self-confidence. He wants to fill us with God-confidence. The Holy Spirit who was *on* Ezekiel externally in 1:3 begins to dwell *within* him internally in 2:2.

[3] The Hebrew word *gōyīm* in 2:3 is plural, so it literally refers to *nations*. Ezekiel would prophesy to the survivors of both the northern and the southern kingdoms, in addition to their pagan neighbours.

[4] The Lord uses the Hebrew words *mārad* and *merī*, meaning *to rebel* and *rebellion*, seven times in 2:3–8. The root problem that Ezekiel needs to address is that God's subjects are in rebellion against his glorious throne.

[5] This is why the Lord tells Ezekiel to *"fill his stomach"* with the Word of God in 3:3. Reading it is not enough. We need to let it fill our hearts, transform our minds and overcome our own desires.

[6] Psalm 19:10 and 119:103. The Lord gives Jeremiah and John similar scrolls to eat, since we must all learn to declare courageously, *"Thus says the Lord!"* (2:4 and 3:11, Jeremiah 15:16, and Revelation 5:1 and 10:8–11).

In 3:4–11, the Lord warns Ezekiel that he will find this again and again.[7] The Jewish exiles will be no more receptive to his message than they were to Jeremiah's. Nevertheless, as Ezekiel meditates on the Word of God, the Lord promises to make him as stubborn a preacher of repentance as his hearers are stubborn practitioners of rebellion. The Lord will make him as hard and unyielding as the blade of a flint knife, using his words as a surgeon's scalpel to operate on the hearts of his sinful people.[8]

In 3:12–15, the Lord begins to transform his man in Babylon from the inside out. Ezekiel confesses that his own spirit still feels *bitter and angry* about all that has befallen him over the past few years. The Holy Spirit therefore lifts him up into his own presence and overwhelms him with such divine purity and strength that all anger is dispelled from the prophet's spirit. As Ezekiel's vision recedes, he returns to Tel Aviv, but the Jewish captives there can tell he is no longer the same man who left earlier to go down and pray by the riverside. Some readers see a link between his seven days of sitting in stunned silence and the seven days that were required for the commissioning of a new priest in Leviticus 8:33. This may well be true, and it gives him a week to reflect on his vision of God's glory and on what it will mean for him to become God's man in Babylon.[9]

In 3:16–27, the Lord breaks Ezekiel's seven days of silence in order to complete his commissioning. He declares that he has appointed him to be a *tsôpheh* – a *watchman*, like those who guarded the lookout towers of ancient cities to sound a warning

---

[7] The Lord is not promising in 3:5–6 that the pagan nations will repent *en masse* when they hear the words of Ezekiel 25–32. He is promising that they will treat Ezekiel's words with greater respect than the Jewish exiles.

[8] See Joshua 5:2–3, Isaiah 50:7 and Jeremiah 17:1.

[9] See also Job 2:13. The Lord can tell that Ezekiel is overwhelmed by his vision of God's glory, so he grants him a recovery week before he completes his commissioning in 3:16–27.

siren whenever hostile soldiers were approaching.[10] If Ezekiel warns the Jewish exiles that further surgery is needed and they refuse to listen to his words, then at least he will have completed the work of a watchman and absolved himself of any part in their slaughter. If he shrinks back, however, from warning them that further surgery is needed then, like a city watchman who fails to sound a warning siren in the face of the enemy, he will be guilty of the sin of murder. If you find these verses pretty sobering, then good – we are meant to! The prophet knows that they don't make for easy reading, but he is being a watchman to us in these very verses. He repeats this warning later, in Ezekiel 33, at the beginning of the second section of his book, because it is our own divine commission too. The Lord has made us *watchmen* and *watchwomen* in our own generation.

Even the atheist TV magician Penn Jillette sees the truth of this.

> *I don't respect people who don't proselytize. I don't respect that at all. If you believe that there's a heaven and hell, and people could be going to hell, or not getting eternal life or whatever, and you think that, "Well, it's not really worth telling them this because it would make it socially awkward" ... how much do you have to hate somebody to not proselytize? How much do you have to hate somebody to believe that everlasting life is possible and not tell them that? I mean, if I believed beyond a shadow of a doubt that a truck was coming at you, and you didn't believe it, and that truck was bearing down on you, there is a certain point where I'd tackle you.*[11]

---

[10] The same Hebrew word is used in 2 Samuel 18:24–27, 2 Kings 9:17–20, Isaiah 52:8 and 56:10, Jeremiah 6:17, Hosea 9:8 and Habakkuk 2:1. The Apostle Paul insists in Acts 20:26–27 that these verses are for us too.

[11] Penn Jillette is one half of *Penn & Teller* (www.youtube.com/watch?v=ZPe3NGgzYQ0).

So let's respond to our God-given calling, like Ezekiel. Let's reflect on the glory of the one who has commissioned us.[12] Let's reflect on the importance of every word we say. For Ezekiel, this would be particularly costly. His seven days of silence are just the start, for the Lord tells him that he will now be mute for seven years, until the city of Jerusalem finally falls in 586 BC.[13] Until then, he will only find himself able to speak when he is praying or prophesying. He is no longer a private citizen who can speak his words at will. He is the mouthpiece of the Lord. Ezekiel has become God's man in Babylon.

---

[12] The Hebrew word *bik'āh* means *valley* rather than *plain*. It is the same word that is used in 37:1–2.

[13] See also 24:25–27 and 33:21–22. This strange disability would serve as a prophetic sign to the Jewish exiles.

Louder than Words
(Ezekiel 4:1–5:17)

"This will be a sign to the people of Israel."

(Ezekiel 4:3)

A famous mime artist was asked if he enjoyed being a silent performer. He shrugged his shoulders and shot back, *"Well, I can't say I complain."*

Ezekiel must have felt the same. It can't have been easy for him to have been struck mute in order to speak only as God's man in Babylon. Jeremiah had made many sacrifices for the Lord, but Ezekiel must have felt that his sacrifice was the hardest. The Lord therefore encourages him by beginning his ministry to the Jewish exiles with a series of prophetic mimes that demonstrate that, often, actions speak louder than words.

The first of Ezekiel's four mimes is bizarre (4:1–3). The Lord commands him to draw a picture of the city of Jerusalem on a large clay tablet and to build models of siege machines around his picture.[1] When the Jewish exiles start to wonder if Ezekiel is going crazy, he is to place an iron baking pan between his face and Jerusalem. Anybody who knows Lamentations 3:44 and Isaiah 59:1–2 will immediately gather that this mimes out the Lord's refusal to listen to the prayers of Jerusalem unless it repents of its many sins.

The second of Ezekiel's four mimes is even stranger (4:4–6). The Lord commands him to lie down on his left side for 390 days! Even allowing for breaks to wash and eat and exercise,

---

[1] This may sound strange to us, but archaeologists have found city maps drawn on clay tablets in the ruins of Babylonia. A famous Babylonian clay tablet map of the world is now on display in the British Museum.

it must have been excruciatingly painful to lie in that position for over a year.[2] To make it even harder, the Lord commands Ezekiel to balance objects on his body that show the Jewish exiles that he is re-enacting 390 years of Israel's sin. This takes us back from 593 BC to the year in which King David committed adultery with Bathsheba.

The Lord knows what he is doing. Actions really do speak louder than words. For the first few days, the Jewish exiles may have ignored Ezekiel. For the next few days, they may have laughed and jeered. But as the prophet stuck to his guns, day in and day out for over a year, even the most cynical observers must have begun to take him seriously. Whether or not they believed his message, they were left in no doubt that he did, so imagine the buzz of excitement when the prophet finally got up from his left side after 390 days – only to lie back down on his right side for forty days more! Since Ezekiel uses the names *Israel* and *Judah* interchangeably for God's people, we are not meant to view these extra forty days as contrasting the sins of the southern and northern tribes, but as a re-enactment of the forty years during which all twelve tribes disobeyed God in the desert. Ezekiel's mime proclaims that rebellion has always been Israel's national story.

Only when his bizarre actions have drawn a crowd does Ezekiel finally open his mouth to prophesy. It is suggested in 4:7–8 that he took off his coat, asked somebody to tie him up with ropes, and shouted a warning to his clay tablet map of Jerusalem. It is suggested by the structure of the book of Ezekiel that what he shouted were the words of chapters 6–7.[3] Suddenly we see the genius of God's decision to make his watchman a mute mime artist. Had Ezekiel simply preached the words of chapters 6–7, he would have struggled to gain a hearing, but now everyone wants to hear what the eccentric prophet has to say.

---

[2] We are told about two of his breaks in 4:9 and 8:1. Otherwise he would have died of bedsores.

[3] The date in 8:1 introduces a new period of his ministry. Ezekiel 6–7 therefore belongs with Ezekiel 1–5.

Ezekiel performed his third mime (4:9–17) on his lunch break during the fourteen months that he spent lying on his side. The Lord told him to eat a tiny vegan meal each day to warn the Jewish exiles that their friends back home in Jerusalem were about to be put on starvation rations.[4] Their city was about to be besieged by the Babylonians. We know from Jeremiah 29 that the exiles believed their friends back home to be the lucky ones, so this mime serves as a graphic illustration to accompany Jeremiah's letter. It declares that Jewish exiles are the lucky ones. They should settle down to enjoy life in Babylon, because the Lord has more radical surgery to perform on the rebellious city of Jerusalem.

When the Lord commands Ezekiel to cook this vegan dinner on a fire made of human excrement, the prophet finally speaks his first recorded words. The Lord has struck him mute, except for when he is praying or prophesying, so he prays a protest prayer for cleaner fuel. Cooking over human excrement would make Ezekiel ceremonially unclean, so the Lord permits him to use cow dung instead (hardly the answer he was hoping for!) but insists that his fuel has to be manure.[5] It is a vivid declaration to the Jewish exiles that their nation is about to be scattered and will have to buy its food from the defiled marketplaces of the pagan nations.

Ezekiel appears to have performed his fourth mime (5:1–4) towards the end of his fourteen months of lying on his side, by which time his hair and beard must have been extremely long. The Lord commands him to take a sharp sword and to shave off everything, collecting the hair and weighing it out into three neat piles next to his clay tablet drawing of the city of

---

[4] 230 g of food and 600 ml of water would only make a tiny meal. Babylonian labour camps served more food than this! The besieged Jews became so crazed with hunger that they ended up eating one another (5:10).

[5] This is evidently how Ezekiel reads Deuteronomy 23:12–14. He sounds very similar to Peter in Acts 10:14.

Jerusalem.[6] He must burn one pile of hair inside the city, as a sign that many Jews will die in its destruction. He must slice the second pile of hair into pieces as a sign that those captured will be slaughtered and their corpses thrown into the Valley of Ben Hinnom. He must throw the third pile of hair into the wind to signify that the remaining Jews will be scattered, their fate left unknown to their loved ones. Ezekiel puts a few stray hairs into the folds of his clothes to represent the 1,577 families that will be dragged off into captivity and who will join his listeners shortly in Babylonia.

In 5:5–17, the prophet finally speaks to explain his mime artistry to the Jewish exiles. That's the genius of the Lord's decision to strike his watchman mute. By the time he finally starts preaching, he has everyone's attention. Everybody listens to his declaration that Judah is even more sinful than its pagan neighbours, since at least the pagans do not pretend to be devoted the Lord. Everybody hears the prophet's warning that the Lord has not yet finished judging their nation. They pay attention when he explains to them why the Lord has called Ezekiel to become his man in Babylon.[7]

None of the Jewish exiles can ignore Ezekiel's solemn warning: *Further surgery is needed.*

---

[6] The Lord's priests were forbidden from doing this in Leviticus 21:5. But Ezekiel has a bigger role to play than merely serving as a priest in Jerusalem. He has become God's man in Babylon.

[7] The Lord will use a variation of this phrase – *Then they will know that I the Lord have spoken* – no fewer than seventy-four times throughout the book of Ezekiel to describe his judgment and his restoration of Judah.

Inconvenient Truth
(Ezekiel 6:1–7:27)

"Disaster! Unheard-of disaster! See, it comes!"

(Ezekiel 7:5)

Robert Schuller, the American TV evangelist, refused to talk about sin in any of his sermons. At least he was honest about why.

> *I don't think that anything has been done in the name of Christ and under the banner of Christianity that has proven more destructive to human personality, and hence counter-productive to the evangelistic enterprise, than the unchristian, uncouth strategy of attempting to make people aware of their lost and sinful condition.*[1]

Robert Schuller's approach has become mainstream for many of us, both in our sermons and in our personal evangelism, but these two chapters warn us that Ezekiel took the opposite approach in Babylon. When the Lord commanded him to break his long silence in 4:7, it was to prophesy against the sins of Jerusalem, and the structure of his book indicates that 6:1–7:27 is a record of what he prophesied.[2] Ezekiel is every bit as blunt as Jeremiah, and he records these two prophecies to warn us

---

[1] From an interview in *Christianity Today* (August 1984).

[2] The structure of Ezekiel is much more chronological than that of Jeremiah. He starts prophesying in August 593 BC (1:1–2 and 3:16) and he receives his out-of-body vision of the Temple in September 592 BC (8:1). This indicates that he spoke the words of 6:1–7:27 at some point between those two dates.

not to hide the inconvenient truth from people ourselves. He points out the sins of Jerusalem because it's how we are to call people to repentance. Ezekiel does not mince his words: further surgery is needed.

In chapter 6, he prophesies against the mountains of Israel since it is there that God's people built *"high places"* – forbidden shrines at which they worshipped foreign idols, and unauthorized altars at which they worshipped the Lord according to their own preferences, instead of travelling to his Temple.[3] Later, Ezekiel will prophesy hope and restoration to these same mountains in chapter 36, but there can be no restoration without repentance, and no repentance without confession of sin.[4] That's why Ezekiel sounds just like Jeremiah, as he prophesies that *"sword, famine and plague"* are about to fall again on the Jewish homeland.[5] It is also why God laments four times in this chapter that a fresh dose of his judgment is required to convince his people *"that I am the Lord."*[6]

I want people to like me. That's why I need Ezekiel to remind me that my calling is not to be the most popular kid in the class. It is to be a watchman who warns the sinners around me that God has set a day of reckoning for their sin. Many of them may hate me for reminding them about the holiness of God and for daring to shine a light on their refusal to worship

---

[3] Most *"high places"* were shrines to foreign idols, but the Lord had also forbidden the building of *"high places"* to himself in Leviticus 17:1–9. He would only be worshipped in his own way.

[4] The Hebrew word *gillûl* in 6:4 means literally *a pellet of dung*. It went on to become a derogatory term for an *idol*. We can tell Ezekiel liked the word, because thirty-eight of its forty-seven Old Testament uses are in the book of Ezekiel.

[5] The trio of disasters listed in 6:11 are also listed together fifteen times in the book of Jeremiah.

[6] Ezekiel 6:7, 10, 13 and 14. A variation of this phrase is used seventy-four times in the book of Ezekiel.

him.[7] But others will be stirred by the Holy Spirit to listen. That's what the Christian gospel does. It convicts some people of their sin and confirms other people in it. Unless what we say to people in God's name runs the risk of maddening them, then there is no risk of it gladdening them. John Cheeseman explains:

> *Evangelism is not a making of proselytes; it is not persuading people to make a decision; it is not proving that God exists, or making a good case for the truth of Christianity; it is not inviting someone to a meeting; it is not exposing the contemporary dilemma, or arousing interest in Christianity; it is not wearing a badge saying "Jesus Saves"! Some of these things are right and good in their place, but none of them should be confused with evangelism. To evangelise is to declare on the authority of God what he has done to save sinners, to warn men of their lost condition, to direct them to repent, and to believe on the Lord Jesus Christ.[8]*

Ezekiel really wants us to understand that this is what it means for us to be watchmen and watchwomen for the Lord. In chapter 7, he therefore records a second example of what he prophesied against Jerusalem while he was lying on his side. This time he speaks inconvenient truth to the land of Israel, rather than to its mountains, but what he says to the land is even starker than what he said to the mountains (7:4–9).

> "I will not look on you with pity;
> I will not spare you."[9]

---

[7] The gospel is more than simply John 3:16. We need to read that verse in the wider context of John 3:16–21.

[8] John Cheeseman says this in his book *The Grace of God in the Gospel* (Banner of Truth Trust, 1972).

[9] Many fool themselves that the Lord will overlook their sins on the Day of Judgment because Christians have never told them that the gospel warns otherwise. That's why we need to read Ezekiel 3:16–21 and 33:1–9 very carefully. The church has many people's blood on its hands.

"Disaster! Unheard-of disaster!"

*"I am about to pour out my wrath on you
and spend my anger against you."*[10]

*"I will judge you according to your conduct
and repay you for all your detestable practices."*

*"Then you will know that it is I the Lord who strikes
you."*[11]

Both of these two chapters do more than expose people's sin. They also expose people's false saviours. Ezekiel does not pull his punches as he confronts the *"detestable idols"* and *"vile images"* of Israel. He warns that they will prove powerless to save Jerusalem from the Babylonian army.[12] Since the ark of the covenant has been turned into a talisman, the Lord will also destroy his Temple when he wages war on the idols of Jerusalem.[13]

If we find Ezekiel a bit intolerant in these verses, could it be because we have forgotten that real gospel-preaching means calling people to turn away from worthless idols, rather than simply to add God to the collection of saviours that already

---

[10] One of the big themes of Ezekiel 1–32 is that the Lord has not yet *fully repaid* the sins of Judah or *fully spent* his anger against their nation. That is to say, further surgery is needed.

[11] This is the tragedy of a watered-down gospel. It tells people that they can know God as their Friend and Saviour without facing up to the fact that unconfessed sin makes him their Enemy and Judge. If what we say does not call people to confess their sin and lay hold of the blood of Jesus, then it isn't the Christian gospel.

[12] Idols are not merely made of gold and silver and wood and stone. Ezekiel warns the Jewish exiles that our trust in earthly wealth and in human leaders can also turn them into idols (7:19–20 and 7:26–27).

[13] The Lord still views his sanctuary as *"the place I treasure"* in 7:22, but all of Jerusalem's idols must fall.

populate their puny pantheon?[14] It is a vice, and not a virtue, to be more tolerant towards sin than God is.

Rather than dismissing Ezekiel's language, we need to learn from it. God wants to teach us through these verses what it truly means for us to be his watchmen and watchwomen.

He wants to warn us that the gospel that brings salvation has not been preached unless sin is named, the cross is explained, and repentance is demanded.

---

[14] Jeremiah 2:13, Acts 14:15 and 1 Thessalonians 1:9.

Moving Day
(Ezekiel 8:1–11:25)

The glory of the Lord went up from within the city and stopped above the mountain east of it.

(Ezekiel 11:23)

One of my friends is in his fifties and he still lives in the house in which he was born. That's pretty unusual for a Londoner, but the Lord was even more committed to living out of one room in Jerusalem. In 2 Chronicles 7:1–2, we are told about the day when he moved into the inner sanctuary of the Temple.

When Solomon finished praying, fire came down from heaven and consumed the burnt offering and the sacrifices, and the glory of the Lord filled the temple. The priests could not enter the temple of the Lord because the glory of the Lord filled it.

For the 366 years since then, the Lord had inhabited that sanctuary, so these four chapters mark a massive milestone for Jerusalem. They describe God's moving day.[1]

The date is 17 September 592 BC, which means that Ezekiel has just finished his 390 days of lying on his left side and is a couple of weeks into his forty days of lying on his right side. He has taken a short break to sit down with some of the Jewish elders who have visited his home, curious to know what else the prophet has to say about their nation. Suddenly, in 8:3,

---

[1] This movement takes place in 9:3, 10:3-5, 10:18-19 and 11:22-23.

the Holy Spirit falls on Ezekiel and takes him on an out-of-body visit to Jerusalem. He finds himself in the gateway of the inner courtyard of the Temple, looking up at the same vision of God's glorious presence that he saw in chapters 1–3.[2] The presence has moved out of the Temple sanctuary, and Ezekiel tells us why. King Josiah removed and destroyed the statue of the Canaanite fertility goddess Asherah that once stood in this gateway, but Ezekiel sees with horror in 8:3–5 that the statue has been rebuilt and reinstalled.[3] No wonder the Lord feels as jealous as a husband coming home to find another man in his wife's bed. God has left his sanctuary because he is leaving home.

Ezekiel is still reeling in horror when the Holy Spirit shows him many other troubling sights in 8:9–18. Seventy of the Jewish elders are worshipping idols together in one of the function rooms of the Temple, led by Jaazaniah, son of Shaphan, the brother of Ahikam and the uncle of Gedaliah. Even the "good figs" of Judah are turning bad![4] Meanwhile, in the courtyards of the Temple, Jewish women are worshipping the Babylonian fertility god Tammuz (8:14–15) and Jewish men are worshipping the sun (8:16).[5] Is it any wonder that the Lord has made it moving day? The Holy Spirit asks Ezekiel, *"Have you seen... Have you seen?"*.

In chapter 9, the prophet hears the Holy Spirit summon seven angels, one to set a mark on the foreheads of anyone who grieves over what is happening in the Lord's Temple, and

---

[2] Since Ezekiel was probably present to hear Jeremiah's *Temple Sermon*, this may be the gateway at which he listened to God's man in Jerusalem preaching a message that he now echoes as God's man in Babylon.

[3] 2 Kings 21:7 and 23:6–7. Asherah is referred to as the *Queen of Heaven* in Jeremiah 7:18 and 44:17–25.

[4] Jaazaniah has betrayed his name as well as his family, since it means *The Lord Hears*. He appears to be calling on the insect and reptile gods of Egypt, in the same way that King Zedekiah called on Pharaoh.

[5] Babylonians believed that the hot and rainless summer was caused by Tammuz spending half the year in the Underworld. They mourned for him publicly each July to "resurrect" him and to bring back the rains.

six to slaughter those who don't.[6] Ezekiel turns to witness God's presence turning its back on the replica cherubim in his sanctuary and moving to the threshold of his Temple (9:3), like a rejected husband waiting for a taxi on the doorstep of his marital home.[7]

In chapter 10, the Lord is on the move again. Ezekiel describes God's glorious presence leaving the threshold of the Temple building (10:4), crossing the Temple courtyards, and waiting at the gateway that leads out of the Temple complex altogether.[8] Once again, we are reminded of a rejected husband waiting for a taxi on the doorstep of his family home. God has finally decided that it is moving day.[9]

In chapter 11, the Holy Spirit invites Ezekiel to listen to what some of the courtiers of King Zedekiah are saying. At the very gateway where God's glorious presence is waiting to abandon their city (11:1), the courtiers are rejoicing that Jerusalem's disasters grant them an opportunity to get rich quick and to climb up the political ladder.[10] The Holy Spirit falls afresh on

---

[6] A ratio of 6:1 indicates that the vast majority of Jews see nothing wrong with this idolatry. Far from saving the city of Jerusalem, the Temple is the very place where its slaughter must begin (9:6). 1 Peter 4:17 and Revelation 7:2–8, 8:2 and 9:4 indicate that the events of Ezekiel 9 are still very relevant to the church today.

[7] Ezekiel is normally silent, but he is so distressed by what he sees that he prays out loud in 9:8.

[8] The four mysterious creatures were not officially identified as *cherubim angels* in Ezekiel 1–3, but now they are. Their *ox* faces are also transformed into *cherub* faces, indicating that the Lord has left behind the earthly replicas of these heavenly realities (9:3, 10:4 and Hebrews 8:5). Lots of things get thrown out on moving day.

[9] The *wheels intersecting wheels* are meant to indicate that God's glorious presence is perfectly mobile. His days of hiding away in a building are over (Jeremiah 3:16). God is on the move.

[10] The Lord is as furious at their self-centred attitude as he was when he witnessed it in Shebna in Isaiah 22:15–19. *Pelatiah* means *The Lord Delivers*, but he no more lives up to his name than Jaazaniah (a different man from 8:11). King Zedekiah was afraid of and led astray by courtiers such as these (Jeremiah 38:24–26).

Ezekiel (11:5) and, still in his out-of-body vision, he begins to prophesy against these wicked courtiers. They are foolish to think that they are the lucky ones. The Lord is relocating his sanctuary to Babylonia because the real *"meat in the pot"* – the true lucky ones – are the ten thousand exiled families through whom he is planning to restore and revive the Jewish nation for the next great chapter in its story.

Suddenly, one of the wicked courtiers drops dead before Ezekiel's very eyes (11:13). Ezekiel stops prophesying and starts praying for the Lord to have mercy on what is left of Jerusalem. The reply he receives is a reminder that the hope of Israel now lies with the exiles in Babylonia and not with the sinful people that they have left behind.[11] Babylon is about to serve as a giant operating theatre. The Lord will use the next seventy years to cut out their stubborn *"heart of stone"* and to replace it with a repentant *"heart of flesh"* (11:19). His Holy Spirit will use the exile to transform the spirits of the Jewish exiles so that they are no longer double-minded over whether to worship the God of Israel or foreign idols, whether or not to follow his commands, and whether or not they ought to rejoice that they are the Lord's people and that the Lord is their God.[12]

Before this glorious promise can be realized, however, further surgery is needed on the land of Judah. The Lord must rid it of the idolaters that Ezekiel has witnessed in its Temple courtyards. In 11:22–23, God's glorious presence therefore leaves the city of Jerusalem and lingers on the Mount of Olives, as if looking back across the Kidron Valley, longing for a better moment in the future when Jerusalem is ready for its God to come back home.

Suddenly, Ezekiel opens his eyes. He is back in his house in Babylonia. The Jewish elders are still sitting there, so he

---

[11] The Lord's description of the Jewish exiles in the Hebrew text of 11:15 can be translated as *"your brothers, your brothers, men who share in your redemption."*
[12] The promise in 11:19–20 is repeated in 36:26–27 and fulfilled in Ephesians 3:16 and Philippians 2:13.

recounts what he has seen. Further surgery is needed on the land of Judah, so the Lord has decreed that it is moving day. He has abandoned Jerusalem to its destruction. Within six years, the city and its Temple will be no more.

reconstric what he has seen. Further surgery is needed on the
land of Judah, so the Lord has decreed that it is moving day. He
has abandoned Jerusalem to its destruction. Within 30 years,

See It, Say It, Sorted
(Ezekiel 12:1–28)

"I have made you a sign to the Israelites."

(Ezekiel 12:6)

British Transport Police have an anti-terrorism slogan that
urges passengers to be vigilant, to report anything unusual and
to leave the rest to them. *See it, say it, sorted.*

I don't know whether their slogan is effective at preventing
terrorism, but I do know that it is helpful when it comes to
understanding the structure of the book of Ezekiel.

Ezekiel 1–12 is all about *see it.*

Ezekiel 1–3	What Ezekiel saw of God
	(31 July to 7 August 593 BC)
Ezekiel 4–7	What the Jewish exiles saw of Ezekiel
	(August 593 BC to October 592 BC)
	Four prophetic mimes, plus some prophetic explanation.
Ezekiel 8–11	What Ezekiel saw of Jerusalem
	(17 September 592 BC)
Ezekiel 12	What the Jewish exiles saw of Ezekiel
	(Late 592 BC)
	Two more prophetic mimes, plus more prophetic explanation.

In 12:1–16, Ezekiel begins to draw this first phase of his ministry to an end by acting out a fifth piece of public mime artistry.[1] Shortly after finishing his fourteen months of lying on his side, he is commanded by the Lord to pack up his belongings by day, in full view of his neighbours, and to dig a hole in the wall of his house that evening so that all of his neighbours can see.[2] He is to let them watch as he passes his belongings out of his house through the hole in the wall and then carries them out of the city. When they ask what he is doing, the Lord prompts him to explain.[3] His mime is a prediction that King Zedekiah will try to flee the siege of Jerusalem by digging a hole in the city walls. But he will be captured and blinded. He will end his days in a Babylonian prison.[4]

In 12:17–20, Ezekiel acts out a sixth piece of public mime artistry. Every time he eats his breakfast, lunch or dinner, he shudders violently with fear, until all of his neighbours are talking about him. When they ask him to explain his strange actions, the Lord inspires him to explain that it is a prediction that those living in Jerusalem and Judah will eat their meals in terror when the Babylonian army invades their land.

If Ezekiel 1–12 is all about *see it*, then Ezekiel 13–32 is all about *say it*. The prophet's mute mime artistry gives way to a series of sermons. They are introduced by Ezekiel's warning in

---

[1] These mimes seem bizarre to us, but they succeeded in piquing the curiosity of the Jewish exiles in 12:9. People who might not have listened to Ezekiel's preaching, start asking questions when he intrigues them with his mime artistry. Preachers take note, since this is also why Jeremiah uses so many visual aids in his preaching – a mouldy belt, a decision not to marry, a smashed clay jar, a yoke and the purchase of a field.

[2] Ezekiel 12 is undated, but 20:1 indicates that he prophesied the whole of Ezekiel 12–19 between October 592 BC and August 591 BC.

[3] Note that the Lord only explains what it means to Ezekiel *after* he has already dug the hole! God does not expect his servants to be very talented, but he does expect them to obey his Word unquestioningly.

[4] Throughout the book of Ezekiel, the prophet refers to Jehoiachin as the *king* and to Zedekiah as a mere *prince*. Nebuchadnezzar had no authority to replace an anointed king of Judah.

12:21–28 that the Jewish exiles must not comfort themselves with the delusion that *"The vision he sees is for many years from now, and he prophesies about the distant future"* (12:27). The Lord is already sharpening the blade of his surgeon's scalpel and he is about to plunge it once more into the corrupted flesh of their sinful nation.

This warning acts as a springboard into a collection of twelve parables and prophecies for Israel, and seven prophecies for pagan nations. There is no more mime artistry in these chapters, because Ezekiel 13–32 is no longer about *see it*. It is all about *say it*.

Ezekiel 13–24

Judgment spoken over Israel
Judgment on false prophets (13)
Judgment on idolaters (14)
The parable of the useless vine (15)
The parable of the adulterous wife (16)
The parable of the eagles and the vine (17)
Judgment on each individual (18)
Judgment on the dynasty of David (19)
The story of Israel (20)
The story of the sword of Babylon (21)
The story of the sin of Jerusalem (22)
The parable of two promiscuous sisters (23)
The parable of the cooking pot (24)

Ezekiel 25–32

Judgment spoken over the pagan nations

We are likely to find the next twelve chapters the hardest-going in the book of Ezekiel, but here's the good news: *See it* and *say it* in the first section of Ezekiel suddenly give way to a second section in which the Lord declares that things are now *sorted*. Because he has been willing to stick the knife into the nation of Judah, the patient will go on to make a full recovery. The survivors will rise up to enjoy the glorious results of surgery.

The book of Ezekiel isn't always easy to read, but I hope this chapter makes its structure easier for you to understand. As we arrive at the end of Ezekiel's period of mime artistry, it helps to grasp where it fits within the three phases of his public ministry. This simple phrase will help us navigate our way through his middle phase in the next few chapters.

The three phases of the book of Ezekiel are: *See it, say it, sorted.*

Look Who's Talking
(Ezekiel 13:1–23)

Even though the Lord has not sent them, they say, "The Lord declares," and expect him to fulfil their words.

(Ezekiel 13:6)

Whenever we are tempted to view the twelve parables and prophecies in Ezekiel 13–24 as a little long and heavy-going, it helps to remember something. They represent pretty much all that Ezekiel was permitted to speak in public for six whole years. His tongue worked when he prayed and prophesied, but otherwise he remained mute until news reached his ears that Jerusalem had finally fallen. Perhaps that's why the first of the twelve chapters confronts the false prophets of Judah, contrasting their hasty tongues with his own tight-lipped reverence towards the Lord. Plenty of people claim to speak for God, but Ezekiel warns his hearers to take a closer look at who's really talking.

We already know from the book of Jeremiah that false prophecy was rife throughout Jerusalem and Judah. In chapter 28, Hananiah thought nothing of adding "thus says the Lord" to his own speculation that King Zedekiah would defeat King Nebuchadnezzar. In chapter 23, Jeremiah complained that his nation might have repented many times over had it not been peddled false hope by people who add "thus says the Lord" to their positive platitudes. Ezekiel addresses the same problem here at the beginning of the second phase of his public ministry. He proclaims God's judgment over anyone who claims to be a messenger from the Lord, but who in reality is nothing of the kind.

In 13:1–16, Ezekiel confronts the Jewish men who are prophesying lies in the Lord's name. In 13:17–23, he confronts the Jewish women. The warning that God gives him for both groups is very similar. They have been inspired by their own sinful spirits, not by the Holy Spirit. Their prophecies are false and their predictions are lies. For all they claim to speak God's message to their nation, the truth is that they are prophesying *"out of their own imagination"* (verse 2).[1] The Lord therefore gives them four reasons why he is about to unsheathe his surgeon's scalpel to remove their deadly influence from the Jewish nation.

First, in 13:3–7, those who proclaim "thus says the Lord" over their own thoughts prove that they care more about sounding good than about doing good. They are like *jackals* amidst the ruins of a city, sniffing around for scraps of human acclamation instead of putting their hand to the hard work of rebuilding. The Lord has seen them for what they are – false prophets in search of false profits – and he will judge them most severely.

Second, in 13:8–16, those who proclaim "thus says the Lord" over their own thoughts inevitably lead people astray. There is no neutral ground when it comes to speaking spiritual words, since every true word spoken brings something of heaven down to earth and every false word spoken drags up something of hell. The Lord accuses these wannabe prophets of having done the spiritual equivalent of skim-plastering over a crumbling wall to hide its cracks from a building surveyor.[2] They know full well that skim-plastering can do nothing to prevent a wall from toppling when the wind blows, so how can they imagine that preaching *"'Peace', when there is no peace"* (13:10) will bring lasting comfort to Jerusalem?[3] When we dress up our own thoughts as God's thoughts, it never leaves

---

[1] To refute their made-up prophecies, Ezekiel declares five times in this chapter that *"This is what the Sovereign Lord says"*.

[2] The Hebrew word *tū'āh* in 13:10 means *to plaster* more than it does *to whitewash*. It forms a play-on-words with *tā'āh*, also in 13:10, which means *to seduce* or *to lead astray*. Paul echoes this verse in Acts 23:3.

[3] These false prophets repeat the lies that were spoken in Jeremiah 6:14, 8:11, 14:13, 23:17 and 28:9.

people as we found them. Offering false comfort to people is always misleading and dangerous.[4]

I find this thought very challenging. I can think of plenty of people whose lives were almost shipwrecked through a careless word of "prophecy". There's the famous story of a well-meaning Christian who told Bono and the Edge that God was calling them to give up music, just before U2 became one of the most influential bands of their generation. But there are also lesser known tragedies that I have witnessed – of couples marrying because "God says we're meant to be together" and of church splits taking place because a faction believes that "God is telling us that we need to do things our way instead". This chapter ought to challenge any would-be prophet to bite their tongue, as Ezekiel did, and to think twice before declaring "thus says the Lord" over anything.

Even more challenging is what this chapter says to preachers, since 1 Peter 4:11 commands that *"If anyone speaks, they should do so as one who speaks the very words of God."* Nobody should dare preach until they are confident that God is truly speaking through them. Until they have this confidence, Peter tells them to pray and get out of the way. Since Ezekiel warns us that one of the surest ways to spot a false prophet or a false preacher is that they proclaim peace and tolerance, while avoiding talk of sin, holiness, judgment and repentance, it is hard not to wonder how much of the preaching that goes on in our churches is truly God speaking. Are we as blind to this as Ezekiel's generation?

Third, in 13:17–23, those who proclaim "thus says the Lord" over their own thoughts invariably incite people to put their hope in something other than the Lord. Ezekiel particularly rebukes the female prophets for doing this, since they were evidently selling lucky charms and talismans – the ancient equivalent of the holy water, the anointed handkerchiefs, the other superstitions that Christian hucksters still peddle today.

---

[4] This is why the Apostle Paul uses building metaphors to describe good church leadership – for example, in 1 Corinthians 3:9–17, Ephesians 2:20 and 1 Timothy 3:15.

Fourth, and most serious of all, those who proclaim "thus says the Lord" over their own thoughts inevitably end up deceiving themselves.[5] It is impossible to speak untruth for any length of time without beginning to believe our own propaganda.

Ezekiel therefore warns those who *"say, 'The Lord declares,' and expect him to fulfil their words"* (13:6) that they had better take a good look at who's talking before they go much further. Jesus tells us in John 8:44 that the Devil is *"the father of lies"* – even of the lies that we tell in God's name.

If you are a prophet, a preacher or a plain old proclaimer of the gospel, then be sobered by Ezekiel's words, but don't be silenced. God says all this because he really wants to speak through you! In order for that to happen, he wants you to grasp how serious it is for any of us to claim "thus says the Lord". There can be no neutral ground after such a statement. If it isn't God speaking, then we are speaking lies, and all lies have a father.

Mike Pilavachi encourages us to take this challenge seriously and to seek God for genuine prophecy.

> *It is God's will and purpose for his Church to move under the anointing of his Spirit... It seems to me that (to use rather outdated terminology) we have largely won the charismatic battle but lost the charismatic war... Lots of churches make space for the gift of prophecy, but how many have moved beyond "I see a waterfall and God says he loves you"?*[6]

---

[5] The lucky charms sold by the female prophets ensnared them, not just their hearers, since the profits blinded them to the fact that they had become unfaithful watchwomen on the walls of God's beloved city.

[6] Mike Pilavachi, the founder of Soul Survivor, said this in an article in *Premier Christianity* magazine entitled "Everyday Supernatural" (November 2016). *Everyday Supernatural* by Mike Pilavachi and Andy Croft (David C Cook, 2016).

Invisible Gods
(Ezekiel 14:1–23)

"Son of man, these men have set up idols in their hearts."

(Ezekiel 14:3)

I love travelling in India. It is one of my favourite countries. Idolatry is everywhere, but at least it isn't hidden. Watching people worship the elephant god Ganesh and the monkey god Hanuman doesn't feel too far removed from what Ezekiel witnessed in the Temple courtyards, when he saw people worshipping Asherah and Tammuz. When I get back home to London, the idolatry is a lot less obvious, which is why I need to read this chapter very carefully. Ezekiel exposes our own invisible gods.

Some of the Jewish elders are paying another visit to Ezekiel's home. Now that the prophet has finished lying on his side, they hope to have a longer conversation with him about Jerusalem. Surely he didn't really mean it when he said that he saw God's glorious presence abandoning his sanctuary to pave the way for the destruction of the city?

Ezekiel makes no small talk. He couldn't even if he tried. His tongue remains mute except for moments when he is praying or prophesying. One of the advantages of this long silence is that it teaches him to listen very carefully to the Lord, who suddenly reveals to him that these elders are a large part of the problem![1] They may not worship statues, like the

---

[1] James 1:19 and 3:1–12 urge us to tame our tongues for this same reason. *"My dear brothers and sisters, take note of this: everyone should be quick to listen, slow to speak."*

idolaters he saw at the Temple, but they are idolaters all the same. *"These men have set up idols **in their hearts**."* In case we miss this, Ezekiel says it again. They have set up *"idols **in their hearts**"*, and invisible idols are the most dangerous of them all.

The sixteenth-century reformer John Calvin spent much of his life fighting visible idols. It was he who pointed out that many of the original missionaries to Europe had not so much destroyed its pagan images as replaced them with Christian-looking ones. A statue of the pagan god of healing had been replaced by the relics of a dead saint who might heal those who touched his bones. Images of gods and goddesses had been replaced by icons of the Apostles and of Mary. But John Calvin also went much further:

> *The human mind is, so to speak, a perpetual idol factory... The human mind, stuffed as it is with presumptuous rashness, dares to imagine a god suited to its own capacity... It substitutes vanity and an empty phantom in the place of God.*[2]

John Calvin grasped that the temptation to worship invisible idols is just as real in our own day as it was in Ezekiel's. It is one of the greatest temptations in every generation. Martin Luther agrees that, *"Whatever your heart clings to and relies upon, that is your God."*[3]

In our generation, we make invisible gods out of marriage and out of sexual freedom. Not all fertility goddesses look like the statue of Asherah in the Temple gateway. We make invisible gods out of popularity and political ideology, as George Bernard Shaw famously observed. *"The art of government is the organization of idolatry... The savage bows down to idols of*

---

[2] John Calvin wrote this in 1536 in his *Institutes of the Christian Religion* (1.11.8).

[3] He argues this in *Luther's Larger Catechism* (1529).

wood and stone: the civilized man to idols of flesh and blood."[4]

Many of us make an invisible god out of money. That's why the writer of Hebrews warns us that the outward chasing of riches is actually a symptom of an inner desire not to have to rely on the Lord to be our daily Helper. It is also why Jesus warns us that it is impossible for love of God and love of Money to co-exist in the same heart.[5]

Others of us turn success and fame and career into invisible idols in our hearts. We are rightfully repulsed by the way that the people of Judah sacrificed their children to the false god Molek, but how many neglected children in our own generation have been sacrificed on the altar of a parent's self-centred ambition?

Most insidious of all is the false version of God that many of us worship in our hearts, who suits our preferences so much better than the holy God of the Scriptures. The actor Morgan Freeman is speaking for so many of us when he muses in his TV series about God that "there is a bit of God in all of us" and that "the best version of me is the god in me".[6]

This may sound quite innocuous to people who have grown up in the West and who are as blind to its idols as many people in India are to their elephant and monkey gods. But Ezekiel warns us that idolatry is still idolatry.

In 14:1–8, Ezekiel warns us that whenever people look like they are seeking the Lord while cherishing invisible idols in their hearts, he refuses to answer them.[7] In 14:9–11, Ezekiel adds that if anybody tells them otherwise and speaks soothing

---

[4] He says this in his *Maxims for Revolutionists* (1903). We witness this whenever Christians get more excited about elections than about Easter, and more interested in political parties than in Pentecost.

[5] Hebrews 13:5–6; Matthew 6:24 and Luke 16:13–15.

[6] Morgan Freeman says this in his TV series *The Story of God* – series 1, episode 2: "Who is God?" (2016).

[7] The Hebrew word *nāzar* is used in the Old Testament to describe people *separating* themselves from the world in order to devote themselves to God (as in the Nazirite vow of Numbers 6). It is with deliberate irony, then, that God uses the word in 14:7 to describe people *separating* themselves from him to worship idols.

words to them in the Lord's name, then *"the prophet will be as guilty as the one who consults him."*[8]

Before the Jewish elders who are sitting in Ezekiel's living room can beat a hasty exit, he declares in 14:12–23 that idolatry lies right at the heart of Judah's sinfulness and rebellion. That's why the Lord has resolved firmly that further surgery is needed. Even if the three great intercessors Job, Noah and Daniel formed a prayer triplet and cried out night and day, they could not change his mind.[9] To emphasize the Lord's resolve, Ezekiel adds a fourth disaster to the deadly trio of *"sword, famine and plague"* that were mentioned fifteen times in the book of Jeremiah. *"Wild animals"* are now added to the list of judgments too, because the Lord will do whatever it takes to cut out the corrupted flesh that is destroying the nation of Judah.

So let's reflect in our own hearts and let's identify the invisible gods that are attempting to turn it into their pagan temple. Let's do as Ezekiel urges us in 14:6. *"This is what the Sovereign Lord says: Repent! Turn from your idols and renounce all your detestable practices!"*[10]

---

[8] We should understand 14:9 to mean that God goads false prophets into speaking such flattering words in order to reveal them to the whole world for the charlatans that they are.

[9] The events of Daniel 1–2 take place in roughly 603–602 BC, so Daniel was near the height of his godly influence in Babylon when Ezekiel prophesied these words in about 591 BC.

[10] This is the first of three great "repentance commands" in the book of Ezekiel. The others are 18:30–32 and 33:11.

Parables
(Ezekiel 15:1–16:63)

"This is what the Sovereign Lord says to Jerusalem…"

(Ezekiel 16:3)

Jesus is not the only preacher of parables in the Bible. Long before the Son of Man ever told his parables to the Jewish nation, the prophet referred to ninety-three times as a *"son of man"* had told several parables of his own. Let's look at two of them together here.

In chapter 15, we have *the parable of the useless vine*. It corrects the idea that Jerusalem is more precious to God than the other cities of the world. Ezekiel reminds the Jewish exiles that Scripture likens their nation to a fruitful vine.[1] If Jerusalem has ceased to bear spiritual fruit for the Lord, then that means it is next to useless. Nobody ever planted a vine so that they could use its wood for furniture! The only thing a fruitless vine is fit for is fuel for the fire. The Lord has already burned Jerusalem and he is about to burn it again.

In chapter 16, we have *the parable of the adulterous wife*. It is the longest chapter in the book of Ezekiel, and perhaps the most surprising. We can easily imagine the parable of the useless vine in the mouth of Jesus, but not this second parable. It is so shockingly vulgar that it makes me think of Martin Luther's excuse for why he used such rough language and coarse imagery in his own polemic pamphlets.

---

[1] Genesis 49:22, Psalm 80:8–16, Isaiah 3:14, 5:1–7 and 27:2, Jeremiah 2:21 and 12:10, Hosea 10:1 and Micah 7:1. Jesus also picks up on this picture in Matthew 20:1–16, Mark 12:1–9, Luke 20:9–16 and John 15:1–16.

I was born to war with fanatics and devils. Thus my books are very stormy and warlike. I must root out the stumps and trunks, hack away the thorns and briar, fill in the puddles. I am the rough woodsman, who must pioneer and make ready a path.[2]

For the same reason, Ezekiel deliberately shocks his listeners in this second parable. He wants to rid them of their misguided confidence that God is duty-bound to protect Jerusalem because of its long history with him. He reminds them in 16:1–6 that it used to be a Canaanite city.[3] It was floundering like an unwanted baby left out to die until the moment he chose it as his new capital and declared his gracious blessing over it: *"Live!"*

Most English Bible translators spare our blushes by toning down the graphic language that Ezekiel uses in the Hebrew text of 16:7–14.[4] He talks about Jerusalem's *nakedness* and *menstrual blood* and *breasts* and *pubic hair* and *wedding presents* and *lovemaking*. It's a pretty shocking way of describing the early days of God's relationship with Jerusalem, but Ezekiel's listeners do need to be shocked out of their fatal complacency. They must grasp that when King David captured Jerusalem and called the nations to come and worship the Lord at his new Tabernacle on Mount Zion, it marked the flowering of their city into womanhood. The city that had been rejected by the Canaanites suddenly became the beautiful, beaming bride of the Living God.

In 16:15–34, the Lord reminds the Jewish exiles how Jerusalem has responded to his grace towards her. She has consistently repaid his undeserved favour with undeserved betrayal. After the death of King David, Jerusalem prostituted herself to the gods of the Canaanites, the Egyptians, the Assyrians

---

[2] He said this in translation in his preface to Philip Melanchthon's commentary on Colossians (*Kolosserkommentar* 1529).

[3] Church history matters. Jerusalem's misguided memory of its past led to misguided actions in the present.

[4] They continue to do so in the rest of the chapter, and throughout its sister parable in Ezekiel 23.

and the Babylonians.[5] She took advantage of the beauty that the Lord had bestowed upon her to play the field with the entire pagan pantheon.[6] She murdered his children on the altar of Molek. She forgot her lowly origins and (shocking language in the Hebrew text again) she *spread her legs* to every passer-by, thinking more of their *large genitals* than of her husband's deep love towards her (16:25–26).[7] Even the proverbially pagan Philistines were horrified by her promiscuity (16:27).

Prostitutes are normally driven by poverty, degrading themselves unwillingly because they need the money in men's pockets. In 16:30–34, the Lord fumes that Jerusalem does not even have this excuse. Her idols demand everything in return for nothing.

In 16:35–58, the Lord therefore tells the Jewish exiles that he will mete out to Jerusalem the judgment that is rightfully hers under the Jewish Law for adultery and murder.[8] She will be stripped naked and stoned. She will be stabbed and burned. How could she not be, in view of her foul history? She has not merely revealed her Canaanite parentage, but she has actually exceeded the depravity of her sister cities, Samaria and Sodom.[9]

It is at this point that the parable shocks us for another

---

[5] The Hebrew verb *zānāh*, which means *to play the prostitute* or *to commit adultery*, is used twenty-three times in its verb or noun form in this chapter in order to emphasize that Jerusalem's idolatry was a repeated action. She didn't even seem to notice that she was paying her lovers, rather than being paid by them.

[6] The repeated accusation in 16:16–20 is *"You took ... you took ... you took ... you took."*

[7] Gratitude is a vital attitude. Jerusalem's sin flowed out of forgetting her lowly origins (16:22 and 43).

[8] Genesis 38:24, Leviticus 20:10 and 24:17, Deuteronomy 22:22 and John 8:3–7.

[9] Sodom is used throughout the Bible as the epitome of sinfulness (Deuteronomy 32:32, Isaiah 1:9–10 and 3:9, Jeremiah 23:14, Lamentations 4:6, Jude 7 and Revelation 11:8). However, Jesus echoes 16:48 by declaring that Israel has managed to make sinful Sodom look a little less unrighteous (Matthew 10:15 and 11:23–24).

reason. Suddenly, we find ourselves dragged into the story. When the Lord enumerates the sins of Sodom in verse 49, we expect him to list some of the things that we are told about in Genesis 19 – gay sex, rape and lynch mobs – but instead, the Lord lists sins commonplace to many of us – pride, complacency and a harsh disregard for the poor. The truth is, we can all fool ourselves, like the Jewish exiles, that the Lord would never apply strong discipline to his church in our own generation. But if the parable fits, we should wear it.

It is only if we face up to the negative parallels between Jerusalem and the church that we can also lay hold of the positive parallels in 16:59–63. The parable does not end with the destruction of Jerusalem. It ends with atonement for sin and with a restoration of the marriage covenant.[10] There is even a promise that Samaria and Sodom will be included in the Lord's new happy family. To put this in our own language, the parable assures us that if we repent of our sins then the Lord will restore and revive our churches. He will not simply bring us back into a deep love relationship with him. He will empower us to reach out to the non-believers all around us and to draw them into his church family too.

Jesus ended several of his parables with the phrase *"Whoever has ears, let them hear"*.[11] As we end these two parables from Ezekiel, he would say the same thing to us here.

So let's read these verses slowly. Let's be shocked by them, let's be grieved by them, let's be humbled by them and let's be revived through them. The church has sinned and she deserves her present punishment – but take heart. Her Husband is calling her home.

---

[10] The Hebrew word for *making atonement* in 16:63 is *kāphar*, which means literally *to cover over*. Unless we bring our sin into the light, it can never be covered over. Frank confession always precedes forgiveness.

[11] Matthew 11:15, 13:9 and 13:43, Mark 4:23, and Revelation 2:29.

Newsflash
(Ezekiel 17:1–24)

*"Son of man, set forth an allegory and tell it to the
Israelites as a parable."*

(Ezekiel 17:2)

It is 22 November 1963. The writer David Lodge is attending a
performance of one of his plays at a crowded theatre. *Between
These Four Walls* stars Julie Christie, and David Lodge is
delighted to see how perfectly she catches the audience up in
the drama that he has written. During one of the scenes, a radio
is switched on to play some background music, when suddenly
a real-life newsreader breaks into the music with a newsflash:
*"Today, in Dallas, Texas, President John F. Kennedy was shot and
killed."* One of the actors rushes to turn off the radio, but it is
too late. The performance is as good as over midway through.
The illusion that held the audience's rapt attention has been
shattered by a few plain words spoken into the drama from the
real world. The theatre begins to empty, as people rush home to
find out about the true drama that is unfolding that day.

The third of Ezekiel's parables is like David Lodge's visit
to the theatre. *The parable of the eagles and the vine* serves as
a newsflash from the real world for Jewish exiles who have
lost track of reality. It explains what is truly happening to their
beloved city of Jerusalem.

In 17:1–4, a mighty eagle swoops down from the sky and
breaks off the uppermost shoot of a giant cedar tree.[1] It flies

---

[1] Don't be confused by the reference to *Lebanon* rather than Judah. The
reference is not geographical. Lebanon simply happened to be world famous
for its giant cedar trees.

away to a land famous for its international marketplaces, where the eagle carefully plants the shoot in a patch of fertile ground.

In 17:5–6, the mighty eagle plants another seedling in a different patch of fertile ground. The seedling puts down strong roots into the well-watered soil beneath it and stretches out its many branches in the direction of the eagle that planted it. It is a vine, nowhere near as strong as the giant cedar tree, but likely to bear much better fruit on its branches.

In 17:7–10, the vine decides that it finds a second mighty eagle more attractive and more desirable than the first one. It pulls up its roots from the well-watered soil beneath it in order to extend them towards this new eagle. Discovering that it now lacks water, it stretches out its branches towards that new eagle too in the hope of absorbing water through its leaves. This is self-evidently foolish: vines cannot absorb water through their leaves. The vine's fickleness will result in unfruitfulness, until the vine withers and dies.

In 17:11–15, Ezekiel explains that this parable is a newsflash from Jerusalem. It warns the exiles not to fall for the positive spin that Hananiah and the other false prophets are putting on King Zedekiah's drama, praising him for daring to stand up to Nebuchadnezzar and for enlisting the help of Pharaoh to throw off the yoke of Babylon. The reality is quite different from that fiction. King Zedekiah has been utterly foolish. He has betrayed Nebuchadnezzar, the first mighty eagle in the parable, who would have prospered him had he remained faithful to the oath of allegiance that he swore to him in the name of the Lord.[2] However, since Zedekiah has ignored God's warning not to rely on Pharaoh, the second mighty eagle in the parable, his city is about to be destroyed.

In 17:16–21, Ezekiel underlines a vital fact from the real world that has been lost amidst the fiction being peddled by the false prophets of Judah. The oath of allegiance that King

---

[2] We might have guessed the identity of the first eagle without any explanation, since Nebuchadnezzar's army is described as an eagle in Jeremiah 48:40 and 49:22.

Zedekiah swore to Nebuchadnezzar was offered in the name of the God of Israel. The Lord sees it as *"my oath"* and *"my covenant"*, which means that Zedekiah has done more than merely betray Babylon. The ease with which he broke his oath is a sign of how much he disdains the name of the Lord.[3] As a result, the God of Israel will take Babylon's side when it comes and lays siege to the city of Jerusalem. Pharaoh will prove to be a false friend. Judah's army will be slaughtered and Jerusalem will be captured. King Zedekiah will be dragged off in chains to Babylon, the land of international marketplaces that is mentioned at the beginning of the parable. There he will die.

In 17:22–24, Ezekiel finishes his newsflash. He takes us back to the beginning of his parable, where Nebuchadnezzar tore a shoot away from the top of the mighty cedar tree of King David's royal dynasty of Judah. Nobody has given much thought to King Jehoiachin since he was dragged off into exile in 597 BC, but Ezekiel's newsflash reveals that the forgotten King of Judah is still a major player in God's real-world drama. Ezekiel emphasizes this throughout his book by constantly referring to Zedekiah as a *nâsî*, which means *prince*, and by reserving the word *melek*, which means *king*, for whenever he mentions Jehoiachin.[4] The surprising message of Ezekiel's parable is therefore that the Lord intends to rebuild Jerusalem through Jehoiachin and his fellow exiles in Babylon, not through the supposed "lucky ones" that they left behind. He will raise up a Messiah to be the Saviour for his exiled people, but he will do so through the forgotten King Jehoiachin, not through the fickle Prince Zedekiah.[5]

Enough of the ancient history lesson. What relevance does all of this have for our own lives today? It invites us to speak

---

[3] 2 Chronicles 36:13. This has a broader implication for our marriages too. It informs us that the vows that we make on our wedding day are made primarily to God, and only secondarily to our spouse.

[4] For example, in 1:2 and 12:10. Ezekiel does not believe that a Babylonian ruler has any authority to depose or install a king of Judah. That authority belongs to the Lord alone.

[5] Note the echo of 17:23 in Matthew 13:31–32.

similar newsflashes to our own generation. Like the real-life newsreader who broke into the theatre performance of David Lodge's *Between These Four Walls*, we are to shatter every fiction that the Devil peddles to people today.

How did Adolf Hitler manage to convince a nation to murder eleven million Jews, gypsies, Slavs and homosexuals in the death camps of the early 1940s? The answer isn't as difficult as it might seem. *"My greatest gift to the Germans is that I have taught them to think clearly,"* he declared. *"When National Socialism has ruled long enough, it will no longer be possible to conceive of a form of life different from ours."*[6] Hitler reframed the German story in a manner that made killing certain groups of people, not just a necessary evil, but a nationalistic virtue. By creating a fictional story about the German race, he convinced people that such *Untermenschen* or non-Aryans must be removed from the human gene pool for the good of humanity. Failure to do so would not be brave and godly, but weak and cruel.

That's the power of the stories that we tell each other. They transform our worldview, which transforms our actions, which is why the Devil loves telling false stories. Ezekiel teaches us through this parable that God has commissioned us to resist the Devil by acting as newsreaders from the real world. We are to break into the fictional drama in which the people around us imagine they are living. We are to tell them the Great Story that transforms every worldview, and therefore every action. We are to proclaim to them the good news that Ezekiel's long-awaited Messiah has come to set every captive free.

---

[6] Adolf Hitler said this in one of his "Table Talk" speeches on 11 July 1941.

What God Wants
(Ezekiel 18:1–19:14)

"Do I take any pleasure in the death of the wicked?
declares the Sovereign Lord. Rather, am I not
pleased when they turn from their ways and live?"

(Ezekiel 18:23)

There was a rumour going round about what God wanted for Judah. We can tell that it was widespread from the fact that it is mentioned in both Jeremiah 31:29 and Ezekiel 18:2. *"The parents eat sour grapes, and the children's teeth are set on edge."* In other words, the present troubles in the land of Judah were not linked to any wrongdoing on the part of the current generation. God was punishing Judah for sins committed decades earlier during the reign of King Manasseh.[1]

There was enough truth in this rumour for Ezekiel not to rubbish it out of hand.[2] Nor would he try to quash it by telling another one of his parables. Parables are a great way of provoking people to start thinking, but they are a poor way of helping people to grapple with the complex questions that they raise. Gospel preaching needs to be accompanied by gospel

---

[1] Manasseh had ruled 697–642 BC. The rumour can probably be traced back to a warning from the Lord that the sins of Manasseh would cause the fall of Jerusalem (2 Kings 23:26 and 24:3, and Jeremiah 15:4).

[2] Under the Old Covenant, people were affected by the sins of their parents (Exodus 20:5 and 34:7), but they were only punished personally for how much they copied them (Deuteronomy 24:16). Ezekiel needed to clarify this for the Jewish exiles. Under the New Covenant, it is made even clearer (Jeremiah 31:29–31).

apologetics, so Ezekiel takes the time to reason with the Jewish exiles. John Stott urges us to take the same approach with people too: *"We cannot pander to a man's intellectual arrogance, but we must cater to his intellectual integrity."*[3]

In 18:1–20, Ezekiel reasons with the Jewish exiles in order to prove to them that what God really wants is *justice*. He will not punish the innocent for the sins of their ancestors. *"The one who sins is the one who will die."* In order to convince them of this, he creates a hypothetical family tree. If a man obeys the Law of Moses, should God punish him as if he didn't?[4] Clearly the answer is "no" – he should be spared.[5] What if that man has a son who rejects the Law? Should the Lord spare his life as if he were a devout believer? Again, the answer is clearly "no" – he should be punished. What if there is a grandson, who obeys the Law like his grandfather? Should he be punished because of his father's sin? Again, it's a clear "no" – he should be spared. *"The one who sins is the one who will die."*

Ezekiel takes his time to prove this because, if the rumour were correct, then it would cause two major stumbling blocks for the present generation of Jews. First, it would make God out to be an unfair bully, rather than a righteous Judge, since it would mean that he desired to punish innocent people for sins committed by others long before they were even born. Second, it would foster spiritual passivity, since it is rather difficult for anybody to repent of another person's sins.

Having proven to the Jewish exiles that God wants justice, the prophet now goes a step further. In 18:21–32, he explains that what God wants even more is *mercy*.

---

[3] Quoted by Paul Little in his excellent manual, *How To Give Away Your Faith* (IVP, 1966). Reproduced with permission of the Licensor through PLSclear.

[4] Ezekiel's summary of the Law in 18:5–9 is very insightful. It is not enough to be able to say of our lives, *I never did anybody any harm*. We need also to be able to say, *I never failed to do anybody any good*.

[5] Ezekiel is not saying here that such a person earns their own salvation, but that only such a person would deserve to be spared amidst the fall of Jerusalem. He is doing what Paul also tells us to do in Romans 3:20.

> *"Do I take any pleasure in the death of the wicked?*
> *declares the Sovereign Lord. Rather, am I not pleased*
> *when they turn from their ways and live? ... Repent!*
> *Turn away from all your offences; then sin will not be*
> *your downfall... Get a new heart and a new spirit. Why*
> *will you die, people of Israel? For I take no pleasure in*
> *the death of anyone, declares the Sovereign Lord. Repent*
> *and live!"*[6]

This is the glory of the gospel. God wants justice, but God wants mercy even more. He wants it so much that he has made a way for guilty sinners to be declared righteous, by sending his own righteous Son into the world to be treated like a guilty sinner for them.

Theologians refers to this as "penal substitutionary atonement". To help the Jewish exiles grasp how much God wants it, Ezekiel writes a poem of lament in 19:1–14. It may not be as beautiful as the five in the book of Lamentations, but its message is every bit as glorious. It proclaims that all of the disasters that have befallen Jerusalem testify to how much God desires to be both just and merciful. Ezekiel picks up on a famous prophecy of Jacob about the Messiah to describe the kingdom of Judah as a mighty lioness.[7] Her first lion cub was King Jehoahaz, who oppressed God's people and was exiled to Egypt in 609 BC (19:1–4). Her second lion cub was King Jehoiachin, who also oppressed God's people and was exiled to Babylon in 597 BC (19:5–9). King Zedekiah is still oppressing God's people, so he will also go into exile in 586 BC (19:10–14). In all of this, the Lord is perfectly just. None of these three sinful kings can blame his fate on King Manasseh. But in all of this, the Lord is also perfectly merciful. Ezekiel's poem may be a funeral dirge

---

[6] This is the second of three great "repentance commands" in the book of Ezekiel. The others are in 14:6 and 33:11.

[7] Genesis 49:8–12 and Revelation 5:5.

for the demise of David's royal dynasty – *"No strong branch is left on it fit for a ruler's sceptre"* (verse 14) – but that demise is an important milestone on the road towards a true and better King of Judah springing forth from the ruined rump of David's dynasty.[8]

So there you have it. What God wants is to be both perfectly just and perfectly merciful. This is what he is achieving through the troubles that have befallen Jerusalem. But Ezekiel has raised a further question through his intense description of God's desire to forgive the guilty in 18:23 and 30–32. It is the one that Rob Bell asks in his book, *Love Wins,* when he asks "If God wants all people to be saved (1 Timothy 2:4), then will God actually get what he wants? Is God big enough to achieve what he desires or just quite great, but not great enough to see all people saved?".[9]

Theologians call this "Christian universalism". It claims that God wants so much to save sinners that he will not punish the guilty forever in hell. It's the flipside of the rumour that was going round Jerusalem. The Jewish exiles believed that God does not want justice: he wants retribution. Rob Bell believes that God does not want justice: he wants mercy at any price.[10] Ezekiel insists in these two chapters that both aspects of the rumour are untrue. God doesn't want justice or mercy. He wants *both* justice *and* mercy! And he has found a way to get what he wants. At the cross of Jesus, his perfect justice and his perfect mercy intersect in perfect love.[11]

---

[8] The fruitless vine in 19:14 connects this poem of lament to other messianic Scriptures – for example, Isaiah 11:1 and 53:2, Jeremiah 23:5 and 33:15, Ezekiel 17:22, Zechariah 3:8 and 6:12, and John 15:1.

[9] Rob Bell in *Love Wins* (2011). See Lamentations 3:33, 1 Timothy 2:4 and 2 Peter 3:9.

[10] Rob Bell's mistake is to think that God would ever force his salvation upon sinners (Luke 7:30). God wants to forgive everybody, but not at the expense of his own justice and respect for their decisions. Sometimes God chooses not to get what he wants in order to get something that he wants even more.

[11] Romans 3:19–26, 4:1–8 and 6:23, and 2 Corinthians 5:21.

Through the work of Jesus, God has got what he wants. He can say to us: *"The one who sins is the one who will die... Therefore... repent and live!"* He can ask us how we want to respond to the fact that Jesus has secured, once and for all, what God wants for us.

History Lesson
(Ezekiel 20:1–49)

"The people of Israel rebelled against me in the wilderness."

(Ezekiel 20:13)

The great Roman orator Cicero argued that, *"To be ignorant of what happened before you were born is to remain a child always."*[1] That's why the prophet Ezekiel gives us a history lesson here. He wants to undo the comforting fiction that the false prophets have been peddling to the Jewish nation. As he does so, he models how we are to speak the truth of God's Word to a world that refuses to acknowledge its sin.[2]

It is 14 August 591 BC. Almost a year has passed since the Jewish elders visited Ezekiel's home and witnessed his out-of-body vision of God's glorious presence abandoning the Temple.[3] The elders visited again in chapter 14 and left with their tails between their legs, so it must be with some trepidation that they return here.

In 20:1–4, the visit begins badly. The Lord does as he promised in 14:3 by refusing to allow his prophet to speak any words in response to their questions. Instead, he inspires Ezekiel to retell the history of Israel, and it isn't what the elders learned at school.

---

[1] Marcus Tullius Cicero said this in 46 BC in his *Orator ad M. Brutum*.

[2] Stephen seems to have used this chapter as his model for retelling the history of Israel to another group of Jewish elders in Acts 7.

[3] Throughout his book, Ezekiel uses the names *Israel* and *Judah* interchangeably. These are therefore the elders of the 10,000 families that have so far been exiled from Judah to Babylon.

In 20:5–9, the Lord corrects their rose-tinted memory of how the Israelites treated him while they were slaves in Egypt.[4] Jewish history teachers made out that the Hebrews separated themselves from their slave masters, but in truth they were avid idolaters. They even clung onto the idols of Egypt after the Lord humiliated them through the Ten Plagues. They did not deserve the Exodus, *"But for the sake of my name, I brought them out of Egypt. I did it to keep my name from being profaned in the eyes of the nations."*[5]

In 20:10–14, the Lord corrects their rose-tinted memory of how the Israelites behaved towards him during their first year in the desert. Jewish history teachers majored on the giving of the Law and on the building of the Tabernacle, but this was only part of the real story.[6] Lawgiving led to Lawbreaking, especially when it came to keeping the Sabbath, which was given to reveal how much the Israelites truly trusted in God and how much they trusted in the work of their own hands. The Lord recalls that he almost destroyed them after catching them worshipping a golden calf. He only relented because Moses reminded him of his own reputation. *"For the sake of my name I did what would keep it from being profaned in the eyes of the nations in whose sight I had brought them out."*[7]

The Jewish elders in Ezekiel's living room are shifting uncomfortably, but before they can slip away, the Lord continues his history lesson. In 20:15–22, he reminds them that the Exodus generation failed to enter the Promised Land. This wasn't because the land was full of giants, but because

---

[4] The Jews prided themselves on the fact that God chose their nation, yet 20:5 is the only reference in the whole of Ezekiel to the Lord choosing Israel – and it is to point out how far short it has fallen of his choice!

[5] Each section of this history lesson follows the same cycle: *revelation, rebellion, wrath* and *reconsideration*.

[6] Ezekiel 20:11 echoes Leviticus 18:5, which is also echoed in Romans 10:5 and Galatians 3:12.

[7] Exodus 32:7–14. Five times this history lesson tells us that God saved the Israelites for the sake of his own name (20:9, 14, 22, 39 and 44), and not because they carried any inherent virtue of their own (Amos 9:7).

their hearts were full of idols.[8] A.W. Tozer observes that *"The essence of idolatry is the entertainment of thoughts about God that are unworthy of him."*[9] Sadly, even when the Lord graciously led the next generation of Israelites into the Promised Land, their hearts remained full of idolatry too. If the Jewish elders are hoping that Israel's history will protect Jerusalem from the Babylonians, then they need to go back to school. It has been an idolatrous nation all the way.[10] *"I withheld my hand, and for the sake of my name I did what would keep it from being profaned in the eyes of the nations."*[11]

In 20:23–44, the Lord begins correcting their rose-tinted memory of Israel's history from that point on. The Israelites exchanged the Law of God for the laws of their idols. They built "high places" everywhere and reaped the curses that are listed at the end of the Law.[12] The Lord fast-forwards to his final conclusion. Since the Israelites have constantly lusted to behave like the pagan nations, it is too late for them to start relying on the uniqueness of their nation to save them from the Babylonians now.[13] *"Go and serve your idols, every one of you! But afterwards you will surely listen to me and no longer profane*

---

[8] The Lord says in 20:6 that he *spied out* the Promised Land long before the 12 spies did so. He wanted to know if they would see what he had seen with eyes of faith, or if their hearts were blinded by idolatry.

[9] A.W. Tozer says this in *The Knowledge of the Holy* (1961).

[10] Five times this chapter tells us that God will *pour out* his wrath. This indicates that the problem has been bubbling away for centuries. Periods of judgment are simply times when God chooses to let it bubble over.

[11] Ezekiel 20:22 and Numbers 14:11–20. Six times in this chapter, God extols his own faithfulness to any oath he swears (*"swore to them"*, *"sworn"* in 20:5, 6, 15, 23, 28 and 42). The negative oath in 20:15 is the one that is mentioned in Psalm 95:11 and Hebrews 3:11.

[12] Paul echoes 20:25–26 when he tells us in Romans 1:24–32 that God still hands people over to their sin today.

[13] This sums up Israel's tragic history – Exodus 19:5–6 and Numbers 23:9 giving way to 1 Samuel 8:19–20.

my holy name with your gifts and idols."[14] Jerusalem will surely fall and Babylon will surely become the sheep pen in which the Lord separates the sheep from the goats within the Jewish nation.[15] Those who persist in idolatry will die in that pagan land, and those who choose to act as God's chosen people will return to rebuild a New Temple and a New Jerusalem.[16] *"You will know that I am the Lord, when I deal with you for my name's sake"* (verse 44).

In 20:45–49, after the Jewish elders have beaten a hasty retreat from his living room, Ezekiel receives further revelation. He is to prophesy against *"the forest of the southland"* – that is, the Jews still living in Jerusalem and Judah, in the south of the Promised Land – and he is to declare God's judgment against them. Although Ezekiel complains that people are not listening to his parables, the Lord insists that his revival plan is working. The survival of sinful Israel has never had anything to do with its own inherent virtue. Their history merely provides the Lord with a catalogue of reasons why he should destroy them. Their survival and their revival is all about *God's passion for his name*.

For the sake of his reputation in the eyes of all nations, the Lord has repeatedly spared his people. For the sake of that same reputation, he will now destroy Jerusalem. And for the sake of his reputation, he will restore and revive the Jewish nation in days to come.

"I will be proved holy through you in the sight of the nations ... You will know that I am the Lord, when I deal with you for my own name's sake" (verses 41 and 44).

---

[14] 20:39. What do you do when the Lord commands you to worship idols? Is it disobedience to do so or disobedience to refuse?! This is the Old Testament equivalent of John 13:27 and Revelation 3:15–16.

[15] The reference in 20:37 to a shepherd sorting sheep with his rod is an ancient equivalent of our picture of a surgeon removing infected flesh with his scalpel. It is echoed by Jeremiah 33:13 and Matthew 25:31–46.

[16] In 20:40, *"my holy mountain"* refers to Mount Zion and promises the rebuilding of God's Temple.

A Tale of Two Cities
(Ezekiel 21:1–22:31)

*"Son of man, mark out two roads for the sword of the
king of Babylon to take... Make a signpost where the
road branches off to the city."*

(Ezekiel 21:19)

The Bible is a tale of two cities, a bitter conflict between Babylon
and Jerusalem. The early chapters of Genesis record the first
attempt to build Babylon, and the final chapters of Revelation
record its fall in order that the New Jerusalem can rise instead.[1]
Babylon and Jerusalem are at loggerheads from start to finish of
the Bible, so we need to read the tale of two cities that is told in
these two chapters in the context of that larger story.

Chapter 21 is *the story of the sword of Babylon*. It consists
of five "sword oracles" that the Lord inspired Ezekiel to deliver
against the city of Jerusalem. Although these oracles are
undated, it seems likely that Ezekiel spoke them after King
Zedekiah reneged on his oath of allegiance to Babylon and
began to stretch out his arms to Pharaoh instead.

The first of these sword oracles is recorded in 21:1–7. Our
sense of shock depends on how well we know the context of
the larger tale of two cities. Babylon is the out-and-out villain in
that story, which is why the final chapters of Revelation use it as
a symbol of sinful humanity united together in rebellion against
God. Jerusalem is the recurring love interest in the story, the city
of God's delight, which is why the final chapters of Revelation

---

[1] *Babel* and *Babylon* are the same word in Hebrew. Although we tend to refer
to "the Tower of Babel", the sin of Genesis 11:1–9 actually begins with a cry:
*"Come, let us build ourselves a **city**."*

present the New Jerusalem as the beautiful, beaming Bride of Christ.

Have you got that? Then you will sense some of the shock that we are meant to feel when reading the first of these sword oracles. The Lord commands Ezekiel to set his face *against* Jerusalem, not towards it. He commands him to preach *against* his sanctuary and *against* the land.[2] This is the moment God was preparing for when he moved out of the Temple back in chapters 8–11. What Ezekiel prophesies to Jerusalem in these verses is meant to horrify us to the core: *"This is what the Lord says: I am against you"* (21:3).

The second of the sword oracles is recorded in 21:8–17. It describes the slaughter of Jerusalem, and it introduces an extra theme. The *"sceptre of my royal son"* (verse 10) refers to King Zedekiah and to the misplaced confidence of the Jewish nation that the Lord would never allow the capital city of David to fall to a foreign army.[3] God replies that Zedekiah's sceptre is nothing more than a fancy stick. It is a false hope for Jerusalem.

The third of the sword oracles is recorded in 21:18–24. It is every bit as shocking as the first one. King Nebuchadnezzar of Babylon will set out south with his army, still undecided on whether he should deal first with the rebellious king of Jerusalem or with the rebellious king of Rabbah, the capital city of Ammon. The Lord commands Ezekiel to help him decide by setting up signposts for him – presumably next to his clay tablet picture of Jerusalem. The Lord's prophet is now working for Babylon against Jerusalem![4]

---

[2] *"Both the righteous and the wicked ... from south to north"* emphasizes that the whole of Jerusalem will fall.

[3] The people of Jerusalem thought nothing of disobeying Scripture, but they confidently quoted 2 Samuel 7:16. They did not understand that its promise would only be fulfilled in the true and better King of Judah (Genesis 49:10, Psalm 2:7–12, 45:6 and 110:2, Isaiah 9:6–7 and Jeremiah 23:5–6).

[4] Nebuchadnezzar is an out-and-out pagan, who seeks direction from his idols by asking soothsayers to examine the liver of pagan sacrifices (see Daniel 2:1–2). Nevertheless, the Lord is sovereign over his pagan divinations. Nebuchadnezzar would go on to destroy Rabbah in 582 BC.

The fourth of the sword oracles is recorded in 21:25–27. Ezekiel always refers to Zedekiah as a *nāsī'* – that is, a *prince* – and reserves the word *melek*, meaning *king*, for the deposed King Jehoiachin. In this oracle, however, he goes a step further by informing Zedekiah that the Lord is stripping him of his crown altogether. It will not be worn by anybody for the next six hundred years *"until he to whom it rightfully belongs shall come."*[5]

The fifth and final sword oracle is recorded in 21:28–32. It informs the city of Rabbah that its reprieve will be short-lived and that it too will fall. These verses grant us a short break from a shocking role reversal in the Bible's tale of two cities, but not for long.

Chapter 22 is *the story of the sin of Jerusalem*. There is very little respite for us here. In the larger tale of two cities, Jerusalem is called the City of the Great King, but here she is instead dubbed the *"city of bloodshed"* and the *"infamous city"*.[6] She has been found guilty of idolatry, murder and all other manner of Lawbreaking. In the tale of two cities, Jerusalem is built with gold and precious stones, but here her people are like the dross left in a crucible after the melting of base metals.[7] In the tale of two cities, Jerusalem is the holy city that brings God's message to the world, but here she is ceremonially unclean and full of false prophets who glibly add "thus says the Lord" to the fabrications of their own minds. The final verses of the story of the sin of Jerusalem (22:30–31) are even more horrifying than the story of the sword of Babylon:

> *"I looked for someone among them who would build up the wall and stand before me in the gap on behalf of the*

---

[5] This prophecy in 20:27 echoes Genesis 49:10, which says the royal sceptre will remain with Judah *"until he to whom it belongs shall come"*. Jesus would not wear a golden crown. His crown would be made of thorns.

[6] The Hebrew phrase translated *infamous* in 22:5 means literally *defiled of name*. Contrast this with 48:35, Lamentations 2:15, Psalm 48:1–2 and 87:3, and Revelation 21:2.

[7] Isaiah 54:11–12 and Revelation 21:9–21.

land so that I would not have to destroy it, but I found no one. So I will pour out my wrath on them and consume them with my fiery anger, bringing down on their own heads all they have done, declares the Sovereign Lord."[8]

These final verses invite us to play our own part in the Bible's tale of two cities. The New Testament informs us that the global church that is descended from the first church in Jerusalem still occupies the same place in the story.[9] It is the beloved Bride of Christ, but woe betide her if she opens the same gap up in her walls to sin and compromise as Jerusalem in the days of Ezekiel. If you sense that she has already done so, then the Lord asks you a question: Are you willing to stand in the gap for the church in your nation? Will you become a person of prayer, acting as a watchman or watchwoman on the walls of the New Jerusalem today, until the Lord restores her to her former glory?

The fourth-century church leader John Chrysostom urges us to say "yes":

The potency of prayer has subdued the strength of fire, it has bridled the rage of lions, hushed anarchy to rest, extinguished wars, appeased the elements, expelled demons, burst the chains of death, expanded the fates of heaven, assuaged diseases, dispelled frauds, rescued cities from destruction.[10]

---

[8] There were plenty of people who might have stood in the gap for Jerusalem – not least, Ezekiel himself! – but prayer has a price. The Lord wants us to pray like Moses in Exodus 32:7–14 and Numbers 14:11–20. There is no dual citizenship between Jerusalem and Babylon, so in prayer we side with one against the other.

[9] Hebrews 12:22–23, Galatians 4:25–26 and Revelation 21:2.

[10] Quoted by Leonard Ravenhill in his classic book *Why Revival Tarries* (© Bethany House Publishers, part of Baker Books, Baker Publishing Group. 1959).

So let's pray. Let's play our own part in the Bible's tale of two cities. Babylon longs to destroy the New Jerusalem and she has given the Lord plenty of reasons to side with Babylon against her. Yet Jesus has stood in the gap for her and today he invites you to join him in standing in the gap in prayer.[11]

---

[11] Praise God, we do not have to do this by ourselves. Ezekiel 22:30–31 points to Jesus as the great Intercessor who fills us with his Spirit so that we can stand with him in the gap to intercede for the New Jerusalem in prayer (Isaiah 59:16, Romans 8:26–27 and 34, and Hebrews 7:25).

Sister Act
(Ezekiel 23:1–49)

"You have gone the way of your sister; so I will put her cup into your hand."

(Ezekiel 23:31)

There have been some lousy attempts to predict the future. There was Ferdinand Foch, the French general, who predicted before World War One that *"Airplanes are interesting toys but of no military value."* There was Thomas Watson, the chairman of IBM, who allegedly predicted that *"There is a world market for maybe five computers."* There is the music executive from Decca Recording Studios who turned down a chance to sign The Beatles in 1962 because he predicted that *"Guitar groups are on their way out."* And then there is the nation of Judah in the days of Ezekiel. Nothing that the prophet said seemed to dent its utter confidence that everything would turn out fine for Jerusalem.

Perhaps that's why Ezekiel resorts to such coarse imagery and language in this chapter. Like his second parable in chapter 16, it is hard to imagine his fourth parable in the mouth of Jesus. *The parable of the two promiscuous sisters* is undated, but the date in the next chapter suggests that Ezekiel told it once King Nebuchadnezzar had set out on the road to Jerusalem to begin his final two-year siege of the city. The prophet doesn't pull his punches, because he knows that he is running out of time to alter people's predictions about Jerusalem. Judgment Day is about to arrive for the Jewish capital.

In 23:1–4, Ezekiel introduces the two main characters in the parable. The younger sister is Jerusalem, so the Lord nicknames her *Oholibah*, which means *My Tent Is In Her*. This recalls the fact that his glorious presence dwelt on Mount Zion for over four hundred years, first in King David's Tabernacle and then later in King Solomon's Temple. The elder sister is Samaria, so the Lord nicknames her *Oholah*, which means *Her Own Tent*. This recalls the fact that the northern kingdom of Israel turned its back on the Lord's Temple in Jerusalem and constructed its own rival temple at Bethel instead.

Despite their slightly different names, the prophet's main point in this parable is that the two cities are very alike. They come from the same mother – the Hebrew nation that the Lord rescued from slavery in Egypt – and they are both married to the Lord.[1] They also share a common lust for foreign idols. Most English Bibles tone down the language that Ezekiel actually uses in the Hebrew text. In these four opening verses, he mentions *prostitution* and *fondled breasts* and *virgin nipples*.[2] If you find his language offensive, then good – the Lord inspired him to choose these words because idolatry really is this offensive to God. It is consistently likened to adultery throughout the Bible because both involve betraying a love relationship consummated by a solemn covenant.

In 23:5–21, Ezekiel catalogues the sordid history of these two sister cities. Samaria worshipped the idols of Egypt and Samaria, so the Lord sent the Assyrian army to destroy her. Instead of learning from her older sister's fate, Jerusalem then ran after those same idols. She went even further by spotting pictures of Babylonian idols on a mural and sending messengers to Babylonia to discover more about its vile pantheon. We are meant to be horrified by this inversion of God's calling for Jerusalem to be a missionary city, proclaiming the Good News

---

[1] As with all parables, we are to focus on the main point rather than getting distracted by the detail. For example, the Lord is not condoning bigamy here. It was just a feature of the Jewish patriarchal story.

[2] The Hebrew verb *zānāh*, which means *to play the prostitute* or *to commit adultery*, is used twenty-two times in Ezekiel 23, communicating that Jerusalem's idolatry was not a one-off thing.

of Yahweh to the world.[3] In case we are not, Ezekiel employs the graphic language of adultery to jolt us to our senses – *virgin nipples* and *lovemaking* and *defilement* and *prostitution* and *nakedness* and *penises like donkeys* and *ejaculated semen like horses*. It isn't hard to see why most English Bible translations tone down some of this language. Jerusalem's betrayal of the Lord is disgusting.

The people of Jerusalem had always prided themselves on being spiritually superior to their northern neighbours. After all, they had the ark of the covenant in their Temple, while the northern kingdom worshipped golden calves. The big shock of this parable is therefore its revelation that the Lord regards Jerusalem's sinfulness as pretty similar to that of Samaria. It's as the song (almost) says: *You say Oholah, I say Oholibah.*

The Jewish exiles do not appear to be listening, so Ezekiel prophesies in 23:22–35 what is about to happen to Jerusalem. He warns them to revise their predictions before King Nebuchadnezzar begins his siege and the city falls. The Lord is about to make Jerusalem drink the same cup of his anger towards sin that Samaria drank in 722 BC.[4] She will be destroyed by the very pagans for whose idols she has lusted. She will suffer the same fate as a drunken woman who goes to bed with a stranger only to discover in the middle of the night that her one-night stand is an axe murderer. The police will need to use dental records to identify what is left of her naked and mutilated body.[5]

In 23:36–49, the Lord inspires Ezekiel to end his parable with a courtroom confrontation. What sentence do the Jewish

[3] The picture Ezekiel uses is meant to conjure up images in our mind of a seedy man sweating over pornographic images and swiping his way through Tinder, while his beautiful wife lies in bed upstairs.

[4] Jeremiah 25 introduced this picture of people being forced to drink *the cup of God's anger*. See also Psalm 75:8, Isaiah 51:17, Lamentations 4:21, Habakkuk 2:15–16, Matthew 26:39 and John 18:11.

[5] Jerusalem will not merely drink from the cup of God's anger. She will chew on its broken pieces too (verse 34).

exiles think Jerusalem ought to receive for her adultery and for sacrificing her children to the false god Molek? The Jewish Law is very clear: she deserves to die.[6] On the very day that her people murdered their own babies to placate Molek, they came into the Temple courtyards and pretended to be devout worshippers of the Lord, like an adulterous wife who gives herself freely to her colleagues at the office Christmas party then goes home and placates her conscience by giving her husband some quick and hurried sex before turning out the light.[7] Did Jerusalem imagine that she could make it up to God through her Temple worship? She merely polluted his Temple with her hypocrisy! She deserves all the Babylonians will do to her.[8]

Ferdinand Foch was foolish. So was Thomas Watson. So was Decca Recording Studios. But none of them was as foolish as those who looked at Jerusalem and predicted that the Lord would deliver her because of his Temple and his history with her.

Time was running out for the city to repent. King Nebuchadnezzar was on the road.

---

[6] Genesis 38:24, Leviticus 20:10 and 24:17, Deuteronomy 22:22 and John 8:3–7.

[7] She has also acted like a wife who uses the perfume and theatre tickets that her husband gave her on Valentine's Day to seduce her next-door neighbour. Compare 23:41 with Exodus 30:22–38.

[8] The Lord would not be thwarted in his purposes. Jerusalem would still proclaim his holiness to the world. She would simply do so when the nations witnessed the furious judgment of her holy God (23:48–49).

Final Words
(Ezekiel 24:1–27)

"I the Lord have spoken. The time has come for me to act."

(Ezekiel 24:14)

It is 15 January 588 BC, the day on which King Nebuchadnezzar finally began his two-year siege of Jerusalem. The Babylonian army is busy pitching its tents around the walls of the city, but hundreds of miles away, God's man in Babylon is receiving a few final words of prophecy for the Jewish exiles before their beloved city falls.

We have already noted the basic structure of the book of Ezekiel – *See it, say it, sorted*. The first phase of his ministry, which took place in chapters 1–12, was essentially a year of prophetic mime artistry. The second phase of his ministry, which takes place in chapters 13–32, consists of twelve parables and prophecies for Israel, followed by seven oracles against its pagan neighbours. This middle section of the book runs as follows:

Ezekiel 13–24
> **Judgment spoken over Israel**
> Judgment on false prophets (13)
> Judgment on idolaters (14)
> The parable of the useless vine (15)
> The parable of the adulterous wife (16)
> The parable of the eagles and the vine (17)
> Judgment on each individual (18)
> Judgment on the dynasty of David (19)
> The story of Israel (20)

Ezekiel 25–32
Judgment spoken over the pagan nations

All of this is to point out that Ezekiel 24 marks a major turning point in the prophet's ministry. Once the Babylonian army pitches its tents around the walls of Jerusalem, a phase of Ezekiel's mission is complete. He speaks a few final words against the city and then turns to warn the pagan nations that they are the next items on the Babylonian shopping list for slaughter.

In 24:1–14, the Lord inspires Ezekiel to tell the last of his five parables.[1] Without the benefit of modern television or text messaging or the internet, none of the Jewish exiles in Babylonia has any idea that the final siege of Jerusalem has begun. Ezekiel prophesies the news and then marks the date clearly on his calendar so that, when the messengers arrive, the Jewish exiles will know that everything else that he has prophesied to them must equally be true.[2]

The parable of the cooking pot is meant to remind us of what the prophet heard King Zedekiah's courtiers saying in the gateway of Jerusalem in 11:3 as God's glorious presence headed out of town – *"This city is a pot, and we are the meat in it."* The Lord turns this arrogant boast back on their own heads as he informs them that he is turning the heat up on Jerusalem. Anyone who has not already been taken into exile and who refuses to obey Jeremiah's call to surrender to the Babylonians

---

[1] Ezekiel complained to God in 20:49 that nobody was listening to his parables. God responds by giving him another parable in 24:3! Fruitful evangelism is less about switching methods than it is about persevering.

[2] When Jerusalem fell on 18 July 586 BC, news only reached Babylonia on 8 January 585 BC (33:21).

is about to be charred to a cinder. Ezekiel employs last-ditch shock tactics, starting out gently, as if sharing a homely cooking recipe, before descending into sudden fire and slaughter! *"I the Lord have spoken. The time has come for me to act. I will not hold back; I will not have pity, nor will I relent."*[3]

In 24:15–24, we discover how much it cost Ezekiel personally to serve as a watchman of the Lord. We are told for the first time that he has a wife. Being struck mute for the past few years, except for when praying or prophesying, must have put a strain on their relationship. So must his obedience to the Lord's command for him to lie on his side for over a year and to cook his dinner over cow manure! Yet Ezekiel evidently loves her, since the Lord describes her as *"the delight of your eyes"* – even as he informs Ezekiel that she is about to die.[4] Ezekiel spends the morning prophesying to the people, then he watches as his wife drops dead later on that evening.[5]

The following day, Ezekiel performs his most painful piece of prophetic mime artistry. Instead of observing any of the noisy mourning rituals of the ancient world, he fails to shed even a single public tear.[6] He turns his own unexpressed grief into a prophetic warning for the Jewish exiles that an even bigger tragedy is just around the corner for Jerusalem. On that day, their Babylonian masters will be watching them too closely for them to dare to weep publicly for the destruction of their rebellious city. They will be forced to hold their broken hearts together in silence on that dire day of national tragedy.

This marks the end of the recorded words that Ezekiel spoke to the Jewish exiles before the fall of Jerusalem. These

---

[3] 24:14. It is madness to believe that the Lord is duty-bound to forgive people on the Day of Judgment simply because he is loving. As we saw in Ezekiel 18, God will not deny his perfect justice in the name of love.

[4] Ezekiel was in his mid-thirties when his wife died, so she probably died very young.

[5] We are not told what Ezekiel did in the afternoon, presumably because he spent it saying whatever goodbyes to his wife a mute prophet was able to say.

[6] See Genesis 37:34 and 50:1–11, 2 Samuel 3:31 and 15:30, Jeremiah 16:5–7 and Micah 3:7.

twelve chapters end with a personal prophecy that he received from the Lord during this time. Having been struck mute after his vision of God's glorious presence in the summer of 593 BC, he has been speechless for the past few years except for whenever he is praying or prophesying. Now the Lord predicts that this ordeal is about to be lifted from him (24:27). On the day a messenger arrives in Babylonia and announces that Jerusalem has fallen, the Lord will restore his speech to him as a sign to the Jewish exiles that his days of prophesying judgment are over.[7] The Lord will use this miracle to reassure them that he has finished operating on the sinful kingdom of Judah. Ezekiel is now free to speak words of comfort to the "good figs" in the basket of Babylon.

The Lord has spoken his final words of judgment over the city of Jerusalem through Ezekiel: *"I the Lord have spoken. The time has come for me to act"* (verse 14).

---

7 Ezekiel 3:24–27 and 33:21–22.

*"You were anointed as a guardian cherub...
I expelled you, guardian cherub."*

(Ezekiel 28:14, 16)

People who skim read the book of Ezekiel don't notice what he is trying to teach us when he starts prophesying to Jerusalem's pagan neighbours that the Lord has set a date for their destruction too. Skim readers assume that these are merely the book-of-Ezekiel equivalent of God's world tour of judgment in Jeremiah 45–51. That's why it pays to read these eight chapters slowly and to look at their structure a bit more thoughtfully.

Ezekiel 25–32

> Judgment against Ammon (25:1–7)
> Judgment against Moab (25:8–11)
> Judgment against Edom (25:12–14)
> Judgment against Philistia (25:15–17)
> Judgment against Tyre and its king (26:1–28:19)
> Judgment against Sidon (28:20–26)
> Judgment against Egypt and its king (29:1–32:32)

When we take a step back like this, it's pretty obvious that God's world tour of judgment in Ezekiel is much more than a mere repetition of the one in Jeremiah. There is an unusual degree of attention given to the kings of Tyre and Egypt, and a surprising lack of any judgment upon Babylon. That's not just because Ezekiel was a prisoner in Babylonia and might have been executed as a troublemaker. It is also to show us that the spiritual power behind Babylon was far bigger than the walls of a single city.

The first four nations on Ezekiel's world tour of judgment are dealt with quickly. Ammon and Moab would be destroyed by the Babylonians in 582 BC, just as Jeremiah predicted.[1] Edom would be destroyed in 583 BC, and Philistia shortly after. The reference to every remnant of the Philistines being annihilated echoes Jeremiah's prediction that neither Edom nor Philistia would be left with any survivors. God's promise in 25:14 that the Edomites will finally be wiped out *"by the hand of my people Israel"* predicts that, after the return of the Jewish exiles from Babylon, the Maccabees would finish off the scraps of Edom that Nebuchadnezzar left behind. There is some impressive detail here.

In the next chapter, we will look at what Ezekiel prophesies about Egypt and its king, so let's spend the rest of this chapter looking at his three chapters of prophecy against Tyre and its king. Although it was an important Phoenician trading city, sending ships from its harbour all across the Mediterranean Sea, it has played no real part in the story of Israel throughout Jeremiah, Lamentations and Ezekiel, which means that it must be given such a surprising amount of attention here for a reason.[2] So, what on earth is it?

Chapter 26 is a declaration of judgment over Tyre that Ezekiel spoke in early 586 BC.[3] He warns the merchant city that the Lord has heard it gloating over the imminent destruction of Jerusalem and plotting how to take over its trade. Its hopes will come to nothing, because the Lord has decreed that they are

---

[1] These two prophecies are undated, but the reference in 25:3 to the Ammonites rejoicing over the destruction of Jerusalem means that Ezekiel must have prophesied these words after August 586 BC.

[2] There are prophecies against Tyre in Isaiah 23 and Amos 1:9–10, but it is not included in the oracles of Jeremiah, Zephaniah or any of the other Old Testament prophets against the pagan nations.

[3] Ezekiel gives the day and year but not the month in 26:1. Early 586 BC fits best with the rest of the chapter.

next on the Babylonian shopping list. Nebuchadnezzar would besiege the mainland section of the city in 585 BC. He would then use its rubble to begin building a causeway half a mile out into the harbour to attack the remainder of the city that was on an island.[4] He would not finish the task of turning it into *"a bare rock ... a place to spread fishing nets"* (26:4–5), but Alexander the Great would complete his causeway and his act of destruction in 332 BC. Tyre would never be rebuilt.

Ezekiel gives us two clues here that he is talking about more than just an ancient trading city in modern-day Lebanon. First, Nebuchadnezzar is described as the *"king of kings"* (26:7), which was Babylonian for "emperor" but which also hints that there was an evil spirit at work behind Babylon, since that name belongs rightly to God alone. Second, the lament at the end of the chapter sounds similar to Revelation 18 – but that describes the fall of Babylon, not the fall of Tyre. Things here are clearly not quite what they seem.

Chapter 27 is a much longer lament over the fall of Tyre. Ezekiel likens the city to one of its famous merchant vessels, so wealthy that even its decks are inlaid with ivory, which hits a storm and sinks to the bottom of the sea.[5] Again the language reminds us of Revelation 18, which describes the fall of Babylon, rather than the fall of Tyre. It is as if the evil spirit that was at work in ancient Babylon was also at work in ancient Tyre.[6]

Chapter 28 prophesies judgment over the king of Tyre and then laments his downfall – except that King Ithobaal III of Tyre was never *"a guardian cherub"* *"in Eden, the garden of God"* (verses 13–14). Nor does it make any sense for the Lord to say to him that *"I expelled you, guardian cherub, from among*

---

[4] The name *Tyre* means *Rock*, and its security was based on its being part island fortress.

[5] *Tarshish* was a port in southern Spain. The other place names in this chapter show that Tyrian ships traded with almost every other major port city in the Mediterranean Sea along the way.

[6] Compare 27:13 with Revelation 18:13. The Spirit of Babylon seeks to enslave souls.

the fiery stones" (verse 16). Tertullian, the third-century Church Father, was the first to popularize the idea that Ezekiel is actually addressing Satan in these verses, as the spiritual force at work behind Ithobaal's throne.[7] If he is right, then Ezekiel is teaching us here that Satan was once a beautiful cherub angel like the ones that he saw in his vision, who became so proud of his own beauty that he could no longer bear to see even the Lord enthroned above him. He tried to usurp heaven's throne, failed, and was cast down to earth where the rest, sadly, is history. Satan was at work behind Babylon and Tyre, and he is still at work in any culture that proudly sets itself up against God.

The chapter ends with an oracle against Tyre's sister city Sidon (28:20–26), but we are still meant to be reeling from the revelation that the rise and fall of earthly empires is part of a far greater spiritual battle that is raging behind the scenes. Ezekiel's aim in these chapters is the same as the Apostle Paul's in 2 Corinthians 2:11, where he urges us to be vigilant, *"in order that Satan might not outwit us. For we are not unaware of his schemes."*[8]

Ezekiel has told us how powerful cherub angels are, so we must not underestimate Satan's work in the world. He has also shown us how subservient cherub angels are to the Lord, so we must not overestimate Satan either. He is merely a creature and therefore no match for his Creator (28:13).[9] He has been thrown

---

[7] He says this in *Against Marcion* (2.10). That would explain why these verses are echoed by Luke 10:18, 1 Timothy 3:6 and Revelation 12:7–12. It would also explain why similar language is used in Isaiah 14:12–17 to describe the spirit at work behind Assyria while it ruled over Babylon, and in Genesis 11:4 to describe the spirit at work behind the builders of Babel. Isaiah 14:12 can be translated, *"How you have fallen from heaven, Lucifer, son of the dawn! You have been cast down to the earth, you who once laid low the nations!"*

[8] The final two verses of this oracle against Sidon are more about Israel and Judah than they are about Sidon. This is a clue for us that these seven oracles are about the war between the Spirit of God and the Spirit of Babylon.

[9] Isaiah 14:16–17 suggests that when we see Satan as he really is, we will be amazed at how much he got away with in his puny brokenness, not awestruck by his colossal power.

down to earth (28:17) and is on his way down to destruction in hell (28:18–19), so the trouble that he causes us is really his last stand. Ezekiel gives us three chapters of prophecy against the king of Tyre in order to open our eyes to the spiritual battle for our cities, so that we can fight alongside the Lord in prayer. There is a work of spiritual warfare for us to do (22:30).

So let's fight for breakthrough, both in the realm we see and in the realm we don't. Let's not just pray *for* cities; let's also pray *against* the forces at work behind them. The old hymn echoes these verses in Ezekiel when it encourages us to believe that *"Satan trembles when he sees the weakest saint upon his knees."*[10]

---

[10] Taken from William Cowper's hymn "What Various Hindrances We Meet" (1779).

Pyramid Scheme
(Ezekiel 29:1–32:32)

"I am against you, Pharaoh king of Egypt, you great monster."

(Ezekiel 29:3)

Most people know better than to put their trust in pyramid schemes. They sound plausible on paper, but they never deliver on their extravagant promises. They are a confidence trick in which someone takes all you have in return for very little.

King Zedekiah had fallen for the ultimate pyramid scheme. He had placed his confidence in the extravagant promises that were made to him by Pharaoh Hophra, the ruler of the great Pyramids of Giza.[1] We saw in chapter 17, in Ezekiel's parable of the eagles and the vine, that Hophra's accession to the throne in February 589 BC was what emboldened Zedekiah to break his oath of allegiance with Babylon and to turn his face and foreign policy towards Egypt instead. Pharaoh Hophra's Egypt is therefore the seventh and final pagan nation to which Ezekiel addresses an oracle of judgment.

Ezekiel prophesied the words of 29:1–16 on 7 January 587 BC, just after the Egyptian army retreated in disgrace, having failed to lift the Babylonian siege of Jerusalem.[2] It depicts

---

[1] Hophra is the name used in Jeremiah 44:30. Most modern Egyptologists refer to him by his throne name Apries instead. He reigned from 589–570 BC.

[2] We were told about this in Jeremiah 37:1–10. Egypt's reputation for letting down its allies was nothing new. The Assyrians spoke words akin to 29:6–7 over a century earlier in 2 Kings 18:21.

Pharaoh Hophra as a *tannīn*, which means more than simply *monster* in Hebrew, because it was used for the fire-spitting cobra that symbolized Pharaoh's power on his crown.[3] You don't have to know much about Bible symbols to spot that Ezekiel is telling us here that Satan is as much at work behind Egypt as he is behind Tyre and Babylon.

Ezekiel declares that Satan is as full of bluster as Pharaoh Hophra. The Devil claims to be the creator and owner of large tranches of the earth, but he is a mere creature. He is deadly to mortal men and women, which is why we dare not underestimate him, but to the Lord he is as easily dealt with as a fisherman hooking an eel. The fish here represent his demons, so the Lord pledges to cast them out into the wilderness with him to be devoured by the birds and wild animals. The mummies, pyramids and tombs of the Egyptians all testify to how much they linked what happened to a person's corpse after they died to what happened to their soul in the Underworld. This is therefore a prophetic picture of Satan and his demons being punished forever by the Lord in hell.

Ezekiel prophesied the words of 29:17–21 on 26 April 571 BC, which means it is the latest of all his prophecies. The Lord warns Pharaoh Hophra not to imagine for a moment that Nebuchadnezzar's difficulties in building a causeway across the harbour of Tyre will make him give up on attacking Egypt. The Lord who sent him to deal with the spirit at work behind Tyre will inspire him to pay his soldiers' salaries by plundering Pharaoh's kingdom. The person most deceived by the Devil appears to be the Devil himself. He actually believes he may yet turn the tables on God, so this oracle laughs off that idea.[4]

In 30:1–19, Ezekiel sings a similar lament over Egypt to the one he sang over Tyre, predicting that the Lord will expose its

---

[3] The same word, *tannīn*, is used in Exodus 7:9–12. Known as an *uraeus*, it was an image of the cobra goddess Wadjet.

[4] The Lord says in 29:21 that, when the Jewish exiles see Pharaoh fall, it will actually help them to believe in Ezekiel's other prophecies about their Messiah. God's promises are never like a pyramid scheme.

gods as powerless idols, just as he did through the Ten Plagues.[5] Sure enough, Hophra would be toppled from his throne in 570 BC and murdered by his former subjects in 567 BC. Egypt would fall with him, slowly recovering its independence but never its superpower status. Hophra and the spirit at work behind his kingdom would be outed as pyramid scheme sellers, as feeble confidence tricksters.

In 30:20–26, Ezekiel speaks a personal prophecy to Pharaoh Hophra on 29 April 587 BC. The "broken arm" in the prophecy refers to the humiliating retreat that he has been forced to make from the walls of Jerusalem. In English, we might say that he received "a bloody nose", but the Hebrew metaphor works particularly well given that one of Hophra's throne names meant *Possessor of a Strong Arm*. Hophra still hoped to recover, just as Satan still hopes to bounce back from his fall from heaven, so the Lord informs both Hophra and the spirit at work behind his kingdom that he is about to break their other arm as well. Their days of flattering the foolish will soon be finished.

In 31:1–18, Ezekiel speaks another personal prophecy to Pharaoh Hophra, this time on 21 June 587 BC. The Lord points out that Assyria looked like a mighty cedar tree until it fell to the Babylonian army because of its pride. Pharaoh must therefore not fool himself that Egypt's history, Egypt's army or Egypt's border fortresses will rescue his kingdom from Nebuchadnezzar. Such pride will come before his own fall too. He and his officials will soon be in the afterlife they discuss so much together, but it will not be the Underworld of Egyptian mythology. They will find themselves in hell, surrounded by Satan and his demons, the true forces at work behind their idols.[6]

In 32:1–16, Ezekiel sings a personal lament over Pharaoh Hophra on 3 March 585 BC. Jerusalem has fallen to the

---

[5] Exodus 12:12 and Numbers 33:4. Here the Lord singles out the Nile god Hapy and the sun god Amun-Ra.

[6] Like the Jews, the Egyptians used the term *"the uncircumcised"* to refer to unsaved outsiders (31:18).

Babylonians due to Egypt's false promises, so the Lord repeats that Pharaoh Hophra is like a *tannīn*, a fire-spitting cobra – both deadly and easily defeated. The Lord has raised him up and allowed him to prosper for a short season so that he can demonstrate his power by defeating him.[7]

In 32:17–32, Ezekiel speaks the last of his seven oracles against Egypt sometime between April 586 BC and March 585 BC.[8] Seizing upon the nation's morbid obsession with the Underworld, the Lord informs Pharaoh that many of the people groups he slaughtered are preparing a welcome party for him in the afterlife – except that it's not the fictional afterlife of Egyptian mythology, but the devastating reality of hell.[9] God talks plainly here about what happens to people who die without a relationship with him. We still need to take this warning seriously today.[10]

He speaks plainly in order to warn us against being hoodwinked by Satan's pyramid schemes. The Devil is real but his boasting has no foundation. Anyone who falls for his trickery today will have eternity to rail against him in hell.

---

[7] Exodus 9:16. This also answers the question why the Lord has not yet fully dealt with Satan. Note the reference in 32:8 to the Ninth Plague, through which God defeated the sun god Amun-Ra.

[8] As in 26:1, Ezekiel gives us the year and day but not the month. *Seven* oracles for the last of *seven* pagan kingdoms speaks of the completeness of God's victory over the evil spirit that is at work behind them all.

[9] The Hebrew verb *nāham* in 32:31 sometimes refers to *repentance*, but here the Lord is merely promising Pharaoh Hophra that his sole *consolation* in his misery will be that his enemies are in hell with him too.

[10] The phrase *"the uncircumcised"* is used ten times in 32:19–32 as an Egyptian way of referring to "the damned". Egyptian culture was full of stories about people's descent into the Underworld, so the Lord warns Pharaoh that his culture has got it wrong. They need to start preparing themselves for heaven or for hell.

Ezekiel 33–48:

The Results of Surgery

Speak Up!
(Ezekiel 33:1–33)

So my mouth was opened and I was no longer silent.

(Ezekiel 33:22)

Many people find the last few chapters of Ezekiel very difficult. I find them glorious. These are some of the most famous chapters in the Old Testament – vivid, odd in places, but deeply inspiring if understood properly. These are the chapters in which God finally puts down his surgeon's scalpel and invites us to reflect on the results of radical surgery.

Jerusalem has fallen. Its walls have been breached, its Temple razed to the ground and its people slaughtered. Ezekiel doesn't know it yet because it took a long time for news to travel in the ancient world, but the Lord knows and he makes it his cue to launch the third and greatest phase of Ezekiel's ministry. The Lord recommissions his mute prophet. He has a vivid way of showing him that the time has come for him to *speak up!*

We are meant to spot at once that 33:1–9 is a repeat of the original commissioning of Ezekiel in 3:16–21. Now that his *Book of Judgment* has come to an end, his *Book of Comfort* begins with a fresh call to serve as the Lord's *tsôpheh* – as his *watchman* on the walls.[1] Now that Old Jerusalem has been reduced to rubble, the Lord can finally commission him to declare the wonders of the New Jerusalem that will be rebuilt in its stead.

Ezekiel's original commissioning came through a private encounter with God, but his recommissioning is much more public. The Lord commands him to declare to the Jewish exiles

---

[1] We saw earlier that this Hebrew word *tsôpheh* is used in 2 Samuel 18:24–27, 2 Kings 9:17–20, Isaiah 52:8 and 56:10, Jeremiah 6:17, Hosea 9:8 and Habakkuk 2:1. We also heard an echo of these verses in Acts 20:26–27.

that he has served God as a faithful watchman. He has no share in the guilt of Old Jerusalem, because he warned its people plainly about their sin, knowing that failure to do so would make him complicit in their murder.[2] He warns the Jewish exiles that they will be responsible for their own deaths unless they take his words more seriously than their fallen city. This is what it means for us to be watchmen and watchwomen for the Lord in our own generation. We mustn't be too self-conscious or too tongue-tied to warn people about their sin. God commissions all of us, as he did Ezekiel, to *speak up!*

This leads into 33:10–20, which is a deliberate repetition of what the Lord said to Ezekiel in 18:23–32. If the Jewish exiles carry on complaining that it is unfair for the Lord to judge Jerusalem, then they will perish with it, but if they trust him when he warns them that they are each responsible for their own response to him, then they can partner with him in the building of his New Jerusalem.[3] They must decide if they are children of Zion or of Babylon, so the Lord appeals to them tenderly: *"As surely as I live, declares the Sovereign Lord, I take no pleasure in the death of the wicked, but rather that they turn from their ways and live. Turn! Turn from your evil ways! Why will you die, people of Israel?"*[4]

One of the most exciting aspects of this recommissioning of Ezekiel is the revelation in verse 10 that the Jewish exiles are finally beginning to feel genuine conviction for their sin. This never seemed to be the case throughout the *Book of Judgment*, in chapters 1–32, so this breakthrough enables Ezekiel to transition into his *Book of Comfort*. The Lord promised King

---

[2] This is sobering. We have not been commissioned to "win converts" or to "find open hearts", but to proclaim the gospel even to those who reject it. See Matthew 28:18–20, Acts 13:46, Romans 1:14 and 2 Corinthians 5:20.

[3] The Lord is not saying in 33:12 that those who are truly saved can lose their salvation, but that those who are truly saved will always show it through their transformed lives (Matthew 3:8 and Acts 26:20).

[4] 33:11. This is the third of the three great "repentance commands" in the book of Ezekiel, after 14:6 and 18:30–32. It echoes Lamentations 3:33, 1 Timothy 2:4 and 2 Peter 3:9.

Solomon after the dedication of his new Temple that *"If my people, who are called by my name, will humble themselves and pray and seek my face and turn from their wicked ways, then I will hear from heaven, and I will forgive their sin and will heal their land."*[5] Ironically, it is only when Solomon's Temple is destroyed that the Jewish exiles finally do so. They humble themselves before the Lord in repentance and turn from their sins, and as they do so they unleash an avalanche of his mercy towards them.

For that to happen, God's mute messenger needs to be released from his seven and a half years of silence. In 33:21–22, as Ezekiel is praying one evening, he suddenly discovers that the Holy Spirit has delivered him of his muteness. Instead of only being able to speak whenever he is praying or prophesying, he now finds that he can speak at will about anything. *"So my mouth was opened and I was no longer silent."*

The following morning, he discovers why. His ministry of judgment is over. The Lord has healed him in order to signal that a new day has now dawned for the Jewish exiles. It is 8 January 585 BC, and the first messengers arrive in Babylonia to announce that the city of Jerusalem has been destroyed.[6] Suddenly, all eyes turn to Ezekiel. His prophecies have been so terribly vindicated that everybody wants to know what he now has to say. He therefore declares in 33:23–33 that there is no hope left for Judah within its borders. Even the survivors amongst the ruins of Jerusalem – who are consoling themselves that their nation came from just one man, the patriarch Abraham, so they can become future patriarchs – are destined to be slaughtered very shortly. The hopes of Judah now lie squarely with the Jewish exiles in Babylon, and even some of them are merely play-acting at repentance, listening to Ezekiel's preaching like

---

[5] 2 Chronicles 7:14.

[6] Don't be surprised that it took four months for news to reach Babylonia after the destruction of Jerusalem in August 586 BC. That's just how long the journey took before the Romans built their roads. See Ezra 7:8–9.

an operagoer enjoying the pleasant sound of songs in Italian without understanding any of the words.[7]

But for the first time, most of them are truly listening. That's the glory of this opening chapter of the *Book of Comfort*. It starts with the Lord telling Ezekiel that the Jewish exiles are *"your people"* (verses 2 and 17), but it ends with his owning them once more as *"my people"* (verse 31). As the exiles begin to humble themselves in repentance, the Lord comes alongside them like a surgeon describing the results of his incisions to a recovering patient. He starts to share the good news about what his scalpel has achieved.

It has brought the *Book of Judgment* to an end and allowed the *Book of Comfort* to begin. It has enabled God's man in Babylon to start prophesying about the New Jerusalem. It has rendered the Lord's messenger mute no more. It has recommissioned him to *speak up!*

---

[7] The Living Bible translates 33:31 very succinctly: *"They talk very sweetly about loving the Lord, but with their hearts they are loving their money."*

"Because my flock lacks a shepherd... I will place over them one shepherd, my servant David, and he will tend them."

(Ezekiel 34:8, 23)

On 22 September 2015, Bayern Munich were losing 1–0 to Wolfsburg in the German Bundesliga. When coach Pep Guardiola responded by taking off his best player, the star Spanish midfielder Thiago, the Bayern Munich fans roared their angry disapproval. Time was running out to score an equalizer, even without such a baffling substitution. But that was the moment when Robert Lewandowski ran onto the pitch and into the annals of football history. He scored five goals in just nine minutes to break four Guinness World Records and to become the greatest substitute in football history.[1]

Soccer pundits still enthuse about the so-called "Munich Nine-Minute Miracle", but Ezekiel begins his *Book of Comfort* with an even greater substitution. The Jewish exiles in Babylon had reacted like Bayern Munich fans when they heard that the city of Jerusalem had fallen. They questioned whether the Lord knew how to manage their nation. He had taken three successive kings of Judah off the football field – Jehoahaz to Egypt, Jehoiakim to the sword, and Jehoiachin to Babylon. Now the news had reached their ears that he had taken a fourth king off the football field too. When they heard that King Zedekiah

---

[1] Buoyed by Lewandowski's turnaround, Bayern Munich would go on to win the Bundesliga that season.

had arrived in Babylon bereaved, blinded and banished, they began to question the Lord's love for their nation. What kind of God would do such a thing and allow the Babylonian army to blow the final whistle over Jerusalem?

In 34:1–10, the Lord points out that these four final kings of Judah were not shepherds to the flock, but ravening wolves in shepherd's clothing. The cutting short of their reigns is an occasion for rejoicing. They were not taken off the football field by Pharaoh and Nebuchadnezzar.[2] Those foreign rulers were merely tools of judgment in the hands of the Lord. God himself called time on those four kings because they had committed so many red card offences against the people of Judah.[3]

In 34:11–16, the Lord echoes the words that he spoke against these four kings in Jeremiah 21:1–23:6. He warns the exiles not to deride his decisions from the football stands, but to trust him that these four final rulers from David's dynasty were not the star players that they pretended to be. The Lord has taken them out of play so that the royal throne of Judah can stand empty for a season. A far better substitute is warming up on the touchline. To the amazement of the Jewish exiles, the Lord reveals that it is himself. The God of Israel is about to run onto the football field to become the true and better King of Judah. He will serve as their Good Shepherd, laying down his life to bring back his scattered sheep and to heal them from the vicious bite marks of their enemies.[4]

Don't miss the echoes of Psalm 23 when God promises to make the Jewish exiles lie down in green pastures while

---

[2] Pharaoh and Nebuchadnezzar are called *"wild animals"* in 34:5, yet it is the four kings of Judah who have Jewish sheep in their jaws in 34:10! Jude 12 echoes these verses in rebuking self-seeking church leaders.

[3] The Hebrew text can either be translated *"I will remove them"* or *"I am removing them"*. Either way, it refers to a work in progress, since King Jehoiachin and King Zedekiah are both still alive in Babylonian prisons.

[4] Jesus appears to be thinking of these verses when he declares that his mission is to *"bring back the lost sheep of Israel"* (Matthew 10:6 and 15:24). See also Matthew 9:36 and 18:10–14.

he ensures that they lack nothing. These verses form the Old Testament background to the famous words of Jesus in John 10:

All who have come before me are thieves and robbers... I am the good shepherd. The good shepherd lays down his life for the sheep... I am the good shepherd... I lay down my life for the sheep... I have authority to lay it down and authority to take it up again.[5]

The book of Ezekiel moves from judgment into comfort because the Lord has stepped in to save his people. He has removed these four final kings of Judah from the football field in order to send his Messiah into play. Having substituted for the sinful kings of Judah, the Messiah will then become a substitute for their sinful subjects, since verse 16 insists that God rules his flock with perfect justice. The Messiah will pay the penalty for the many sins of God's people so that they could become recipients of God's mercy. Unlike Robert Lewandowski, who ran onto the pitch to become a footballing hero, the Messiah will come into the world to be rejected and crucified. He will not be numbered among the *"sleek"* and *"strong"* – those who rely on the human strength that proved the downfall of Old Jerusalem – but among the *"injured"* and *"weak"* – those who admit they need a Saviour.

In 34:17–24, Ezekiel therefore prophesies that the arrival of the Messiah will separate the sheep from the goats within Israel. Not all who are Jewish by birth are the people of God by belief. Some of them are the children of Babylon. Jeremiah 33:13 and Ezekiel 20:37 both hinted at this, but now Ezekiel states it more explicitly.[6] The Good Shepherd will prove to be the Judge

---

[5] God is portrayed as a shepherd in Genesis 49:24, Psalm 23:1, 28:9 and 80:1, Isaiah 40:11, Micah 2:12 and 5:1–4, Luke 15:3–7 and 19:10, John 10:11–30, Hebrews 13:20, 1 Peter 2:25 and 5:4, and Revelation 7:17.

[6] Jesus states this even more explicitly in Matthew 25:31–46, and in Revelation 2:9 and 3:9. "Fat" and "lean" sheep has nothing to do with dieting. It reminds us that true Christians live for others, not for themselves.

of Israel as well its Saviour. Having driven out the self-centred shepherds of Israel, he will also drive out any self-centred sheep who remain.[7]

In 34:25–31, the Lord rejoices over what his radical surgery will achieve for those who say "yes" to his Messiah. They will live under the New Covenant that the Lord will make with his people, which will offer them protection, blessing, freedom and fruitfulness. They will know God as their Good Shepherd and hear him speaking lovingly over them: *"You are my sheep, the sheep of my pasture, and I am your God"* (verse 31). Even their non-believing neighbours will be forced to recognize that God dwells among them, when the repeated refrain that cursed God's people throughout the *Book of Judgment* – *"then they will know that I am the Lord"* (verse 30) – is transformed into a promise of their glorious restoration.

Football fans still hail Pep Guardiola as a genius for his bafflingly brilliant substitution of Thiago for Robert Lewandowski, so let's not demean Almighty God by celebrating his far greater genius any less. He removed the four final kings of Judah from the football field of history so that he could run onto the pitch personally. He destroyed Old Jerusalem in order to pave the way for the rebuilding of the New Jerusalem.

What a wise God. What a Substitute. What a Good Shepherd. What a Saviour.

---

[7] Ezekiel 34:23–24 echoes Psalm 78:70–72 by linking David's original job as a shepherd-boy to his ultimate calling to become God's shepherd-king. Ezekiel prophesies that Jesus will be both *over* his people as God (34:23) and *among* his people as a man (34:24). See Romans 8:29 and Hebrews 2:11.

Three Names
(Ezekiel 35:1–36:23)

"It is not for your sake, people of Israel, that I am going to do these things, but for the sake of my holy name."

(Ezekiel 36:22)

If you want to understand the sudden change of tone as the book of Ezekiel transitions from judgment to comfort, then you need to grasp what three names mean.

The first name is *Mount Seir*, in chapter 35. Although this normally refers to the land of Edom, the Lord has already pronounced judgment upon that nation in 25:12–14. We are therefore meant to view it here in spiritual terms, as representing anybody who hardens their heart towards the Lord. The Edomites were descended from Isaac's son Esau, so they ought to have acted kindly towards Israel, but instead they took advantage of the fall of Israel and Judah to renew an *"ancient hostility"* towards God's people.[1] They knew full well that the Lord dwelt in his Temple in Jerusalem, yet they invaded the Promised Land to plunder its riches and to sell its survivors to their enemies.[2] Ezekiel prophesies that the Lord will always judge such hard-heartedness towards him. *"I will make myself*

---

[1] Examples of this ancient hostility can be found in Genesis 27:41, Numbers 20:18–21, 1 Samuel 14:47, 1 Kings 11:14, Psalm 137:7 and Lamentations 4:21. As a result of this persistent hatred towards Israel, God uses *Edom* as shorthand for all the hard-hearted enemies of God's people in Isaiah 34:5 and 63:1–6, and Malachi 1:1–4.

[2] *"I the Lord was there"* (35:10) looks back to Ezekiel's visions of God's glorious presence and it looks forward to God's glorious final promise in 48:35.

known among them when I judge you ... Then they will know that I am the Lord."

The second name is *the mountains of Israel*, in 36:1–15. If you have been reading carefully then you will remember that this is the name that the Lord used for the people of Judah when he pronounced terrible curses over them back in chapter 6. He used the same name again at the start of his *Book of Comfort*, in 34:14 and 35:12, when he promised to replace those curses with blessing. Ezekiel uses the same name here to expand on that promise. He says that the Lord will once again make the mountains of Israel very fruitful. Their towns and cities will be rebuilt. Their fertile fields will be ploughed and sown. They will become more populous and more prosperous than ever. How can this be, given that many of the Jewish exiles are still questioning God's wisdom and merely play-acting at repentance?[3] The answer to that question lies in the third name.[4]

In 36:16–38, the Lord explains his motivation for restoring the fortunes of Israel. These are some of the most important verses in the whole book of Ezekiel because they tell us what has guided the surgeon's scalpel throughout the whole operation.

The third name isn't Israel or Judah. It is *the name of the Lord*. Ezekiel warns the Jewish exiles that God has not decided to restore their fortunes because he has forgotten their sin. He still finds it as repulsive as a bloodied menstrual rag (36:17).[5] He has operated on the Jewish nation because his own name

---

[3] This is indeed an amazing turnaround. The God who told the Israelites *"I am against you"* in 13:8 and 21:3 now tells them literally in 36:8–9, *"Mountains of Israel ... behold ... I am for you."* The God who said negatively in 6:7, 10, 13 and 14 *"Then you will know that I am the Lord"* now speaks those same words positively in 36:11.

[4] The Lord told Ezekiel to *set his face against* the mountains of Israel in 6:2. He can now reverse this because he *set his face against* Mount Seir in 35:2 instead. This should be the church's comfort whenever her enemies appear to triumph over her. It provokes the Lord to stand by her side to vindicate the honour of his name.

[5] The Lord uses similarly shocking language in the Hebrew text of Isaiah 64:6. See Leviticus 15:19–33.

is tied up with theirs. He couldn't bear the way that the pagans assumed from their idolatry and self-assertiveness that the God of Israel must be no better than their own pathetic deities.[6] He therefore judged them, but even as he did so he was aware that he was giving those pagans a different reason to reject him, since now they would conclude that he was weaker than the gods of those who overthrew Jerusalem. *"Wherever they went among the nations they profaned my holy name, for it was said of them, 'These are the Lord's people, and yet they had to leave his land.'"*[7]

Suddenly, we see why God uses a variation of the refrain *"then they will know that I am the Lord"* seventy-four times in the book of Ezekiel. The ancient world divided everything into two categories. Something was either *hôl* – that is, *common* or *profane* – or it was *qâdôsh* – that is, *holy* or *set apart* or *in a different league*. Ezekiel explains to the Jewish exiles that the Lord judged their nation's sins because they made him appear *hôl* to the pagan nations, and that now he will restore their nation so that his judgment will not make him appear *hôl* instead.[8] His primary motivation for redeeming and restoring the Jewish exiles is not that they have done anything new to warrant his attention. His motivation is his steely determination to vindicate his name before the eyes of a watching world. *"I had concern for my holy name, which the people of Israel profaned among the nations ... The nations will know that I am the Lord, declares the Sovereign Lord, when I am proved holy through you before their eyes."*[9]

---

[6] *Bloodshed* and *idolatry* in 36:18 represent a breaking of the entire Jewish Law. The people of Israel and Judah sinned both against each other and against God.

[7] 36:20. Ezekiel 36:20–23 echoes Isaiah 52:5 and is echoed by Romans 2:24. Israel had been called to represent God to the world (Exodus 19:6). Tragically, they had *mis*represented him (2 Kings 18:33–35).

[8] We see this motivation again in Isaiah 6:3 and Revelation 4:8. God is *qâdôsh qâdosh qâdôsh* – in such a league of his own that even many things that this world regards as *qâdôsh* are *hôl* next to him.

[9] 36:21, 23. We need to grasp that it is God's deep-seated desire to reveal himself as *qâdôsh* to the world by making us *qâdôsh* too. Jeremiah 23:6 leads to Jeremiah 33:16, just as John 8:12 leads to Matthew 5:14.

Some readers don't see this as good news. They question whether it is right for God to be so jealous for his own name, since such an attitude in us would be called pride. John Piper responds that:

> God is the most glorious of all beings. Not to love him and delight in him is a great loss to us and insults him. But the same is true for God. How shall God not insult what is infinitely beautiful and glorious? How shall God not commit idolatry? There is only one possible answer: God must love and delight in his own beauty and perfection above all things.[10]

It is wonderful news for us that God delights in his own name. If his chief motivation for saving us were our need, then he would be an unpredictable God. How could we ever know for sure if we were needy enough to attract his pity? If his chief motivation for saving us were our repentance, then we would have a God who is as fickle as our own feelings. How could we ever find assurance of our salvation when our hearts are so easily drawn back into pride? When we give it thought, it is far better for us that God's chief motivation in saving us is far more solid and endurable than anything that we could ever bring to the party – that he is motivated by nothing less than his own fiery, passionate, unflinching and inexhaustible passion for the honour of his name.

This divine motive that undergirds our salvation is tougher than titanium.[11] It is a solid rock on which to place our feet. God's passion for his own glory affords us a far firmer hope than any

---

[10] John Piper in *The Pleasures of God* (Desiring God, 1991). The book of Ezekiel begins with a vision of God's great glory and then reveals his people's great sin. Praise God that his glory is so great that it engenders great salvation.
[11] God first preaches the gospel, in Genesis 3:15, not to Adam and Eve, but to the snake. We are caught up in the story of his name, and we downgrade the story of our salvation when we act as if he is caught up in ours.

merit of our own. That's why it's such good news when Ezekiel reveals what always motivates the Lord's hand whenever he wields his surgeon's scalpel.

"I want you to know that I am not doing this for your sake, declares the Sovereign Lord.... I the Lord have spoken, and I will do it... Then they will know that I am the Lord." [12]

Heart Surgery
(Ezekiel 36:24–38)

"I will remove from you your heart of stone and give you a heart of flesh."

(Ezekiel 36:26)

If you google the first successful heart transplant operation, you will be told that it was performed on Louis Washkansky by Dr Christiaan Barnard on 3 December 1967 in Cape Town, South Africa. But that is out by two and a half thousand years. Ezekiel informs us that the Lord performed the first successful heart transplant on the Jewish exiles during their seventy years in Babylonia. In 36:26–27, he prophesies one of his greatest promises:

> *I will give you a new heart and put a new spirit in you; I will remove from you your heart of stone and give you a heart of flesh. And I will put my Spirit in you and move you to follow my decrees and be careful to keep my laws.*

That's fantastic news for a number of reasons. First, it deals with the great deficiency of the priesthood at Solomon's Temple in Old Jerusalem. Ezekiel came from a priestly family, so don't miss the priestly language that he uses in verse 25 to describe the Lord wiping away Israel's sin.[1] The priests in Old Jerusalem were able to sprinkle clean water on people and to wash away their outward impurities, but the Lord promises to cleanse the

---

[1] Ezekiel 36:25 deliberately echoes Exodus 30:18–21, Leviticus 14:49–53 and Numbers 19:18–20.

parts that they could never reach. He will place his Holy Spirit inside his people to purify them from the inside out. When the River of God enters them and flows out from their inner beings, he promises to do away with the superseded, outside-in rituals of the Temple. This is one of the Old Testament passages that Jesus has in mind when he tells the crowds in John's gospel that, *"the water I give them will become in them a spring of water welling up to eternal life"* and that *"Whoever believes in me, as Scripture has said, rivers of living water will flow from within them."*[2]

Second, it reverses the great tragedy that Ezekiel witnessed at the start of his book when he saw God's glorious presence leaving the Temple in Old Jerusalem. The Lord explains that he moved out because he was making plans to build a new and better Temple in which his presence would dwell forever. The Messiah would be born to the returning Jewish exiles and he would pour the Spirit of God into the hearts of his people. He would fulfil the promise in Jeremiah 3:16 that *"In those days ... people will no longer say, 'The ark of the covenant of the Lord.' It will never enter their minds or be remembered; it will not be missed, nor will another one be made."* The returning Jewish exiles would rebuild Solomon's Temple, but their descendants would become God's New Covenant Temple![3]

Third, it is great news because it deals with the greatest weakness that prevented the Jews of Old Jerusalem from truly following the Lord. Although they were able to read what the Law of Moses told them about serving God, they discovered that their hearts were too stubborn to do so. Try as they might to motivate themselves through external religious activity, they lacked the inner desire and the inner power to do so. Note the way, therefore, that verses 26–27 echo 11:19–20 and 18:31,

---

[2] John 4:14 and 7:38. We will look at this promise in more detail when we come to Ezekiel 47:1–12.

[3] These verses form the Old Testament background to the Apostle Paul's teaching in 1 Corinthians 3:16–17, 2 Corinthians 6:16 and Ephesians 2:19–22. See also Ezekiel 11:16.

as the Lord promises to bring such days of outside-in religion to an end. When he pours out his Holy Spirit into the hearts of his people, he will so unite his Spirit with their own spirits that they will find themselves impassioned and empowered from the inside out to do whatever he tells them to do.[4]

These two verses form the Old Testament background to the promise in 1 Corinthians 6:17 that *"whoever is united with the Lord is one with him in spirit"* and to the promise in Philippians 2:13 that *"it is God who works in you to will and to act in order to fulfil his good purpose."* These verses prophesy that the New Covenant will bring, not just forgiveness *for* sin, but freedom *from* sin too.[5] When God's Spirit comes to dwell within his people, he will perform a heart transplant on them.[6] Their frustrated days of finding that outside-in religion is too feeble to transform anyone will finally come to an end.

Dr Christiaan Barnard spent over five hours operating on Louis Washkansky, but the patient died eighteen days after he went under the surgeon's scalpel. Perhaps that's why the Lord took seventy long years to operate on the hearts of the Jewish exiles in Babylon. He was determined that their hard hearts would be transformed for the long haul into tender hearts towards him by the time they returned to the Promised Land. He wanted to ensure that the Jewish nation lost its taste for sin and gained a long-term longing for holiness, so that the mountains

---

[4] Ephesians 2:2 says the Devil is the spirit at work in people's hearts until they are filled with the Holy Spirit, who quickly displaces the squatter. People who hesitate to surrender their lives to Jesus because "I don't think I could keep up a Christian life" have missed the point. God not only forgives us; he also empowers us.

[5] The language of 36:24 likens the return from captivity in Babylon to a Second Exodus. This promise applies to those whom God delivers from spiritual captivity as much as to those he delivered from ancient Babylon. See Isaiah 11:11 and 49:9–10, and Jeremiah 16:14–15.

[6] All attempts to sanctify ourselves through human willpower are doomed to fail (Colossians 2:23), but when God fills us with his Holy Spirit, he begins to sanctify us from the inside out. See Exodus 31:13, Romans 8:1–17, 1 Thessalonians 5:23, 2 Thessalonians 2:13, Galatians 5:16–23 and Titus 2:11–12.

of Israel could become pure and prosperous and populous once again.[7] He wanted to reassure them for the long haul that *"you will be my people, and I will be your God."*[8]

Strangely, this chapter ends by likening the restored Jewish nation to the flocks of sheep that were brought into Jerusalem to be slaughtered at her great religious festivals. This is not an indication that this radical turnaround in its fortunes would be the result of its own sacrifices for God, but a reminder that the Messiah will be the Lamb of God. He will perform this heart transplant that will finally make the Jewish nation want to serve the Lord.

The sacrifice will be his so that the glory will be his too. When the pagan nations hear the gospel, they will confess that none of their national deities would have done the same. Ezekiel repeats that this is the Lord's primary motivation in our salvation:

> *I want you to know that I am not doing this for your sake, declares the Sovereign Lord ... The nations around you ... will know that I the Lord have rebuilt what was destroyed and have replanted what was desolate. I the Lord have spoken, and I will do it.*[9]

That's the glory of the Christian gospel. Not just forgiveness *for* sin, but freedom *from* sin – and all for the glory of God's holy name.

---

[7] Although these verses do not use the phrase *New Covenant*, they rank alongside Jeremiah 31:31–34 as one of the great Old Testament descriptions of what the Christian life ought to be like – as *the garden of Eden* (36:35).

[8] Ezekiel 36:28 echoes 11:20, 14:11, 34:30. It also looks forward to 37:23 and 27.

[9] 36:32, 36. God refused to let the hard-hearted Jewish nation enquire of him in 14:3, 20:3 and 20:31. Once they have a new heart, however, he promises literally in 36:37 that *"I will once again be enquired of by the house of Israel."*

New Life
(Ezekiel 37:1–28)

He asked me, "Son of man, can these bones live?"
(Ezekiel 37:3)

If you enjoy messing around on boats, then you may have heard the same chilling sound that I heard a few years ago while out on the Solent. I was on a glorious eight-man yacht, basking in the freedom of feeling the wind in my hair and the sea air in my lungs, when suddenly I heard the pop-pop-pop spluttering of the engine. The hull was spotless white and the decks were gleaming, but the yacht was completely out of fuel. I might have tried to fool myself that I looked the part of an expert mariner, but I was all adrift at sea.

The Lord decides to teach Ezekiel a similar lesson in this chapter. The Holy Spirit descends powerfully on his prophet and transports him back to Jerusalem in a second out-of-body vision.[1] After slaughtering the inhabitants of Jerusalem, the Babylonians had piled up their corpses in the Valley of Ben Hinnom.[2] The birds and animals have been busy, because by now all that is left of them is a pile of dry and disconnected

---

[1] Ezekiel tells us seven times that *"the hand of the Lord was on me"* (1:3, 3:14, 3:22, 8:1, 33:22, 37:1 and 40:1). This metaphor for being anointed with the Holy Spirit is also used in Ezra 7:28 and Nehemiah 2:8.

[2] Since the Hebrew word *biq'āh* is used to describe Ezekiel's vision on the *plain* in 3:22–23 and 8:4, many readers assume that this vision also took place in Babylonia. However, *biq'āh* also means *valley*, so it makes more sense to see it as an out-of-body visit to the bones of Jerusalem's dead in the Valley of Ben Hinnom.

bones.[3] The Lord asks Ezekiel the same question that he has asked many church leaders over the ages. *"Son of man, can these bones live?"*

Ezekiel is honest. God only knows how to transform this valley of dry bones from a mortuary into a maternity ward. Ezekiel can see that Jerusalem is finished. Dry bones speak of utter lifelessness. Their exposure to the elements speaks of divine judgment, since death without burial was regarded with great horror by the ancient world.[4] Jerusalem can only be rebuilt and restored through a mighty miracle from the Lord.

But that's precisely why God asked his prophet the question. He wants him to prophesy to the lifeless bones of Old Jerusalem. When he does so, he discovers that even death itself cannot defy a direct command spoken by a servant of the Lord. With a loud noise, the bones of the dead come back together and are joined together by fresh tendons and muscles and skin. They still lie there on the floor of the valley, but God has begun to reconstitute his fallen people.

As yet, however, they are still a bit like my boat on the Solent. They look impressive on the outside but they are dead on the inside. None of them have any breath in their lungs. The Lord therefore commands Ezekiel to prophesy a second time – this time to the *rūach*, which means *wind* or *breath* or *spirit*.[5] When he does so, the reconstituted corpses are raised to life and stand to their feet as the new Spirit-filled army of the Lord.[6]

The Lord still asks the same question of us, as we gaze out over our churches today. *"Can these bones live?"* We may not

---

[3] Ezekiel does not give us the date of this vision, but it was sometime between 585 BC (33:21) and 573 BC (40:1). Several years may have passed since the fall of Jerusalem.

[4] Jeremiah 8:1–2, 9:22, 15:3, 16:4, 22:19, 34:20 and 36:30, and Ezekiel 6:5, 29:5, 32:4–6 and 39:4.

[5] *Rūach* is the main word used in the Hebrew Old Testament for the *Spirit* of God. It means *Spirit* in 37:1 and 14, and *breath* eight times in 37:5–10. This chapter is therefore an illustration of what was promised in 36:26–27.

[6] In Genesis 2:7, the Lord needed to breathe his breath into Adam's body for him to become a living soul. In the same way, he has to breathe his Holy Spirit into people to be born again (John 3:3–8).

enjoy reflecting on the spiritual deadness of our generation, but it is essential that we do so, because God's resurrection power is reserved for corpses. Ezekiel might have pleaded that Leviticus 21:1–12 forbade priests such as him from touching a dead body, yet he faces up to the facts by walking back and forth among the bones. He might have accepted the spiritual status quo – *"Sovereign Lord, you alone know"* (37:3) – yet he acts to overturn the status quo.[7] He might have protested that the Lord's command to preach to dry bones made no sense, since ears have many bones but bones have no ears. He might have resigned himself to the sorry situation that he saw, like the Jewish exiles in verse 11: *"Our bones are dried up and our hope is gone; we are cut off."* He might even have been satisfied with the reconstituted corpses of the dead. But he wasn't. He didn't merely want the exiles to return to the Promised Land. He wanted nothing less than the revival of Israel.

Nor must we. When Jesus tells us in the Gospels that he has given us authority to speak commands in his name to sickness and to demons and to death itself, he is commissioning us as he did Ezekiel. We may feel as foolish as the prophet in the valley of dry bones when we obey, but if we resolve to listen to the voice of God rather than to the voice of our rationalistic and materialistic culture, then we will witness similar mighty miracles of our own. We will see the promise of this chapter played out in our own churches. They will be reconstituted, resurrected, renewed, revived and reunified.

Yes, that's right. *Reunified*. The final surprise of this chapter is that the northern kingdom of Israel and the southern kingdom of Judah are reunited in 37:15–28 by the power of God's Spirit. The Lord does not merely pledge to breathe new life into the corpses of Old Jerusalem. Nor does he merely extend the promise that he made in 36:26–27 to the fallen people of Judah. He pledges to pour out his Spirit on the survivors of the ten northern tribes too. Ezekiel expresses this through another

---

[7] It is far easier to lament than to act, far easier to hide behind the sovereignty of God than to lay hold of it.

of his prophetic mimes, connecting two sticks together as a picture of what will happen to God's people when he pours out his Holy Spirit on them.[8] They will live under a new covenant and enjoy God's glorious presence in a new way together, resulting in a new holiness that flows from the inside out. They will enjoy a new unity and a new fruitfulness under a new King, their long-awaited Messiah, who will transform sinners from both the north and the south into one holy people.[9] They will become God's new Temple together.[10]

With such new life available to them through the Holy Spirit, it would be tragic for the Jewish exiles to be satisfied with a mere return from captivity. It would be equally tragic for us to satisfy ourselves merely with crowded churches. We dare not be satisfied with reconstituted corpses. We must cry out to him until he transforms the dry bones of our churches into the Spirit-filled marching army of the Lord.

The Lord therefore invites us to look at our churches and to answer his question: *"Can these bones live?"* Through Ezekiel's example, he encourages us to believe that resurrection and revival are only ever a few faith-filled prayers away.

---

[8] 37:15–28. *For ever* in verse 25 hints that these promises will only be partially fulfilled through the Jewish return from exile and completed later when the Messiah finally comes. When Zechariah repeats Ezekiel's prophetic mime over fifty years later, he also hints at this by breaking the sticks as a prediction that many Jews will reject their Messiah, paving the way for many Gentiles to be saved (Zechariah 11:4–17 and 12:1–14:21).

[9] Jesus not only justifies us from the penalty of sin. Through his Spirit, he also sanctifies us from the pollution of sin (37:23 and 28).

[10] *The mountains of Israel* in 37:22 link this promise back to 36:1–15. *The shepherd* in 37:24 links it back to 34:1–31. *The sanctuary* in 37:26–28 links it back to Ezekiel's vision of God's glorious presence leaving the Temple in 8:1–11:25, and links it forward to the promises of Ezekiel 40–48. The Apostle Paul appears to quote from 37:27 when he tells us in 2 Corinthians 6:16–17 that the church is the new covenant Temple of God.

New Victory
(Ezekiel 38:1–39:29)

*"In days to come, Gog, I will bring you against my
land, so that the nations may know me when I am
proved holy through you before their eyes."*

(Ezekiel 38:16)

When the army of God is raised up onto its feet, the Devil rarely
takes it lying down. Hot on the heels of Ezekiel's vision of the
revival of God's people in the valley of dry bones, the Devil
launches a demonic invasion of the Promised Land.

A lot of readers become confused by these two chapters
about Gog and Magog. They are full of apocalyptic imagery,
which Daniel 12:10 tells us God used during periods when Israel
was living under foreign rule so that *"None of the wicked will
understand, but those who are wise will understand."* This ought
to caution us against dismissing the final chapters of Ezekiel
as too baffling for us to bother with. They are not meant to be
straightforward, but nor are they are meant to be unintelligible
to anyone but the wicked. The Lord speaks cryptically in order
to hide his secrets from unfriendly eyes, but he gives believers
several clues to help them understand what he is saying here.

Nobody knows what the name *Gog* means and nobody
has ever convincingly connected him to a specific individual in
history.[1] We are told that he rules over Magog, but this offers us
little help because it simply means *The Place of Gog*.

---

[1] One of the most popular candidates among commentators is King Gyges of
Lydia, in modern-day Turkey – yet Gyges never tried to invade Israel and he
died in about 652 BC, long before Ezekiel ever prophesied!

The first clue we have to his identity is the fact that Genesis 10:2 mentions Magog, Meshek and Tubal as the ancient ancestors of the Greeks who ruled over the western coastlands of modern-day Turkey. This led successive generations of Jews to identify Gog as Alexander the Great, as the Seleucids and as the Romans. It also led European Christians to identify Gog as the Turks, as the Goths and even as the Soviet Union during the Cold War.[2]

The second clue is that Gog leads a coalition of nations that extends far beyond western Turkey. Ezekiel mentions *Persia* (modern-day Iran), *Cush* (modern-day Sudan), *Put* (modern-day Libya), *Gomer* and *Beth Togarmah* (modern-day Armenia, Azerbaijan and southern Russia). You don't have to be good at geography to spot that each of these represents one of the four points of the compass from western Turkey, which is a second clue that Gog represents something bigger than any single individual or nation.[3]

The third clue comes through the reappearance of Gog and Magog in Revelation 20:8. The Apostle John predicts that, throughout AD history, the Devil *"will go out to deceive the nations in the four corners of the earth – Gog and Magog – and to gather them for battle."* Put together, these three clues indicate that these chapters describe the constant attacks on God's people throughout history from their invisible, spiritual enemies.[4]

Ezekiel is therefore using *Gog* in 38:1–23 in the same way that he used *Edom* in 35:1–15.[5] Whenever the Devil sees a

---

[2] They argued that *rō'sh*, the Hebrew word for *chief*, sounds a little bit like *Russia*, and that *Meshek* also sounds like *Moscow*. Yet the USSR never ruled western Turkey, nor did it ever attempt to invade Israel!

[3] Literalists insist that *north* must mean north and *army* must mean army, so these chapters predict an actual invasion of the modern state of Israel. However, to be consistent, *arrows, spears, shields* and *swords* must also mean arrows, spears, shields and swords – weapons that a modern army would be very unlikely to use.

[4] John also hints at this in Revelation 9:13–19 by saying that the army comes from Iraq, and not from Turkey. For more on this and on *"the thousand years"* of Revelation 20:7, see my book *Straight to the Heart of Revelation* (2010).

[5] The Battle of Armageddon in Revelation 16:16 echoes these verses as another description of the Devil's repeated attacks throughout church history.

spiritual revival, he stirs up the enemies of God's people against them.[6] Whether through a government crackdown or a foreign invasion, Ezekiel reassures us that the Lord permits it in order to reveal the glory of his name.[7] Gog may believe that he is hatching plans, but in reality he is inspired by the Devil.[8] The Devil may believe that he is succeeding in his puppetry, but in reality he is also a mere extra in God's great salvation drama. The Lord allows his people to be attacked by their enemies because it offers him the perfect opportunity to display his supreme power.[9]

> *I will bring you against my land, so that the nations may know me when I am proved holy through you before their eyes ... I will show my greatness and my holiness, and I will make myself known in the sight of many nations. Then they will know that I am the Lord.*[10]

Ezekiel repeats this promise in 39:1–29. Whenever God's people experience a spiritual revival, he allows the Devil to stir up non-

---

[6] The Jewish exiles rebuilt their walled cities (36:35), so the lack of walls in 38:11 hints that this is a prophecy about God's people after the coming of his Messiah (Zechariah 2:4–5). So does the description of the Jewish exiles as *"the people gathered from the nations"* in 38:12. An even greater gathering from the nations would follow.

[7] The Hebrew text of 38:17 asks literally: *Are you the one I spoke of in former days by my servants the prophets of Israel?* If this question demands the answer "yes", then God is boasting that he foretold the Devil's doom. If it demands the answer "no", then he is promising that no new Nebuchadnezzar will destroy his New Jerusalem.

[8] Evil spirits stir up thoughts in Gog's mind in 38:10. This is the satanic counterfeit of 37:10 and 14.

[9] Since Revelation 9:18 tells us that the chief weapons of this army are *fire* and *sulphur*, Ezekiel 38:22 is reassuring us that the Lord will turn the Devil's own weapons back on him.

[10] 38:14, 23. Attacks on God's people often seem disastrous at the time, but Ezekiel urges us to trust the Lord to transform each supposed setback into an opportunity to shatter the teeth of our enemies on our armour.

believers against them in order to showcase his glory by leading his people to a new victory.[11] Each time the Devil comes against them, the Lord grants them such a decisive breakthrough over the forces of darkness that Ezekiel pictures them heating their homes for seven years with the chopped up spear shafts of their enemies![12] It also takes them seven months to bury the corpses of their enemies after the birds and animals have stripped them down to dry and disconnected bones, just like the ones that Ezekiel saw in the Valley of Ben Hinnom in chapter 37.[13]

The Lord therefore ends these two chapters with a prophetic declaration that echoes his earlier declaration in 36:16–38. When God judges his people, it makes non-believers assume that the God of Israel is too weak to defend his people, so the destruction of Gog's horde serves to set the record straight. It clarifies that the Lord is not *too weak* to support his people, but *too holy* to support their behaviour.

> *I will display my glory among the nations, and ... the people of Israel will know that I am the Lord their God ... I will be zealous for my holy name ... I will be proved holy through them in the sight of many nations ... for I will pour out my Spirit on the people of Israel, declares the Sovereign Lord.*[14]

So don't let your eyes glaze over when you read about Gog and Magog. Don't skim-read these verses and dismiss them as too

---

[11] In 39:6, even those left behind in the safety of Magog are caught up in the judgment that befalls its army.

[12] The number *seven* speaks here of complete victory. *The Valley of the Hamon Gog* in 39:11 and 15 means *the Valley of the Hordes of Gog*. It stands in deliberate contrast to the Valley of Dry Bones because the Lord's revival army will completely conquer the Devil's.

[13] Don't miss the deliberate symmetry. In Ezekiel 37, the Lord turns the dry bones of Jerusalem into a living army. In Ezekiel 39, the Lord turns the living army of Gog into dry bones.

[14] 39:13, 22, 25, 27, 29.

difficult to understand. When the Lord revives his people, it invariably provokes the Devil to attack them. God permits such satanic onslaughts so that he can transform each fresh attack into a new victory for his people. Whenever the church appears beleaguered, God is planning to display the glories of his holy name to the nations of the world.

New Presence
(Ezekiel 40:1–43:12)

"Son of man, describe the temple to the people of Israel, that they may be ashamed of their sins. Let them consider its perfection."

(Ezekiel 43:10)

The nine final chapters of Ezekiel are widely regarded as the weirdest in the Bible. They appear to describe a Temple that was never built, a priesthood that was never needed and resettlement of the Promised Land that can only be a metaphor. As a result, many people skim-read these chapters quickly, while others ignore them altogether. But don't tune out here. Give these nine chapters your full and undivided attention, because there is rich treasure buried here for those who are willing to do a little digging.[1]

Ezekiel was visited in power by the Holy Spirit on 28 April 573 BC and transported back to Jerusalem in a third and final out-of-body vision. In his first such vision, in chapter 8, he had witnessed God's glorious presence leaving the old Temple. In his second out-of-body vision, in chapter 37, he had spoken new life into the bones of Jerusalem's dead that were piled up in the Valley of Ben Hinnom. In this third out-of-body vision, he is granted a visit to the new and better Temple that God is planning to rebuild.

That's the first thing we need to note if we want to understand these chapters. Only God can build the Temple that

---

[1] Remember Daniel 12:10. God speaks in apocalyptic language so that *"None of the wicked will understand, but those who are wise will understand."* These chapters may be cryptic, but God wants you to understand them.

Ezekiel witnesses in his vision, because he makes it impossible for human hands to build. It stands on the same site as the old Temple (*"he took me there"*) and yet it lies in the shadow of *"a very high mountain"*. Every Jewish exile knew that the city of Jerusalem was nowhere near any high mountain. The Mount of Olives is little more than 800 m above sea level. That's barely a quarter as tall as Mount Hermon, in the north of Israel, and not even a tenth as tall as Mount Everest. This is meant to convey to us that this vision describes a spiritual reality. It goes alongside Psalm 48:2, which extols the loftiness of Mount Zion (even though it isn't lofty), and alongside Psalm 46:4, which praises Jerusalem's river (even though it doesn't have one). These verses are descriptions of the New Jerusalem that only God can build.[2]

Ezekiel's vision is full of big-picture imagery but short on architectural detail. We are told in 40:3 that the angel holds a massive ruler in his hand but, apart from in 40:5, he never uses it to give us any 3D measurements that could be followed by a builder.[3] As a result, Zerubbabel and the returning Jewish exiles ignored these chapters and rebuilt a Temple that was a mere fraction of its size.[4] The angel explains in 43:10 that this vision has a bigger purpose. Ezekiel is to *"Describe the temple to the people of Israel, that they may be ashamed of their sins. Let them consider its perfection."*[5] This is a vision of God's glorious New Covenant Temple, which is intended to convict the Jewish exiles

---

[2] See also Isaiah 2:2, Ezekiel 17:22, Micah 4:1, Zechariah 14:10 and Revelation 21:9–15.

[3] The angel gives us lengths and widths, but the only height he gives us is in 40:5. God gave 3D instructions to Moses and Solomon because they were builders, but God is the Builder of this New Covenant Temple.

[4] Ezra 3:12. The angel tells Ezekiel in 40:4 that this is a Temple for the Jews to *hear* about, not attempt to build.

[5] The *"man whose appearance was like bronze"* cannot be the Lord himself since he is standing next to Ezekiel in 43:6 when God speaks to him out of the Temple. He is an angel like those described in 9:2. A *measuring rod* was used to measure short distances and a *measuring line* was used to measure longer ones.

of their sin and of their dire need for the Messiah to come and be their true and better Zerubbabel. It prefigures the great New Testament declaration: *"Don't you know that you yourselves are God's temple and that God's Spirit lives in you?" "For we are the temple of the living God."*[6]

In 40:5–42:20, we discover that the Messiah will build a Temple that is far more glorious than that of Solomon.[7] Its outer courtyard is quarter of a kilometre long and wide, which makes it over three times larger than the one destroyed by the Babylonians. The Temple building is only slightly larger than that of Solomon, but it possesses a large west wing and a vast accommodation complex for the priests, which the Old Temple never had. The thick wall that towers high around the courtyard and the guardrooms at each of its gates express the utter holiness of this new Temple. No unclean thing may ever enter it.[8] The requirement to climb all those steps – seven to the outer courtyard, eight to the inner courtyard and ten more to the Temple building – expresses God's call for his people to embrace ever-increasing holiness with each deeper experience of his presence. So does the way in which the gateways get smaller the closer we get to the inner sanctuary.[9]

You don't have to know much about Solomon's Temple to spot a massive difference in this New Covenant Temple.[10]

---

[6]   1 Corinthians 3:16, 2 Corinthians 6:16–17, Ephesians 2:19–22 and 1 Peter 2:4–10.

[7]   The blood sacrifices offered in 40:38–43 are prophetic pictures of the cross of Jesus.

[8]   Ezekiel 42:20 is echoed by Revelation 21:27, which also describes the glories of the New Jerusalem.

[9]   Ezekiel 40:6, 22, 26, 31 and 49 are Old Testament precursors to the promise of 2 Corinthians 3:18. Ezekiel 40:48 and 41:2–3 are precursors to Hebrews 12:14. The Greek Septuagint text of 40:49 describes *"ten steps"*.

[10]   Like Solomon's Temple, this new Temple is decorated with pictures of palm trees and cherubim, which look back to the paradise of the Garden of Eden. Unlike Ezekiel's earlier visions, the cherubim angels pictured here have only two faces – those of a man and a lion, but not those of an ox or an angel or an eagle.

The promise of Jeremiah 3:16–17 has been fulfilled. There is no ark of the covenant in the inner sanctuary of the Temple.[11] The post-Pentecost people of God have no need for a special box in a special room in a special building, because their very bodies have become the new and better sanctuary of God.[12] They belong to the Spirit-filled army of believers that is predicted in Ezekiel 36:26–27 and 37:1–14.

This leads to the great crescendo of this description of God's New Covenant people. In 43:1–12, Ezekiel witnesses the sudden return of God's glorious presence to his Temple. Having left through the east gate towards Babylonia in 10:19, God now returns through the east gate to fill his new Temple with his presence once again.[13] He calls out to Ezekiel from within the Temple to promise that his Spirit-filled people will no longer be half-hearted in their worship and defiled by sin.[14] They will be transformed from the inside out to become carriers of his holy presence to the world. *"I will live among them for ever"* (43:7).

So don't skim-read these strange chapters. Ezekiel isn't bewildered by his vision. He recognizes what it means. He falls flat on his face and worships God for these results of his radical surgery. Such new enjoyment of his presence was worth all the pain.[15]

---

[11] Nor is there any mention of the Sea of Cast Metal or of the golden lampstands (1 Kings 7:23 and 49), since the Holy Spirit has become those things to God's New Covenant people. He sanctifies us, guides us and empowers us to pray.

[12] The Hebrew words translated *most holy* in 43:12 – *qōdesh qādāshīm* – mean literally *Holy of Holies* or *Most Holy Place*. The entire Temple and its courtyards are now home to God's presence (Hebrews 10:19–23).

[13] Ezekiel echoes his earlier visions by likening God's voice to *"the roar of rushing waters"* and his glory to the radiant sun (1:24 and 10:4). See also Isaiah 60:1–3, Malachi 4:2, Luke 2:9, Acts 26:13, and Revelation 1:15, 14:2, 19:6 and 21:23.

[14] The storerooms that surrounded Solomon's Temple shared a partition wall with its sanctuary, yet the Jews used them as shrines for their idols (8:7–16 and 43:8, and 2 Chronicles 33:4–7). Ezekiel warns us here that, as God's New Covenant Temple, we must not defile ourselves with any form of sin.

[15] Ezekiel falls on his face before the Lord, just as he did in 1:28, 3:23, 9:8 and 11:13. He has not allowed his many visions of God's glorious presence to make him overfamiliar with God. Nor must we.

New Authority
(Ezekiel 43:13–46:24)

"The priests are to present your burnt offerings and fellowship offerings on the altar. Then I will accept you, declares the Sovereign Lord."

(Ezekiel 43:27)

Ezekiel was a priest. He had been born into the priestly family of Zadok and he would have started serving at the Old Temple on his thirtieth birthday had the Babylonians not carried him off into exile. He therefore understood the calling of a priest of Israel as it is described in Malachi 2:7, *"The lips of a priest ought to preserve knowledge, because he is the messenger of the Lord Almighty and people seek instruction from his mouth."*

Modern readers tend to think of Israel's priesthood purely in terms of slaughtering sacrificial animals. They therefore get confused when Ezekiel's vision talks about *altars* and *priests* and *sacrifices*, since these seem out of place in a description of the New Covenant Temple. We need to remember that the primary calling of Israel's priests was to act as God's anointed ambassadors to the people.[1] Ezekiel's final vision therefore uses priestly terminology to predict the *new authority* with which we can now speak for him.

The Israelites believed that Solomon's Temple was the earthly footstool of God's heavenly throne. The Lord picks up on this when he declares in 43:7 that his New Covenant Temple will

---

[1] See Jeremiah 18:20, where the prophet describes his priestly calling to stand between God and the people.

be *"the place of my throne and the place for the soles of my feet."*[2] Being filled with the Holy Spirit is not just about enjoying greater intimacy with God. It is also about wielding greater authority from God. Each of the prophetic pictures in these chapters is meant to encourage us that, when the Messiah commissions his followers to offer prayers and issue commands in his name, God will treat it as if the Messiah prayed and commanded those things personally. The Lord will make his people on earth a visible outpost of his invisible control room in heaven.

In 43:13–27, Ezekiel describes the sacrificial altar in the inner courtyard of God's new Temple that he mentioned very briefly in 40:47. Although it stands in the same place as the bronze altar built by Solomon, it is larger.[3] It consists of three perfectly square slabs placed on top of one another, like an Egyptian pyramid, predicting that the blood sacrifice of Jesus will be perfect.[4] In Ezekiel's vision, the Lord commands him to serve as a priest from Zadok's family, so that his sacrifices can also prefigure the perfect sacrifice that will one day be offered by the greater *Son of Man* who is to come.[5]

In 44:1–31, the angel carries on speaking about the new authority that the Messiah will convey upon his followers. He takes Ezekiel back to the east gate of the Temple courtyards,

---

[2] 1 Chronicles 28:2, 2 Chronicles 9:18, Psalms 99:5 and 132:7, and Lamentations 2:1.

[3] The altar of Moses was 2.5 m wide x 2.5 m deep x 1.5 m high (Exodus 27:1). The altar of Solomon was 9 m wide x 9 m deep x 4.5 m high (2 Chronicles 4:1). At its base, this new altar is 10.5 m wide x 10.5 m deep, getting smaller as it rises up like a pyramid to 5.2 m high.

[4] The Most Holy Place was shaped like a cube in Moses' Tabernacle and in Solomon's Temple, its equal width, depth and height testifying to the perfection of the *holy, holy, holy* God. The same thing is signified here by these three perfectly square blocks, which decrease in size so as to create a perfect pyramid.

[5] In 43:18, the Lord speaks literally about *the day on which the altar will be built* – that is, the day of Jesus' crucifixion. Zadok led the godly clan of Eleazar, as opposed to the sinful clan of Ithamar, so his clan alone serves in the Temple as an expression of the total purity of God's New Covenant people (40:46 and 43:19).

through which the Lord left in 10:19 and returned in 43:4, and informs him that the gate must remain closed to everyone except *"the prince"* who is to come.[6] Overwhelmed by the thought of this Messiah, and catching a fresh glimpse of God's glorious presence filling the Temple, Ezekiel falls face down in breathless worship (verse 4).

From within the Temple, the Lord calls out to his prophet that the Messiah's followers will enjoy a far greater priesthood than the one that Ezekiel left behind in Old Jerusalem. The Messiah will be a better high priest and his followers will be a nation of better priests under him.[7] They will no longer abdicate their God-given authority to those who know nothing of the Lord.[8] They will no longer permit the dirty feet of the spiritually uncircumcised to sully the holy courtyards of God's Temple.[9] To illustrate this promise, the sinful clan of Ithamar is demoted from serving as priests to serving as mere Levites in the Temple courtyards. The godly clan of Zadok recommits itself to following the Lord's instructions to his priests about what to wear, how to look, what to eat and drink, whom to marry and what to touch.[10] By practising what they preach, they will convince the world that the Lord is holy. *"They are to teach my*

---

[6] 44:3. The reason given is reverence for a gateway that has been used by the Lord, but this also promises that God's glorious presence will never leave his New Covenant Temple in the way that it did the Old Temple.

[7] See Exodus 19:5–6 and 1 Peter 2:4–10. Hebrews 3:1, 4:14, 8:1–2 and 9:11 will lead to Revelation 1:6 and 5:10.

[8] We must ensure that this is true. Every time in history that non-believers have been entrusted with leadership positions within the church, the Lord has disciplined his church as he did Israel and Judah.

[9] *"No foreigner uncircumcised in heart and flesh"* (44:9) echoes Deuteronomy 10:16 and 30:6, and Jeremiah 4:4 and 9:25–26. It is echoed in turn by Romans 2:28–29 and Colossians 2:11–12.

[10] Numbers 3:10 had already barred the Levites from entering the Temple, on pain of death, so the Lord cannot merely be repeating this in 44:10–14. He must be demoting the priests of Ithamar to the status of Levites, as a fulfilment of the curses on Eli and Abiathar (1 Samuel 2:30–36, 1 Kings 2:26–27). The name *Zadok* means *Righteous*, and this serves as a prophetic picture of the church's utter purity.

people the difference between the holy and the common and show them how to distinguish between the unclean and the clean."[11]

Sin drove the Jewish exiles from the Promised Land, so we discover in 45:1–8 that the repentant Jews will have authority to reallocate the land. The language here is clearly symbolic, since it splits Israel into thirteen strips of land that run from east to west, like the hoops on a rugby shirt – one for each of the twelve tribes of Israel and one for the prince, priests and Levites.[12] The *"sacred district"*, which is split equally between the priests and Levites, forms a perfect square to symbolize the perfection of our inheritance in Jesus, the true and better Joshua who leads his people into a better Promised Land.[13]

In 45:9–46:24, Ezekiel's vision explains how all of this is possible. It moves from talking about the justice of the Prince of Israel's rule to talking about the blood sacrifices that the Prince of Israel will offer to the Lord. The Messiah will make atonement for God's people by fulfilling what was prophesied through the burnt offerings, grain offerings, drink offerings, sin offerings, guilt offerings and fellowship offerings listed in the Law of Moses. His death on the cross will grant to his people the peace that was prefigured by all the Sabbath-rests and festive holidays that are stipulated by the Law.

The results of God's radical surgery have come in, and the prognosis is very good. It has achieved for us a new heart, a new life, a new victory, a new experience of his presence, and a new authority to serve as priests – earthly ambassadors of the Majesty in heaven.

---

[11] 44:23. Don't be surprised by the Old Covenant language in this chapter. God uses the commitment of Eleazar's clan to purity as a picture of our New Covenant holiness (Numbers 25:7–13 and 1 Kings 1:7–8).

[12] The priests will not own their tracts of land, but will simply steward them for the Lord (44:28). A clue that the language in these verses must be symbolic is that the Temple is no longer in the city of Jerusalem.

[13] The *"sacred district"* measures 25,000 cubits by 20,000 cubits. The "Jerusalem district" measures 25,000 cubits by 5,000 cubits. Together, they form an 8-square-mile piece of territory. See also 47:13–48:35.

New Power
(Ezekiel 47:1–48:35)

The man brought me back to the entrance to the temple, and I saw water coming out from under the threshold of the temple.

(Ezekiel 47:1)

Great cities consume great amounts of water. That's why most of them are built on rivers. London has the Thames, Paris has the Seine, Rome has the Tiber, New York has the Hudson, Delhi has the Yamuna, and Shanghai has the Huangpu. Go to almost any major city and you will find a major river.

Except for Jerusalem, that is. Unlike the other major cities of the ancient world, it had no river at all. Its citizens were forced to rely on the Gihon spring outside the city walls, and this made the city weak. David captured Jerusalem by sending his men up its water shaft. It was an urban anomaly, a town planning nightmare and a military embarrassment – until one day the sons of Korah prophesied something radical. They declared in Psalm 46 that the Lord had deliberately chosen a riverless city to express where the true power of his people lay. *"There is a river whose streams make glad the city of God, the holy place where the Most High dwells. God is within her."* They insisted that the rushing river that watered Jerusalem was none other than the Holy Spirit of God.[1]

This insight provides the background to the two final chapters of Ezekiel. So far, the *Book of Comfort* has prophesied

---

[1] Psalm 46:4 built on David's earlier prophecy in Psalm 36:8. See also Joel 3:18 and Zechariah 14:8.

about a new King (34:1–31) who will bestow a new heart on his people (36:24–38) through the new life that comes from his Spirit (37:1–28). This will grant them a new experience of his victory (38:1–39:29), of his presence (40:1–43:12) and of his authority flowing through them (43:13–46:24). Now, as we come to the end of Ezekiel's final vision, we are told that the new King of Judah will also grant his people a new experience of his power. At the heart of the New Jerusalem, Ezekiel witnesses what the sons of Korah sang about. He witnesses the River of God in all its glory.

In 47:1–12, the angel promises Ezekiel that a day is coming when the River of God will transform the world. It will proceed *from* God (since its source is his sanctuary within the Temple) but it will also *be* God (since it flows through parts of the Temple that are forbidden to anyone but God and his Messiah).[2] This must be one of the Old Testament passages that Jesus has in mind when he declares in John 7:37–39 that *"Whoever believes in me, as Scripture has said, rivers of living water will flow from within them."*[3]

The angel uses his measuring line to promise Ezekiel that God's people will have an ever-deepening experience of his Holy Spirit. The returning Jewish exiles will paddle in the River of God. After the Day of Pentecost, the Messiah's followers will go *"knee-deep"* and *"to the waist"* in the River of God, because its powerful flow will remain restricted, first to Jerusalem, then to the Roman world. In time, however, the Messiah's followers will be swept away by the River of God to every nation of the world. Don't miss how very different this is to many of our assumptions today. The angel responds to those who think that Christians can no longer expect to have the same experience of the Holy

---

[2] Ezekiel 44:1–3 and 46:1–2. The parallel passage in Revelation 22:1–5 speaks even more explicitly about the Trinity, *"Then the angel showed me the river of the water of life … flowing from the throne of God and of the Lamb."*

[3] John explains in verse 39 that, *"By this he meant the Spirit, whom those who believed in him were later to receive."*

Spirit as Christians in the book of Acts: *"Son of man, do you see this?"*[4]

Ezekiel prophesies that the Holy Spirit will overflow to reach the entire world by assuring us that even the Dead Sea will become a fertile fishing lake.[5] The River of God is so brimming with life that any tree on its riverbanks will bear fruit monthly. There is no person, no place and no people group too lost for its healing waters to transform.[6]

I love the whole of the book of Ezekiel, but there are few passages so inspiring as this picture of the Holy Spirit flowing out through the people of God to transform the world. It is such a far cry from the static view that we can often have of church, imagining that it is enough for our non-believing friends and neighbours to "know where we stand" and to know that "all are welcome" at our Sunday gatherings.

In 47:13–23, Ezekiel underlines the dynamic, missionary nature of God's people by describing boundaries of the Promised Land that are very similar to those promised to Moses and enjoyed by Israel under King David and King Solomon.[7] There are two big differences. First, there is no mention of the land east of the River Jordan where the tribes of Reuben, Gad and Manasseh settled as a sinful act of compromise. Second, the Promised Land is shared with many foreigners who have converted to the God of Israel. The River of God will empower God's people to become truly pure and truly global.[8]

---

[4] 47:6. God saves the best till last (John 2:10). We should expect the church's experience of his Spirit to deepen, not to lessen, as we near the final decades of world history.

[5] The Dead Sea is the lowest place, the saltiest place and one of the least fertile places on earth. Yet the River of God bears fruit even in the most barren places. See Jeremiah 2:13, and John 15:5 and 16.

[6] The *salt* that remains in 47:11 is presumably to enable the Temple sacrifices that are described in 43:24.

[7] Numbers 34:1–12, 1 Kings 8:65 and 1 Chronicles 13:5. Sinful Israel and Judah never ruled all this territory.

[8] Numbers 32:1–42 and Ephesians 2:11–22. The parallel vision in Revelation 22:1–5 emphasizes this by upgrading leaves that heal in general in 47:12 to leaves that *"are for the healing of the nations."*

In 48:1–29, Ezekiel underlines this further by repeating in more detail what he told us in 45:1–12 about the new division of this Promised Land.[9] The thirteen horizontal strips of land, running from east to west like the hoops on a rugby shirt, that are allocated to the tribes of Israel are clearly meant to be taken figuratively. So is the *"sacred district"*, a perfect square of land in verse 20, measuring eight miles by eight miles.[10] These represent the riches of God's inheritance for his people through the death and resurrection of their Messiah.[11]

In 48:30–35, Ezekiel ends his vision with a final description of the New Jerusalem.[12] Having witnessed the departure of God's glorious presence from the Temple in Old Jerusalem, he ends his book with a final promise that the New Jerusalem will be so full of God's glorious presence that it will be nicknamed *Yahweh Shammah –The Lord Is There*.[13] God's presence will become the defining feature of God's people.[14]

So don't be satisfied with your own present experience of God's Spirit. It's fine to begin with a trickle, as at the start of

[9] Ezekiel 48:11 also repeats 44:10–16, which demoted the sinful priestly clan of Ithamar to the status of Levites and of servants to the faithful priestly clan of Zadok.

[10] The twelve tribes are not even the same in 48:1–29 and 30–35. *Levi* replaces one of the two tribes of Joseph.

[11] Ephesians 1:3, Philippians 4:19, Romans 8:32, 1 Corinthians 1:30 and 2 Corinthians 1:20. Modern Jews have no record of their tribal ancestry, so the language here has to be symbolic. It speaks less about the return of the Jewish exiles in 516 BC than about the church that would emerge from their resurrected nation through its Messiah. Romans 4:13 upgrades our "Promised Land" to encompass the whole world.

[12] The Apostle John is also granted a tour of the New Jerusalem by an angel with a measuring stick (Revelation 21:15–21). Not only are its gates named after the twelve tribes of Israel, but its foundations are also named after the twelve apostles. Consequently, the city that John sees is 1,000 times wider and 1,000 times longer than the city seen by Ezekiel.

[13] Other nicknames for the New Jerusalem can be found in Isaiah 1:26, 60:14 and 62:1–4, Jeremiah 3:17 and 33:16, and Zechariah 8:3.

[14] The final verses of Ezekiel respond to the great prayer of Moses in Exodus 33:15–16: *"If your Presence does not go with us … What else will distinguish me and your people from all the other people on the face of the earth?"*

chapter 47, but it isn't fine to stay there. God wants to catch you up in his plan to transform every nation of the earth through the life-giving power of the River of God flowing out through his people. That's why the Lord wielded his surgeon's scalpel so determinedly when he operated on the sinful hearts of Israel and Judah. It is also why he still disciplines his church today. He wants to catch us up in the River of his Holy Spirit, enduing us with supernatural power to transform the world.

Conclusion:
Only Radical Surgery
Can Save This Patient

*"I looked for someone among them who would build up
the wall and stand before me in the gap on behalf of
the land so that I would not have to destroy it."*

(Ezekiel 22:30)

The Lord explained to Jeremiah and Ezekiel that he was looking
for a person who would willingly embrace his surgeon's scalpel.
He lamented in Ezekiel 22:30 that *"I looked for someone among
them who would build up the wall and stand before me in the gap
on behalf of the land so that I would not have to destroy it"* – adding
sorrowfully, *"but I found no one."*

Then one day, after centuries of hunting, the Lord finally
alighted upon the one that he was looking for. When a carpenter
from Nazareth was baptized in the River Jordan, God's voice
boomed out from heaven with pleasure: *"This is my Son, whom I
love; with him I am well pleased."*[1]

Almost immediately, the obedient Son of God was led into
the desert by the Spirit of God. In that dry and arid land, as he was
tempted by the Devil, he was sustained by the River of God that
flowed out from within him. When he faced the same temptations
that scuppered ancient Israel and Judah, he repeatedly submitted
himself to the surgeon's scalpel. Drawing on the Scriptures, he
raised a battle cry against the Devil: *"It is written."*[2]

---

[1] Matthew 3:17. Matthew begins his gospel with a family tree that emphasizes
that Jesus was the descendant of King Jehoiachin of Judah. He was the better
King promised by Jeremiah and Ezekiel.

[2] Matthew 4:4, 7, 10.

Jesus even submitted to God's surgeon's scalpel in the loneliness of the Garden of Gethsemane. Although perfectly sinless, he chose to die on a cross as the sin offering that takes away the sin of the world. He sweated drops of blood as he agreed to stand in the gap for sinners by surrendering his body to God's operating table. When he prayed, *"Father ... not as I will, but as you will"*, he enabled his Father to write a new ending to Ezekiel 22:30 – *I looked for someone who would stand before me in the gap so that I would not have to destroy my people. **And I found the perfect Intercessor.***[3]

Jesus surrendered his body to crucifixion because he understood the message of Jeremiah and Ezekiel. Only radical surgery could save God's people from their sin. Their souls were so riddled with its cancer that the only remedy was death and resurrection – first his own, as the atoning sacrifice for their sin, and then theirs, through water baptism, as an expression of their repentance towards the Lord. Jesus might have cried out in self-pity from the cross the words of Lamentations 1:12: *"Look around and see. Is any suffering like my suffering that was inflicted on me, that the Lord brought on me in the day of his fierce anger?"* Instead, the gospel writers tell us that he kept his eyes fixed on the results of his painful surgery. He looked down from the cross at his crucifiers and he prayed in Luke 23:34, *"Father, forgive them, for they do not know what they are doing."*

After Jesus rose from the dead on the third day, he called his followers to submit to God's surgeon's scalpel too. Peter had saved his own skin on the night that Jesus was arrested by denying three times that he knew him. On the Day of Pentecost, however, as the River of God began to flow out through him, he confronted the city of Jerusalem with the same courage as Jeremiah and Ezekiel. Three thousand Jews were immediately baptized in water as an expression of their willingness to submit to God's surgeon's scalpel. Through the Spirit-filled Peter, the Lord began to build the New Jerusalem.

---

[3] Matthew 26:36–44 and Luke 22:39–44.

A few years later, a respected Jewish rabbi submitted to God's surgeon's scalpel to become one of the despised and hated followers of his Messiah. Saul of Tarsus gave up everything to become the Apostle Paul – his friends, his family, his reputation and eventually his life – but as he lay down on God's operating table, he experienced what Ezekiel promises us in his *Book of Comfort*. Paul received a new heart and a new experience of God's Spirit that endued him with new authority and power to spearhead the advance of the gospel to the pagan people groups of the Roman Empire. In his final letter, written while on death row, he revelled in the results of his surgery. *"I have fought the good fight, I have finished the race, I have kept the faith. Now there is in store for me the crown of righteousness, which the Lord, the righteous Judge, will award to me on that day."*[4]

The past two thousand years of church history have continued that same story. Every time God's people have committed the same sins that infected ancient Israel and Judah, the Lord has lovingly operated with his surgeon's scalpel. The prophecies of Jeremiah and Ezekiel still provide the commentary for the many ups and downs of God's people throughout AD history. As we end this book together, each of us therefore needs to reflect on our own situation. Where is there sin and compromise in our own lives and in our churches? In what ways is God seeking to operate on our own hearts today?

Over the past two thousand years, there have been many occasions when God's people have responded to the Lord with the same repentance that brought the Jewish exiles back to the Promised Land in 516 BC. Many Jews have received Jesus as their Messiah and found salvation through him. Many Christians have admitted that the church's failures and flounderings are not a proof that God has lost his power, but a proof that the words of Ezekiel 20 remain true: *"for the sake of my name I did what would keep it from being profaned in the eyes of the nations ...*

---

[4] 2 Timothy 4:7–8.

For their hearts were devoted to their idols."[5] These have been the periods that church historians term "revivals" – times when the church confesses how much it looks like Old Jerusalem and pleads with the Lord to forgive its sins, to fill it with his Holy Spirit and to transform it into his New Jerusalem.

So let's end our study of Jeremiah, Lamentations and Ezekiel by praying together for a fresh revival in our own day. Let's be like Evan Roberts, whose prayers helped to launch the great Welsh Revival of 1904–05.

> *For a long time I was much troubled in my soul and my heart by thinking over the failure of Christianity – oh! it seemed such a failure – such a failure and I prayed and I prayed and I prayed ... I was taken up into the divine fellowship ... and I saw things in a different light and I knew that God was going to work in the land, and not this land only but in all the world.*[6]

After a hundred thousand people were converted in Wales, and several million more around the world, Evan Roberts was asked to share his secret for transforming churches. He shot back: *"There is no secret! Ask and ye shall receive!"*[7]

So let's ask and receive. Let's confess that only radical surgery can save our churches, and let's believe that God has found a Saviour to embrace the surgeon's scalpel for us. Let's ask for revival in our own day, for the glory of the God of Jeremiah and Ezekiel!

---

[5] Verses 14 and 16.

[6] Evan Roberts in an interview with W.T. Stead in *The Bruce Herald* (28 March 1905).

[7] Quoted by Arthur Wallis from an account of the Welsh Revival in his book, *In the Day of Thy Power: The Spiritual Principles of Revival* (1956).